MARLBOROUGH'S OTHER ARMY

The British Army and the Campaigns of the First
Peninsular War, 1702–1712

Nicholas Dorrell

'This is the Century of the Soldier', Fulvio Testi, Poet, 1641

Helion & Company

Helion & Company Limited
Unit 8 Amherst Business Centre
Budbrooke Road
Warwick
CV34 5WE
England
Tel. 01926 499 619
Email: info@helion.co.uk
Website: www.helion.co.uk
Twitter: @helionbooks
Visit our blog at http://blog.helion.co.uk/

Published by Helion & Company 2015. 2nd edition corrected and with new plates 2019
Designed and typeset by Serena Jones
Cover designed by Paul Hewitt, Battlefield Design (www.battlefield-design.co.uk)
Printed by Henry Ling Limited, Dorchester, Dorset

Text © Nicholas Dorrell 2015, 2019
Illustrations open source
Colour artwork by Mark Allen © Helion & Company 2019
Maps drawn by George Anderson © Helion & Company 2015, 2019

Cover: The Battle of Almansa, by Balaca.

ISBN 978-1-911628-40-8

British Library Cataloguing-in-Publication Data.
A catalogue record for this book is available from the British Library.

For details of other military history titles published by Helion & Company
Limited, contact the above address, or visit our website: http://www.helion.co.uk

We always welcome receiving book proposals from prospective authors.

Contents

List of Illustrations & Maps

Maps

Introduction

In the later part of the seventeenth century the power and influence of France had grown, provoking a reaction by other states that felt threatened. This culminated in the War of the League of Augsburg or Nine Years' War of 1688–1697. In this war a coalition of powers headed by Britain, Holland and Austria tried to defeat, or at least limit the power of, France. With the help of a group of other states, these powers fought a war of attrition against France with limited success. French armies were still dominant on the battlefield but France did not have the resources or manpower, despite a greatly expanded army, to defeat such a powerful coalition. The war petered out indecisively in 1697 but few believed that the war had solved anything. Another major war was likely and perhaps just waiting for a cause to spark it.

An obvious spark for renewed conflict, amongst other possibilities, was the throne of Spain. Spain had formerly been a major power but was declining by this time. It was still powerful and a useful addition to either side in future confrontations. What made Spain a possible cause for a renewal of the contest between France and her enemies was that the Spanish king, Charles II, was childless and in poor health. There was no obvious clear-cut heir but two of the strongest claims were Philip of Anjou, the grandson of the French king, and Archduke Charles, the brother of the Austrian emperor. Whichever became king would place Spain, and the considerable Spanish resources and manpower, in one or other of the rival camps.

On 1 November 1700 Charles II died and it emerged that he had named Philip of Anjou as his successor. Louis XIV realised that this could cause another war but could not resist trying to take advantage of it. Louis XIV moved quickly to get Philip crowned as Philip V of Spain in an attempt to pre-empt objections from other states. Yet many of the other European states could not tolerate this increase in French power and influence. Britain, Holland and Austria did not accept the enthronement of Philip of Anjou on the Spanish throne. Instead they put forward Archduke Charles as an alternative candidate and again mobilised for war to enforce this choice. Other smaller states supported the two sides in this war to, in theory, decide who would be the next Spanish king. The identity of this king was therefore the cause that the war was fought for, although the greater aim for the Confederates was to try to check French ambitions.

The War of the Spanish Succession was fought over many fronts in Europe and the wider world. The main focus of interest, in the English-speaking world at least, has been the campaigns of the Duke of Marlborough. These .

campaigns, mainly in the Flanders area with a brief visit to Southern Germany in 1704, have been widely written about. With four great battlefield victories under a British commander, featuring British troops, and with a lot of material on the events available in English, it is not surprising that this should be the case. Yet the focus on this front detracts from the often interesting and important events of this war on other fronts.

This is perhaps surprising in the case of what has been dubbed the first Peninsular War in Portugal and Spain. Physical possession of Spain was a prime objective of the Confederate cause as this was probably the best way to ensure that Charles, the Confederate candidate, would become king. The British war slogan 'No peace without Spain' encapsulated the perceived importance of this theatre to the war. The British contingents in Marlborough's army and Iberia varied considerably over time. Overall around half of the British units sent overseas went to Spain and Portugal and because of the smaller number of allied units there the British units were usually a bigger percentage of the army than in Marlborough's army. Similarly the senior commanders in this theatre were also often British. It should be a campaign of interest to the English-speaking world but has been often overlooked.

1. Archduke Charles, future Emperor Charles VI. Austrian School, late 17th century.

The lack of Confederate success in this theatre, compared to Marlborough's efforts, is the obvious reason why this is so. The lack of information about this interesting theatre of war is another factor. This work is an attempt to give details of the Confederate forces in Spain and Portugal and an overview of the campaigns. Where possible details have been given of all the Confederate forces involved in the campaign, not just the British, although because of the lack of information on some of the contingents present this is not always possible. What little coverage this theatre has received largely focuses on the 1707 campaign and the 'decisive' Battle of Almansa. Yet this was just a part of the various campaigns of the war in Spain and Portugal and this work covers all of these. I hope that it will encourage further interest in the war in this area and provide an interesting contrast to Marlborough's activities in the same war.

Weapons and Tactics

The armament of the troops involved in this campaign was similar no matter which army they came from. Although of course slight differences existed between the precise weapons used, they were all of similar type. The bulk of the infantry were armed with a flintlock musket and bayonet. They also usually had a short sword of poor quality. In the early part of the war some nations still had a proportion of the men in a unit armed with pikes. From the available evidence it seems likely that many of the foreign troops that went to Iberia did not take their pikes, if they were using them at the time that they were sent to the theatre. Portuguese units, and possibly the Spanish as well, used pikes in the early part of the war, possibly up to 1707. Officers and non-commissioned officers were usually armed with a variety of polearms and similar weapons. The grenadiers were supposed to carry grenades with them on campaign but unless defending or assaulting a position it is likely that these were not carried in the field. Cavalry were armed with a sword, two pistols and a carbine. It was common practice for protective headwear to be worn, often of a type called a 'secret'. 'Secrets' were protective headwear that was hidden under the normal hat of the wearer. In a similar manner some units or individuals could have breastplates but these were also commonly worn underneath coats and so out of view. Finally the armies were supported by artillery equipped with standard pieces of the time. Field guns of three pounds and upwards were used, along with a small number of howitzers and mortars.

There were some differences between the tactics used by different armies during this period, although whether these differences were significant in reality is more of a problem. There is little reliable evidence that any of the tactics discussed here and used by the armies in this campaign, and indeed in the war generally, were actually an advantage or disadvantage. There were differences of detail between different national armies using in theory the same tactics but in general two styles of infantry tactics were used at this time in Western Europe. The first was the older style and could be considered the standard tactics of the period. The other was a newer system developed by the Dutch and British.

For infantry the standard tactics of the period were to deploy in four or five ranks, although it was normally four by this time, and use ranks to fire. That is, a rank or ranks of the formation would fire independently. Those that had fired would then reload while the other ranks took their turn to fire. Most commonly, a single rank would fire each time but it was also possible that two or three ranks could fire together. The alternative to this tactic was to deploy in three or four ranks and for all the ranks of sections of the units frontage to fire a salvo together. The frontage of the line would be divided into a varying number of platoons. The platoons or groups of platoons would close up their ranks so that two or three ranks could fire a salvo together. After firing the platoon would open ranks again and load, meanwhile the other platoons in the unit would fire. It was common practice under both systems for one rank not to fire and to be kept as a fire reserve.

Prior to this war it was only the Dutch and British armies that generally used the 'platoon firing' system. Even in these armies, rank firing continued to be used in some circumstances. The Austrian army also used platoon firing but only in theory when fighting against the Turks. In theory the Austrian units were supposed to use a rank firing system against other opponents. During the war more nations started to use the platoon firing system, mainly because they were being paid to fight by the Dutch and British and they wanted them to use this system. Often it is not clear which system the armies actually used. The rank firing system was in effect the default system of the time, and except for the Dutch and British units in Spain all other units involved in the campaign in Iberia probably used it. Yet the Dutch and British paid for the

Portuguese and Palatine units in the Confederate army. Similar units to these in Flanders were often required to use the platoon firing system. There is no record that these units did convert to this firing system but possibly they also were required to change over. There is also an example of an Austrian unit using platoon fire during the campaign. Therefore Austrian units may have used platoon firing generally, contrary to expectation. This raises the possibility that Spanish units in the Confederate army may also have used platoon fire. The Spanish army generally followed Austrian practice.

Cavalry tactics in the west were divided into three main systems. Once again there were minor variations in the exact method used but we can identify three schools of tactics – the French, German and Anglo Dutch schools. Key elements of a successful charge were high speed and good order. All of these tactics were compromises that sacrificed one or more key elements of a successful charge. The cavalry at the time were less effective in charges than cavalry charges were to be later in the century.

The French-style tactics were to charge in at the gallop, but in considerable disorder when compared to other tactics. The units advanced slowly on the enemy before breaking into a gallop when a short distance from their opponents. They would sometimes also fire just before breaking into a gallop but not in all cases. It was high-speed attack, which was good, but also with a high level of disorder, which was bad. The German school of tactics also fired but then charged in at the trot to keep disorder to a minimum. This school was low on speed, which was bad, but also low on disorder, which was good. The tactics of both of these schools in theory involved firing before charging home against the enemy. The main aim of this fire was to cause disorder in the target. However they also risked causing disorder in their own unit and/or slowing it down. In practice it was common for units using these tactics to dispense with firing and just move straight in with the sword only. Anglo-Dutch style tactics did not require firing for this reason. Units using this school of tactics charged in at the fast trot and were perhaps medium speed and disorder when compared to the others in use. Thus all of the tactics used were compromises and in practice there was little to choose between these various tactical schools. Once again it is not always clear which tactics were used by the various contingents. The British and Dutch units, not surprisingly, used the Anglo-Dutch school of tactics. The pro-French Spanish and French troops used French tactics and it is possible that the pro-Confederate Spanish units also did. The Imperialist and Palatine units used the German school. What tactics the Portuguese used is completely unknown, and it is possible that any of them were. It is possible that units paid for by another state used the tactics of the state paying for them; this was not the case in Flanders but that does not mean it was not the case in Iberia. The Spanish units were also officially part of the Imperial army and so could have used Imperialist tactics, for example.

One problem the Confederate cavalry faced in Iberia, particularly Portugal, was finding suitable horses. When the main phase of campaigning started in 1704 the British and Dutch sent their cavalry units without horses: the plan was for the Portuguese to supply mounts for these units but they were unable to do so. In the initial campaign, there was a severe shortage of horses, particularly good quality ones, partly because before the Portuguese entered the war many of the available animals had been bought by the opposing Bourbon armies. Agents of these armies had bought all of the best mounts available and many of the others, so it took a long while to find any at all. Perhaps because of the initially poor quality of Portuguese horses the British and Dutch decided that they were not strong enough to carry heavy western troopers. This was not, in fact, true and Portuguese horses, like Spanish ones, were used to the conditions in Iberia and so better able to survive and flourish in them. Yet it was also true that often there were not enough horse to meet the needs of the armies. The horse shortage of 1704 was the start of a long search for what the British and Dutch considered suitable mounts.[1] Moroccan, Irish and horses from various other places were sent to the theatre but they all proved inferior to the native ones. Imported horses were usually bigger and stronger than native ones, but they were not used to the difficult conditions in Iberia and soon began to suffer from the conditions. The French discovered that their horses also soon became ineffective or worse, and turned to the good-quality and acclimatised Spanish horse.

Artillery in this period was standardised in use in western Europe at this time. The pieces were very heavy and the much of the support staff was civilian. This meant that once the pieces were deployed it was usually difficult to move them. Most commonly they were placed in small groups or batteries at vantage points to support an attack. In defence, they could also be in batteries or spread across the front to support the units, usually infantry. Some modern writers believe that small 'battalion' or 'regimental' guns were in use at this time. These were, they argue, light enough to be able to move with the infantry and support them. While these kinds of guns were certainly in use later in the century there is no reliable evidence that they were regularly used at this time.

Finally it should be noted that battles were generally rare occurrences in wars of this period. Warfare at this time was dominated by sieges to take control of, or retain control of, the fortresses in an area. Fortresses were vital to the operations of armies and control of an area. There were many more sieges, whether successful or not, than battles, and the losses from a siege were often at least as much as from a battle. The other major causes of casualties at this time were desertion and sickness: even in the most favourable conditions armies would lose far more men to these than from active warfare. In Spain and Portugal conditions were often very far from ideal and so these kinds of loses could be major factors.

General Notes on Uniforms

Across Europe at this time there was a great uniformity in military dress and it was the same in Iberia. Some troops such as grenadiers and dragoons sometimes had different headwear or other changes to the standard dress. There were also some differences due to the type of troops – cavalry generally wore riding boots, and the infantry walking boots, for example. Yet except for a relatively small number of occasions the uniforms of all the armies were overall very similar. There were of course minor variants such as more or less lace, etc., but in general the same style of uniform was worn by all nations.

---

1   J.A.C. Hughill, *No Peace Without Spain* (Oxford: Kensal Press, 1991), pp. 65–66.

The general dress of the time consisted of a three-cornered hat, a tricorne, normally in black and sometimes with coloured lace around the edges. A long coat was worn with a lining, often in a different colour to the coat itself. The ends of the sleeves of the coat and sometimes the collar were turned or folded back to expose the lining colour. Under the long coat was worn a shirt and usually a waistcoat. On the lower part of the body breeches were worn and for infantry stockings. Finally boots of the right kind for the type of soldier completed the outfit.

1

The British Army

Until 1707 the British army did not exist. Before this time the various units belonged to the English or Scottish armies. Because of this before 1707 referring to the British army, British regiments, etc, is not technically correct. For the sake of simplicity I will use 'British' at all times in this works.

The British contingents sent to Iberia were not usually the largest contingent in the Confederate forces. Yet despite this they were a vital part of the effort to secure the Spanish throne for the Confederate candidate. The British were the driving force, and increasingly the paymasters, for the Iberian campaigns. For the ruling pro war faction of the British government the slogan "No peace without Spain" soon became their rallying call and the core of their war aims. The war in Spain and Portugal was always a coalition effort but the views and wishes of the British would dominate in the period up to the Battle of Almansa in 1707. In the aftermath of the disastrous 1707 campaign and with the huge increase in troops directly loyal to Archduke Charles, the Confederate-backed candidate for the Spanish throne, the dominance of the British waned a little. Yet even in this period the views of the British could not be ignored as they were still the main paymaster. The British then enjoyed something like a shared dominance with the Imperial faction.

British Organisation and Tactics

Infantry
In the British army the standard infantry unit was the regiment, but in contrast to many other armies of the period a regiment usually only had a single battalion. A few units in the army fielded more than one battalion but none of these were involved in the campaigns discussed here. All of the British infantry units involved were therefore a single battalion but there were numerous small changes or variation in the organisation of a battalion. Standard organisation was 13 companies of 63, or a little more, men plus 15 or a little more in the regimental staff. One of the companies was of grenadiers. This gave an official total of between 834 and 876 men per battalion. The units increased in size slightly over time.

Battalion/Regiment Organisation

Battalion Staff: 15+ men
1 company of 63+ grenadiers
12 companies of 63+ men
Total: 834 to 876 men

Of course it would be extremely rare for a unit to actually have this number of men in reality. Even if the unit was near to full strength at some point it would soon dwindle down in size through desertion, sickness, etc. British units always suffered from the sea crossing to the theatre of war and from the very different climate in Iberia. The conditions in Spain and Portugal were harsh while replacements and new recruits were scarce. This meant that units were often a shadow of their full strength. Units in the field would be lucky to number 600 men and in Spain and Portugal even this would be rare. Periodically replacements were sent to the Iberian fronts and on these infrequent occasions the units could reach this kind of size.

In addition to the above some units were short of this theoretical strength in the first place. Some units at the start of the war only had 12 companies and/or had reduced strength companies of around 55 men. Over time these units received an extra company and/or extra men per company to make them up to the standard organisation, although this is unlikely to have made much difference to field strength. Units which were on the Irish establishment during the earlier part of the conflict seem to have normally had only 12 companies of reduced strengths. When sent to this theatre some of these units recruited themselves up to the full establishment used in other parts of the army or received an additional company and men from units that were to remain in Ireland. Yet it is clear that this was not always the case so variations would remain.

Other units were sent as part of a combined unit, often with fewer companies than a standard battalion. An example of this is the combined Guard battalions fielded. In 1702 this had nine companies from two of the guard regiments. Finally it was also common for units in this theatre to be 'reduced' and then typically used for light duties. It is not entirely clear what being 'reduced' actually entailed but it seems in general to be that the unit was too small to take the field. Often they seem to have been little more than a skeleton force. Perhaps when a unit was reduced this involved the bulk of the remaining personnel in a small unit being used as replacements for other units and leaving only a skeleton force. Sometimes units in Spain or Portugal returned to the British Isles to be built up. They could then return or be assigned to other duties. On other occasions reduced units were never rebuilt and were eventually disbanded altogether.

British infantry in this period fought in three ranks and were trained in the use of platoon fire. This was a system of firing which proponents of it say was superior to others in use at this time. There is a lack of reliable evidence that it did in fact have an edge at this time. In addition, while it is true that the infantry were trained to use this system there is little evidence of them actually doing so in the field and growing doubt that it could be maintain for long if it was used. After this time platoon firing may have conferred a tactical advantage but on balance it is difficult to a significant advantage at this time.

At the start of the war most British units still had a strong contingent of pikemen. Walton says that there were 14 ordinary pike men per company.[1] So there would be 168 ordinary pike men per battalion and in addition officers, sergeants, musicians, etc. Some units such as fusilier and marine battalions never carried pikes and during the war the other units replaced their pikes with additional muskets. Unfortunately in general we are lacking details of when this change over happened. Yet many of the details we do have are for units being dispatched to Spain or Portugal. We do not have details about all the units sent to Spain or Portugal but we do have a reasonable proportion of them, especially when compared to those sent to the Low Countries. See the sections dealing with individual campaigns below for details. In general we can see that in the 1702 campaign the units involved were armed with pikes. After this time many of the units sent to Iberia are specifically noted, and so presumably contrary to normal practice, as being sent to Iberia without their pikes. This strongly suggests that it was normal practice for units sent to Spain or Portugal after 1702 to go without pikes. These units would replace any pikes they had with extra muskets.

Cavalry

British cavalry was organised into regiments of Horse (heavy cavalry), and Dragoons. Generally Horse regiment had three squadrons and Dragoon regiments had four squadrons but the regiments could have a varying number of squadrons. In Spain and Portugal the units that the British sent generally had two squadrons. The other two squadrons, one for Horse regiments, remained behind to provide recruits and replacements for the squadrons in the field. The exception to this seems to have been the Royal Dragoons in 1704. These seem to have initially sent all four of its squadrons to Portugal. The harsh conditions and losses in Iberia meant that unit strengths were difficult to maintain. Indeed on occasion units would consolidate their dwindling strength into a single squadron.

A squadron was composed of two troops and a small number of headquarters staff. Most sources give a troop of 70 to 75 men and therefore a squadron of about 150 to 160 men with the squadron staff. Yet there are some problems with these figures. First of all the details of the squadron composition are very general and lacking in details. Secondly when we have numbers for full size units, or can deduce them from other information, is seems clear that they were officially larger than this. The details of this are covered in the sections dealing with the campaigns. They give a confusing picture but seem to suggest that at full strength a squadron was supposed to be something like 200 to 220 men. This number would of course rapidly decline, assuming it was ever actually reached in the first place, once active campaigning started. Once this

---

1   C. Walton, *History of the British Standing Army, 1660–1700* (London: Harrison and Sons, 1894), p.428.

was the case then squadrons often did number circa 150 men and this may be the origin of this figure for squadron sizes.

British cavalry charged at the trot with sword in hand without firing their pistols or carbines. This was certainly an improvement on the tactics used previously. In the previous war the British cavalry had been second rate compared to their opponents but these tactics allowed the cavalry to achieve parity. The tactics were still a long way from effective full-blooded charges but they were a step in the right direction.

Artillery

As with all armies of this period artillery organisation into standard batteries was not used. Instead artillery was deployed on an ad hoc based as needed. It could therefore be grouped into one or more batteries, strung along the battle line individually or in small group or directly attached to the support of specific units. Often combinations of these were used.

Chandler and followers of his view think that the British, and others, were using 'Regimental' or 'Battalion' guns at this time. Certainly all nations used light guns in these roles later in the century. The evidence for this is questionable and it seems likely that this view is incorrect. Whether or not they were used generally there is no evidence for their use by the British in this theatre.

Horses

Horses were to be a continual problem for the British and other forces operating in Spain and Portugal. At the start of the main campaign in 1704 there were severe shortages of horses. The Portuguese had agreed to provide not only their own army's horses but also horses for the arriving British and Dutch cavalry. Unfortunately Portugal did not prove capable of providing enough horses even for their own army who were desperately short of horses. Portugal did not have large numbers of horses available and their enemies had done their best to remove what they could before Portugal joined the war. This meant that for the opening campaigns mounted cavalry was in short supply. Horses remained difficult to obtain in Portugal though the whole war as there was always a high demand for them.

In addition their British and Dutch allies often rejected the horses the Portuguese did provide. To western eyes, the same applied to the French operating in Iberia, the native horses, particularly the Portuguese horses, looked weak and not capable of being used by big western troopers. As Francis[2] argues the British and Dutch failed to understand the conditions in Iberia: "They looked for large fine horses fit for a cavalry charge, but such horses did not survive campaigning in peninsular conditions for very long; small hardy mounts were often better; they were useful for transport and could survive, where their betters perished." This attitude meant that the British and Dutch tended to undervalue the contribution and quality of the Portuguese and Spanish cavalry. It also meant that they continued to look for alternative sources for horses during the war. They "tried to remedy their

---

2   D. Francis, *The First Peninsular War 1702–1713* (London: Ernest Benn, 1975), p.204.

Infantry Uniforms

Unit	Later ID	Coat	Facing	Waistcoat	Breeches	Notes
All Guards Units	1st, Coldstream, Scots Guards	Red	Royal Blue	Red	Royal Blue	Yellow Lace
Bellasis', Portmore's	2nd Foot	Red	White		Grey	Yellow Hat Lace
Churchill's	3rd Foot	Red	Buff	Buff	Buff	White Buttons/Hat Lace
Seymour's Marines	4th Foot	Red	Yellow	Red	Grey?	
Pearce's	5th Foot	Red	Yellow Green		Green	
Columbine's, Rivers', Southwell's, Harrison's	6th foot	Red	Yellow			
Royal Fusiliers	7th Foot	Red	Blue			
Stewart's	9th Foot	Red	Blue			
Stanhope's, Hill's	11th Foot	Red	Yellow	Yellow	Yellow	
Livesay's	12th Foot	Red	White		Blue	
Barrymore's	13th Foot	Red	Yellow	White	White	White Buttons/Hat Lace
Blood's	17th Foot	Red	Grey			
Erle's	19th Foot	Red	Yellow		Yellow	White Hat Lace. Brown gaiters
Hamilton's, Newton's	20th Foot	Red	White			
Whetham's	27th Foot	Red	Blue			
Mordaunt's	28th Foot	Red	Yellow			
Farringdon's	29th Foot	Red	Yellow		Blue	White stockings
Saunderson's, Wills' Marines	30th Foot	Red	Yellow			
Villiers', Churchill's Mar.	31st Foot	Red	Yellow			
Fox's, Borr's Marines	32nd Foot	Red	Green			White lace
Duncanson's, Wade's	33rd Foot	Red	Yellow		Yellow	White stockings
Hamilton's	34th Foot	Red	Grey	Grey	Grey	White hat lace
Donegal's, Gorge's	35th Foot	Red	Orange			
Charlemont's, Alnutt's	36th Foot	Red	Green			
Breton's	-	Red	Willow Green			
Stanwix's	-	Red	Yellow			
Montjoy's	-	Red				
Lepell's, Richard's, Stanhope's	-	Red	White	White	White	

weakness by importing horses from Morocco, Ireland, or even Holland or Germany, but this was a long, costly, and difficult business".[3]

The native horses were usually, in practice, better for the conditions the armies faced. Francis says "This was often a mistake, for the local *Rosinantes*, in spite of a miserable appearance, were often better fitted to subsist and to stand the climate." The Spanish horses were generally superior to Portuguese horses and were arguably the best overall. They were as tough as the Portuguese horses but larger, stronger than them and better able to perform close actions.

British Uniforms

Not all of the uniforms of the units involved in the Iberian campaign are know to us. This is a common occurrence when discussing this period as often the details of the uniforms were not recorded. This is especially true for units which were disbanded during the war or at the end of it. The following are the known uniforms of the units from this campaign.

Cavalry Uniforms

Unit	Later ID	Coat	Facing	Waistcoat	Saddle Cloth	Notes
Harvey's Horse	2nd DG	Red	Buff	Buff	Buff edged White	White hat lace
Royal Dragoons	1st Drag	Red	Blue			
Lloyd's, Carpenter's Dragoons	3rd Drag	Red	Blue	Blue	Blue edged Yellow	Yellow hat lace
Essex's Dragoons	4th Drag	Red	Light Green	Light Green	Light Green edged White	White hat lace
Cunningham's, Killigrew's, Pepper's Dragoons	8th Drag	Red	Yellow	Buff	Yellow edged white	White hat lace/buttons
Pearce's Dragoons	-	Red	Yellow			
Peterborough's, Nassau's, Stanhope's Dragoons	-	Red	White	Yellow		White hat lace

Artillery Uniforms

Unit	Coat	Facing	Waistcoat	Breeches
All Units	Red	Blue	Blue	Blue

---

3 *Ibid.*, p.88.

2

The 1702 Campaign: Cadiz and Vigo

In 1701 active campaigning in the war was restricted to Italy, and so 1702 was the first year of general campaigning. The Confederates would be fighting Spanish troops on various fronts but they wished to strike directly against Spain, yet they did not have any suitable bases to do this. Therefore it was decided to organise an amphibious assault to capture a suitable base in the area to use in future campaigns. The target for the operation was the important Spanish port and fortress of Cadiz. A fleet of 50 English and Dutch ships of the line were assembled under the command of Admiral Rooke, the Dutch were under the command of Van Allemond. This force was to accompany and support an expeditionary force of English and Dutch troops under the Duke of Ormond, with Spaar in charge of the Dutch contingent. This force would land and capture Cadiz.

The land forces totalled one understrength cavalry regiment, 10 infantry battalions and seven marine battalions. The units involved in this operation were as follows.

British Troops
The bulk of the forces involved in the expedition were from Britain. Troops from one cavalry regiment, two Guards infantry regiments, eight line regiments and four marine regiments took part. These were formed into a single cavalry unit and 12 infantry units.

These were the units involved:

Type	Unit Name	Later Identity
Cavalry	Lloyd's*	3rd Dragoons
Infantry	Guards**	1st & Coldstream
Infantry	Bellasis'	2nd Foot
Infantry	Churchill's	3rd Foot
Infantry	Columbine's	6th Foot
Infantry	Fusiliers (O'Hara)***	7th Foot

Type	Unit Name	Later Identity
Cavalry	Lloyd's*	3rd Dragoons
Infantry	Guards**	1st & Coldstream
Infantry	Bellasis'	2nd Foot
Infantry	Churchill's	3rd Foot
Infantry	Columbine's	6th Foot
Infantry	Fusiliers (O'Hara)***	7th Foot
Infantry	Erle's	19th Foot
Infantry	Gustav Hamilton's	20th Foot
Infantry	Lord Donegal's	35th Foot
Infantry	Lord Charlemont's	36th Foot
Marine	Seymour's	4th Foot
Marine	Villiers'***	31st Foot
Marine	Fox's	32nd Foot
Marine	Lord Shannon's	Disbanded 1713

* Only a detachment of two troops from the regiment was involved.

** Detachments from two Guards unit formed a single battalion - two companies from the 1st Guards, six companies from the Coldstream Guards and one combined grenadier company.[1]

*** Only three companies of the Fusiliers and five companies of Villiers' unit participated, they fought as a combined unit.

The following is a detailed breakdown of the units involved:[1]

Unit Name	Officers	Sgts.	Cpls.	Mus.	Serv.	Eff. Men	TOTAL	Dalton*
Lloyd's	25	5	15	22	23	185	275	185
Guards	35	30	30	20	40	600	755	755
Bellasis'	41	25	36	24	50	658	834	834
Churchill's	41	25	36	24	50	658	834	834
Columbine's	40	24	36	24	50	550	724	724
Fusiliers (O'Hara)	50	50	36	21	62	633	833	313
Erle's	40	24	36	24	50	550	724	608
Gustav Hamilton's	40	24	36	24	50	550	724	616
Ld. Donegal's	40	24	36	24	50	550	724	600
Ld. Charlemont's	40	24	36	24	50	550	724	633
Seymour's	41	25	36	24	50	658	834	834
Villiers'	Included in numbers for Fusiliers above							520
Fox's	41	25	36	24	50	658	834	834
Ld. Shannon's	41	25	36	24	50	658	834	838
Eng's & Train								312
TOTAL	515	330	441	303	625	7,458	9,653	

1 D. MacKinnon, *Origin and services of the Coldstream Guards*, vol. 1 (London: Bentley, 1833), p.281.

An Impartial Account of all the material transactions of the Grand Fleet and Land Forces[2] agrees with the total given by MacKinnon but gives an additional 10 men in total.

It must be stressed that these are very much theoretical full strengths of the units at the time. It is possible that given that this was very early in the war and one of the first actions that the units at least started with something like these numbers of men. Yet sickness, desertion, etc, would soon reduce these numbers drastically. The figures given by Dalton perhaps reflect, in some cases, the reduced real strength of some of the units involved. But more likely they reflect the varied official strength of units in this early stage of the war.

From the Calendar of State Papers we see that the Dragoons took 235 horses, not including the senior officers.[3] This is probably a good indication of the full strength of the dragoons. From the same source it is also clear that the infantry used in this expedition still carried a proportion of pikes. This says that on the expedition there will be "eight complete regiments of foot, according to the new establishment. Each soldier in these regiments is to have a musket, besides the usual proportion of pikes. Four more regiments which are to come from Holland are to be provided with muskets and pikes in the like manner."[4]

Dutch Troops

The Dutch contribution to the attack came from three of their regiments. Two of the regiments were marine units and appear to have had two battalions each. The third regiment was a standard infantry unit with a single battalion.

St. Amant's Marine regiment (two battalions)	(NL 5)
Torsay's Infantry Regiment (one battalion)	(NL 46)
Swansbel's Marine regiment (two battalions)	(NL 24)

Note: The Dutch regimental numbers refer to those used in *Uniforms and Flags of the Dutch Army And The Army of Liege 1685–1715* by Robert Hall, Iain Stanford and Yves Roumegoux, 2013.

The *Impartial Account*[5] says that the Dutch 'Rank and file, besides Officers, etc.' were 3,924 men.

Artillery

The expedition had 20 heavy siege guns, 16 mortars and 10 field guns.[6] It could also of course rely on massive fire support from the accompanying fleet.

---

2   Anonymous, *An Impartial Account of all the material transactions of the Grand Fleet and Land Forces* (London: Gibson, 1703), pp.26–27.

3   R.P. Maffey (ed.), *Calendar of State Papers, Domestic Series, of the Reign of Queen Anne Volume 1 1702–03* (London: HMSO, 1916), p.17.

4   *Ibid.*, p.11.

5   Anonymous, *An Impartial Account of all the material transactions of the Grand Fleet and Land Forces*, pp.26–27.

6   A. Parnell, *The War of Succession in Spain: 1702–1711*, pp.22–23.

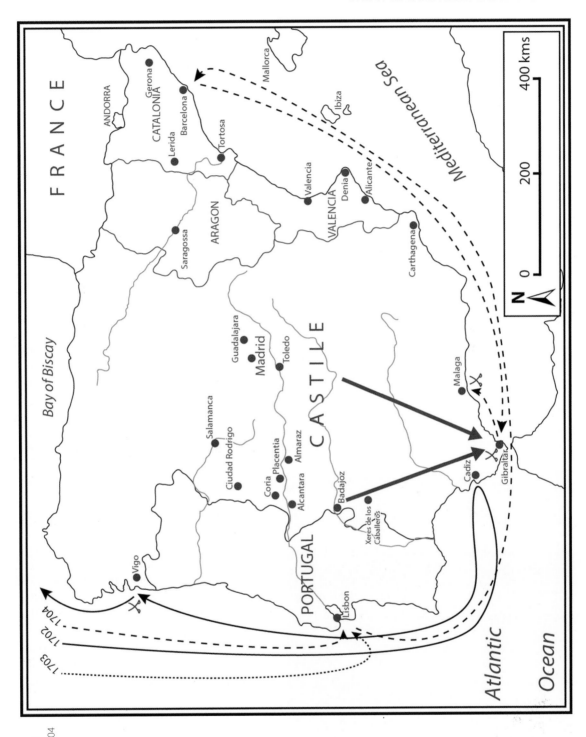

Map 1
General area of
operations, 1702–04

Cadiz

The expedition arrived at Cadiz, and on August 15 1702 started to disembark. The landing was to be in three waves and was a short march from the port. 1,200 combined British and Dutch grenadiers taken from their parent units spearheaded the descent.

Landing at Cadiz

Spearhead: Combined British/Dutch Grenadiers: 1,200 men under Lord Donegal and Brigadier Palandt

1st Wave: Under Bellasis, Lord Portmore, Baron Spaar and Brigadier Matthews

Five battalions – Guards, Bellasis', Churchill's, Seymour's, Torsay's

2nd Wave: Under Sir Charles O'Hara and Brigadier Hamilton

Seven battalions – Columbine's, Fusiliers (Hara), Erle's, G. Hamilton's, Fox's, Swansbel's regiment (two battalions)

3rd Wave: Under Brigadier Lloyd

Five battalions – Lord Donegal's, Lord Charlemont's, Lord Shannon's, St. Amant's regiment (two battalions)

A small force of Spanish cavalry attacked the grenadiers who landed first shortly after landing but these were easily driven off. The entire force then started the long process of disembarkation. It was now discovered that the Spanish fortress had a strong garrison and was not interested in surrendering or switching sides. The Confederates had hoped that substantial parts of the Spanish nobility and population would rally to their cause when given the chance. To aid in this objective strict orders were issued, and at first enforced, against Confederate soldiers looting and committing other abuses common when in enemy territory. Despite this very little Spanish support was received and regular military operations commenced.

2. James Butler, 2nd Duke of Ormonde, by Michael Dahl. (National Portrait Gallery)

The disembarkation took some time but once complete the Confederates marched towards Cadiz. They were attacked again by a small group of Spanish cavalry and captured a number of minor positions on the way. By the end of August Ormond's army was closing on Cadiz and wished the navy to enter the harbour to assist him. This the navy was not keen to do this until an outer work called 'Matagorda' had been taken by the army. Therefore a battery was raised to attack 'Matagorda' and on 2 September infantry also moved on this position. The Spanish position was strong, on marshy, difficult to bombard, ground, and so progress was slow. Meanwhile looting, drunkenness and other abuses were growing and becoming a major problem within the Confederate forces.

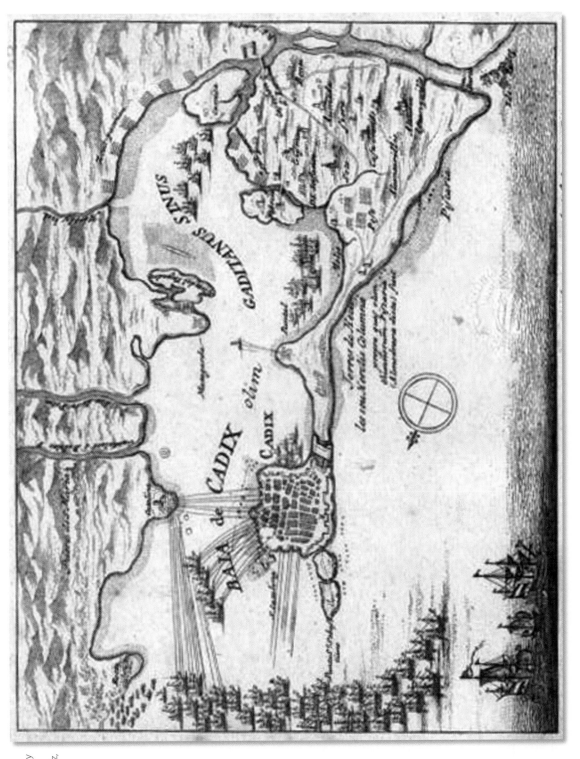

3.
Contemporary
map of the
Battle of Cadiz,
1702

4. The Battle of Vigo Bay, 23 October 1702

The behaviour of the troops had disgusted the local population and turned them against the invaders. It was clear that the attempt to win the Spanish over had failed. Even worse there were growing signs of an enemy force assembling to drive off the disheartened Confederates. Clearly the attempt to take Cadiz had failed and so on 13 September the Confederates marched away from Cadiz to re-embark. The Spanish forces shadowed their move but they did not seriously attack.

The expedition had failed and heading back home when they received some interesting news. They heard that an enemy naval forces and part of the Spanish treasure fleet, the fleet that brought gold and silver from the Americas to Spain, were in the port of Vigo. This port was close and on the path home. The news also offered a face-saving chance for the commanders of the expedition to achieve something concrete. The commanders of the expedition quickly made the decision to attack the enemy forces in the port of Vigo.

The 50 British and Dutch warships heavily outgunned the enemy fleet of 16 French and three Spanish ships of the line in the harbour. The French and Spanish ships wisely decided not to sail but remained in the harbour. The harbour was protected by some galleons that had been chained across the entrance as part of a boom to block passage. The port also had two strong batteries of guns covering the entrance to the harbour. It was agreed that the Confederates would attack and force their way into the harbour to get at the enemy.

By this time four of the British battalions had already been sent to the West Indies by a detachment of the fleet. These were the Erle's, Gustav Hamilton's, Lord Donegal's and Lord Charlemont's regiments. The following forces undertook the landings.

Landing at Vigo[7]

Spearhead: British and Dutch grenadiers under Lord Shannon
First Brigade: Under the Duke of Ormond and Brigadier Hamilton
Four battalions – Guards, Churchill's, Columbine's and Fox's
Second Brigade: Under Lord Portmore and Brigadier Lloyd
Four battalions – Bellasis', Seymour's, Fusiliers and Lord Shannon's
Dutch: Unknown number of units under Baron Spaar and Brigadier Pallandt

2,500 men were involved in this operation but this may just be a figure for the British. The attacks were successful, both on land and on the water, with little losses or incident. The Confederates captured or sank over 40 enemy ships, including some from the Spanish treasure fleet. These last proved to be mainly empty but still the Confederates acquired quite a lot of loot and could now claim the expedition as a success. It was certainly a partial success but it was also a wasted opportunity. The capture of a major base would have been a lot more significant than what was achieved.

---

7   Anonymous, *An Impartial Account of all the material transactions of the Grand Fleet and Land Forces*, p.31.

3

The Dutch Army

The Dutch army was the core of Marlborough's armies in Flanders but was usually of lesser importance to the armies in Iberia. The Dutch accepted the need to support the armies in Iberia but not with any great enthusiasm. They had a powerful enemy army on their borders and so were understandably not keen to reduce their forces located in that area. For these reasons the Dutch contribution to the Iberian armies was not as large as it could have been. Over the period of the war the size of the Dutch contingent dwindled as lost units were not replaced. Yet the Dutch did send regular and large contingents of replacements. In addition they seem to have left many of the personnel of units which left the area behind to boost the size of the remaining units. This meant that the Dutch units retained their experienced personnel and were probably overall the best units in the Confederate armies.

The Dutch regimental numbers I will use to identify the units refer to those used in *Uniforms and Flags of the Dutch Army and the Army of Liege 1685–1715* by Robert Hall, Iain Stanford and Yves Roumegoux.

Dutch Organisation and Tactics

Infantry

As with the British army in the Dutch army it was usually the case that a regiment consisted of just a single battalion. There were some exceptions but all of the Dutch units involved in these campaigns are normally listed as single battalion units. Despite this there is clear evidence that at least some of the Dutch infantry units actually fielded two battalions. Dutch marine regiments in particular are often noted as having two battalions or about twice as many men as other units, depending on the nature of the source, in the Iberian campaigns.

Dutch infantry battalions had twelve companies but the exact organisation changed in 1705.

Infantry Battalion (pre-1705):[1] Battalion staff of eight men, 12 companies of 71 men. Total 860 men.

Infantry Battalion (1705 and after):[2] Battalion staff of 13 men, one company of 66 grenadiers, 11 companies of 66 men. Total 805 men.

The Dutch used a number of marine regiments in this theatre. These were a similar size to the infantry units but with a different organisation. Also as already noted they could have two battalions per regiment.

Marine Battalion (1705 and after):[3] Battalion staff of 15 men, 10 companies of 84 men (eight in each company were grenadiers). Total 855 men.

As with all units in this period it would be rare for units to be at or near to full strength.

The Dutch army fought in three ranks and perfected the form of platoon firing tactics used at this time. The British army and other Dutch allies then took up this tactic. Many older works claim that this system of firing gave the users of it a significant advantage but more recently work suggests that this was not the case. Certainly, there is no evidence for the alleged superiority of this system in Iberia. Instead traditional factors such as morale, experience, leadership, etc., appear to account for any superiority or otherwise of particular units.

As with the British army the traditional view of the Dutch army is that it started the war with only a few pikes within a battalion. These supposedly obsolete troop types were, according to this view, replaced by musket-armed troops in the first few years of the war. As with the British army, for which similar views exist, this view has been challenged in recent times. It now seems that at least some of the Dutch units, as with the British, used pikes for considerably longer than originally thought. Yet this is probably not important as far as this topic is concerned. So far, no details have emerged but it seems likely that as with the British infantry, the Dutch sent to Spain and Portugal went without any pikes they might have. Dutch marine units would in any case not have pikes, assuming others units did have them. While as it seems likely that the Dutch infantry units would, like the British, not have taken their pikes with them. The Dutch and British armies usually acted tactically in the same fashion and so if the British left their pikes behind it seems likely that the Dutch would also. Therefore it seems likely that the Dutch units in Iberia were without pike, although it must be emphasised that there is no evidence for this.

---

1   C.A. Sapherson, *The Dutch Army of William III* (Leigh-on-Sea: Partizan Press, 1997), p.23.

2   C.-P. Golberg, *Die Vereingten Niederlande Heft 3* (Kaltenkirchen: Golberg, 1993), p.8.

3   Ibid., pp.9–10.

Cavalry

There were two basic types of Dutch cavalry regiments, horse and dragoons. Overall the Dutch army had more horse regiments than dragoon regiments, but despite this more dragoons than horse were sent to Iberia. Dutch horse regiments generally had two squadrons and dragoon regiments four. There were some exceptions to this but this was true for all the Dutch units sent to Iberia. Often the full units were not sent initially but they eventual all arrived, often to later return partially or in whole. As with the Dutch infantry the organisation of the cavalry regiments changed in 1705.

> **Horse Regiment (pre-1705):**[4] Regimental staff of eight men, two squadrons of 201 men, three companies of 67 men per squadron. Regimental total of 410 men.

> **Horse Regiment (1705 and after):**[5] Regimental staff of 16 men, two squadrons of 159 men, three companies of 53 men per squadron. Regimental total of 334 men.

> Dragoon Regiment (pre-1705)[6]: Regimental staff of six or seven men, four squadrons of 160 men, two companies of 80 men per squadron. Regimental total of 646 or 647 men.

> **Dragoon Regiment (1705 and after):**[7] Regimental staff of 16 men, four squadrons of 144 men, two companies of 72 men per squadron. Regimental Total of 592 men.

> Dutch cavalry charged at the trot with sword in hand in a similar manner to British cavalry.

> **Artillery:** The notes about British artillery also apply to the Dutch artillery, however there is no evidence that any Dutch artillery participated in the campaigns in Spain and Portugal.

Dutch Uniforms

Not all of the uniforms of the units involved in the campaign are known to us. The following are the known uniforms of the units from this campaign:

---

4   C.A. Sapherson, *The Dutch Army of William III*, p.8.
5   C.-P. Golberg, *Die Vereingten Niederlande Heft 3*, p.11.
6   Sapherson, *The Dutch Army of William III*, p.20.
7   C.-P. Golberg, *Die Vereingten Niederlande Heft 3*, p.12.

Cavalry Uniforms

Unit	ID	Coat	Facing	Waistcoat	Breeches	Saddle Cloth
Rhoo, Drimborn Horse	C15	Grey	Green	Green	Red	Green edged White
Schlippenbach Dragoons	D 2	Red	Blue	Blue	Blue	Blue edged White
Mattha Dragoons	D 4	Blue	Red	Blue	Blue	Red edged White

Infantry Uniforms

Unit	ID	Coat	Facing	Waistcoat	Breeches	Stockings
Welderen	3	Grey	Blue	Blue	Red	Blue
Bruhese	4	White	Red	Red	Red	White
St. Amant	5	White	Blue	Blue	Blue	White
Holstein-Norberg	13	White	Red	Red	Red	White
Noyelles en Falais, Verpoorten	17	White	Red	Red	Red	White
Swansbel, Palm, Leefdael	24	Blue	Yellow	Red	Red	White
Waes, Keppelfox	33	Pearl Grey	Red	Pearl Grey	Pearl Grey	Pearl Grey
Fagel	42	Red	Yellow	Red	Red	Red
Torsay	46	Red	Red	Red	Red	White
Friesheim	51	White	Blue	Blue	Red	Blue
Vicouse	53	Blue	Orange	Blue	Red	White
Lislemarais	54	Grey	Yellow	Grey	Yellow	Grey

4

1703: Portugal Enters the War

After the failure of the 1702 Cadiz expedition to secure a base in Iberia there was no active campaigning in the area in 1703. Instead, the Confederates turned to diplomacy to further their aims. The obvious target for their efforts was neutral Portugal. Because of its strategic geographic position it would be difficult for Portugal to remain neutral: both sides were attempting to get it to join their side by diplomatic means but could be tempted to attack if they thought it would join their opponent. Therefore, there was a lot of pressure for Portugal to join one side or the other before the choice was taken out of its hands. Initially the Portuguese King Pedro II favoured joining the French side; the Spanish allies of France were in the best position to intervene militarily in Portugal. Yet the Portuguese were as worried as many other states by the potential growth in power of their Spanish neighbours by the unification of the Spanish and French crowns. In addition, the Confederates offered financial help to fund and enlarge the Portuguese army. The British and Dutch also pledged to send a 12,000-strong expeditionary force to fight alongside the Portuguese army. Finally, the Portuguese were promised parts of Spanish Extremadura and Galicia at the successful conclusion of peace.

For these reasons, Pedro II of Portugal was persuaded to join the Confederates and help them to secure the Spanish throne for their candidate. In December 1703 the Portuguese signed a treaty which brought them into the war as allies of the British, Dutch and their allies. This treaty stated that none of the parties would make peace until Archduke Charles the Confederate candidate secured the Spanish throne. The treaty also contained the phrase "No peace without Spain", which became the rallying call of the pro-war faction in Britain. It was too late to start campaigning in 1703 but the Anglo-Dutch troops promised they would arrive for the 1704 campaign. The Portuguese pledged to commit 15,000 men to the cause, about 12,000 infantry and 3,000 cavalry, and to raise an additional 13,000 auxiliaries with funds from Britain and Holland.

The Portuguese Army

Information about the Portuguese army of this period is difficult to find and often confusing. There is a general lack of information and what there is can often not be linked together. Part of the reason for this is that the Portuguese continued to use the names of the commanders of the units as the unit name, rather than switching to some other more permanent naming system. This makes it difficult to trace units when the commander changes, especially so as the form of name used can also vary. For example, and using more familiar names, a unit commanded by "John Smith, Duke of Somewhere" might be called "John Smith's" regiment or the "Duke of Somewhere's" regiment. Such a unit might easily be actually commanded by another, more junior, officer because John Smith might be in command of a higher formation, or sick or absent for some other reason. In addition to this, various other circumstances have caused problems.

First of all, at the time Portugal joined the war the army was in a terrible state and totally disorganised. The process of organising the army was chaotic and further complicated by the loss of units in the 1704 and other campaigns. In 1706 the bulk of the original Portuguese army was cut off from Portugal when it marched to join its allies in Madrid. This meant that a whole new army had to be raised in Portugal. At the same time the units of the original army were disbanded, combined into fewer units or otherwise disappeared as unable to get replacements the units dwindled. At around the same time in 1707 there was a major reorganisation of the army during which the units changed from a very 17th century organisation to the model current at the time. There are more details on this below. All of these combined to make it very difficult to study the Portuguese army of this period.

5. Pedro II, King of Portugal, by Maria Paula Marçal Lourenço

The Portuguese army was a major contingent of the Confederate forces in Iberia and indeed was often the largest single contingent. The bulk of the army in Portugal was of course Portuguese but also a sizeable contingent joined the army in Spain and Catalonia in 1706. This force dwindled over time but was still a considerable proportion of the army for some time.

Portuguese Organisation and Tactics

At the time of Portugal's entry into the war the army was still organised into units of 17th century origin. The infantry were organised into 'Tercios'

(*Terços* in Portuguese) and the cavalry into 'Trossos' (*Troços* in modern Portuguese). A 'Trossos' was a cavalry regiment in the 17th century-style. In 1707 the army was reorganised into more contemporary organisation of the period. Both cavalry and infantry were formed into regiments with fixed organisation and similar to those of other nations of the time.

Infantry

Tercios were originally 2,000 to 3,000 strong but during the 17th century their size had steadily declined. By the time of Portugal's entry into the war the tercios were generally around 1,000 men strong, although with some variations and always a lot smaller in practice. These units had 10 companies of 100 men. A company had 10 to 15 pikes and the tercio also had some grenadiers. In July 1704 the tercio was standardised at 800 men. As the real strength of both the 1,000-strong and 800-strong units was generally 500 to 700 men this made little difference in practice. The new 800-strong tercios seem to have had a grenadier company but the other details are not known. It seems likely that the organisation was 10 companies of 80 men.

In November 1707 this distinctly old-fashioned organisation was changed. The infantry units now became regiments with a single battalion. A regiment had 681 men at full strength – 12 companies of 56 men, with one of the companies being grenadiers. Up to this point in time the Portuguese infantry retained a proportion of pike-armed men within the unit and some matchlock muskets were also in use. From this time on an effort was made to replace the pikes and matchlock muskets with modern firearms. This process does not seem to have been completed until 1715, after the war finished. Probably frontline units rarely used the out of date weaponry after 1707.

> **Tercio (up to July 1704):** 1,000 men in 10 companies of 100 men. 10 to 15 pikes per company. one company possibly grenadiers.[1]

> **Tercio (July 1704 to November 1707):** 800 men. Probably in 10 companies of 80 men with up to 15 pikes per company. one company grenadiers.[2]

> **Infantry Regiment (November 1707 and after):** 681 men in 12 companies of 56 men plus regimental staff. one company was grenadiers. In theory there would be no pikes.[3]

Very little is known about Portuguese tactics. It seems likely that at the time Portugal entered the war it was using rank firing and fighting in four or five ranks. They probably then continued fighting in this manner throughout the war, probably switching to just four ranks at some point. It is also possible that the Portuguese could have switched to using the same system as their British and Dutch allies – i.e. using platoon firing and in three ranks. In the

---

1 P. Condray, *The Portuguese Army during the War of the Spanish Succession (1704–1715)* (Alexandria, VA: Editions Brokaw, 1992), p.5.

2 J.V. Borges, *Conquista De Madrid 1706* (Lisbon: Tribuna, 2003), p.31.

3 P. Condray, *The Portuguese Army during the War of the Spanish Succession (1704–1715)*, p.5.

Low Countries it was normal for troops fighting with the British and Dutch to start using the tactics that their allies used. It is therefore possible that the Portuguese would also have adopted the tactics of the British and Dutch they fought alongside.

Cavalry

Initially the cavalry were organised into 'Trossos'. A 'Trossos' was a grouping of varying numbers of cavalry companies or troops. This was the way that 17th century cavalry regiments were often organised. The cavalry companies were, at full strength, between 80 and 120 strong. The companies were themselves constructed from smaller units, sometimes called squads, which seem to have been around up to 50 men. A 'Trossos' could have any number of companies but usually numbered from 1 to 6. 'Trossos' probably averaged about two or three companies per unit.

In 1707, as part of the major reform of the Portuguese army, the composition of the cavalry units was standardised. Cavalry units were now called regiments. Each regiment now consisted of 12 companies of 40 men and a regimental staff of six men. Heavy cavalry regiments had three squadrons and each squadron had four companies. Dragoon regiments had four squadrons and each squadron had three companies.

> **Trossos (Up to November 1707):** one to six companies of 80 to 120 men each.[4]

> **Heavy Cavalry Regiment (November 1707 and after):** Regimental staff of six men, three squadrons of 160 men, four companies of 40 men per squadron. Regimental total of 486 men.

> **Dragoon Regiment (November 1707 and after):** Regimental staff of six men, four squadrons of 120 men, three companies of 40 men per squadron. Regimental total of 486 men.[5]

As with the Portuguese infantry little is known about the tactics of the cavalry. Initially they would have used one of the various versions of cavalry tactics involving firing before closing. Portugal's neighbours, the Spanish, used a very aggressive charge at the gallop in disorder, sometimes preceded by a volley before the charge, essentially a version of the French tactics of the period. Perhaps the Portuguese used similar tactics to these. Similar to the infantry it is possible that the cavalry adopted British and Dutch style tactics of charging sword in hand at the trot. Yet, this seems unlikely, as these tactics were not widely adopted by other contingents fighting with the British and Dutch. Unfortunately, as with the infantry, the lack of information precludes us knowing more.

---

4   J.V. Borges, *Conquista De Madrid 1706*.

5   P. Condray, P., *The Portuguese Army during the War of the Spanish Succession (1704–1715)*, p.6.

Trying to determine Portuguese cavalry tactics is complicated by their history during the war. At the start of the war the cavalry was in a deplorable state, as was the rest of the army, and desperately short of horses. The Portuguese needed horses not only for their own forces but they had also agreed to supply horses for the allied British and Dutch troops that were coming to Portugal. The first contingent of British and Dutch cavalry came without any horses. Yet before the Portuguese entered the war the French had secretly bought all the Portuguese horses they could, perhaps anticipating a Portuguese entry into the war. The Portuguese needed large numbers of good quality horses but none were to be obtained. As loyal allies they provided the British and Dutch with the best of the available horses at the expense of their own forces. The result of this was that in the first year or two of active campaigning the Portuguese cavalry was very badly mounted and their battlefield performance reflected this. These initial problems were overcome but the reputation for poor battlefield performance followed the Portuguese, in English language sources at least, during the rest of the war. Sources that are more balanced suggest that the performance of the Portuguese cavalry was generally good once they had horses, or at least the units of the original army. These units fought well when they joined the main Confederate army in 1706 and afterwards, but they were often used as the scapegoat for setbacks suffered by this army. This means that the positive contribution of the Portuguese cavalry and the tactics they used are overlooked.

Artillery

As with the rest of the army, information about the Portuguese artillery is scarce. It appears to have consisted of standard artillery of the period and as with the other armies involved in these campaigns there is no evidence of 'regimental' or 'battalion' guns.

Army Composition

We are lacking in details about the numbers of units that the army had. At the time of Portugal's entry into the war the army is usually said to have been 15,000 strong, consisting of 12,000 infantry and 3,000 cavalry. In addition to these forces the Portuguese undertook to raise a further 13,000 troops as auxiliaries to the original army. The auxiliaries seem to all have been infantry. They were intended to act as garrison troops and for other second line tasks, thus freeing the rest of the army for active campaigning. It seems likely that generally this was what they did until the crisis of 1707.

The original army seems to have had 20 or 21 tercios of infantry. Condray indicates that there were 21,[6] Borges 20.[7] The Calendar of State Papers contains an interesting entry[8] that for 1 May 1704, indicating there were

---

6   *Ibid.*, p.5.
7   J.V. Borges, *Conquista De Madrid 1706*, pp.33–34.
8   C.S. Knighton (ed.), *Calendar of State Papers, Domestic Series, of the Reign of Queen Anne*, volume 2, 1704–05 (Woodbridge: Boydell Press, 2005), p.125.

34 infantry regiments and 13 foot companies with 23,511 officers and men in Portugal. This is interesting because deducting the 14 British and Dutch regiments that were present this gives 20 Portuguese regiments with the 13 foot companies unaccounted for. Possibly these foot companies account for the additional unit given by Condray, but many other explanations are possible and it is impossible to say. One possible piece of evidence is that in 1706, when the Portuguese field army marched to Madrid, it also had 20 tercios, and so once again these may have been the original 20 units. Finally in 1715, after the war, the army was reorganised again into what would be its peacetime strength, and this was again 20 regiments. In the same entry of the Calendar of State Papers mentioned above there are details of the probable composition of the auxiliary force at this time. This states that there were 33 regiments and one company of foot and auxiliaries with 18,106 men in garrisons. It seems likely that these were the new units that the Portuguese had agreed to raise for the war.

Therefore, it seems likely that the original army was 20 tercios of infantry, while the 'new army' was the 33 regiments mentioned. This appears to be confirmed by later events, and in particular the 1707 reorganisation of the infantry into 34 regiments. Superficially this does not seem to make sense, but it perhaps does if we look at the details. In 1706 20 tercios marched to Madrid. Nineteen of these units then joined the main Confederate army and became separated from Portugal. They fought the rest of the war away from Portugal. They dwindled in size over time and frequently were combined into new units until eventually being totally disbanded. Because of this they probably were not covered by the formal reorganisation of 1707. It seems more likely that the 34 units reorganised into regiments in 1707 were the 33 'new army' regiments along with the one 'old army' which did not get cut from Portugal. They were not all of the army but only those that were operating in Portugal and that there were others still fighting with the army in Spain which were not covered by the reorganisation.

These units became the army defending Portugal from 1707 and eventually the post-war army. This in turn leads to another conclusion. The Portuguese units of the later period retained the names and traditions of the pre-war units. As some or all of the original units must have been disbanded when they were cut off from Portugal this must mean that other units must have been renamed with the old names of other units. This adds to the already confusing picture when trying to identify units during the periods.

For the cavalry we are in a similar situation to the infantry. We can arrive at a general picture but getting a detailed view is more difficult. Condray states that there were 80 Portuguese cavalry companies.[9] Once again the Calendar of State Papers, in the same entry as mentioned above, provides possible clarification. It states that there were 108 troops of cavalry with a total of 5,807 men on 1 May 1704. Of these 24 troops, or possibly a few more, were British or Dutch and so 84, or a few less, would be Portuguese.

---

9   P. Condray, *The Portuguese Army during the War of the Spanish Succession (1704–1715)*, p.6.

The usual strength given for the Portuguese cavalry during the war is around 3,000 to 4,000. The Portuguese army when it entered the war was around 3,000 cavalry for example, possibly around 4,000 cavalry at full strength. The problem is that if the Portuguese had 80 or so companies/troops with a theoretical full strength of around 4,000 men then the companies/troops would be around 50 at full strength. This suggests that in fact the 80 Portuguese units were actually squads rather than companies. Once again the composition of the Portuguese army that marched to Madrid in 1706 suggests that this is true. This force had 39 'squadrons' which was most or all of the Portuguese cavalry available at the time. These seem to have numbered around 100 men. It seems likely they are probably most or all of the 80 or so Portuguese cavalry units of around 50 men organised into larger units.

In 1707 the Portuguese cavalry were reorganised into 20 new-style regiments. Yet, as with the infantry, by this time most or all of the original units had been cut off from Portugal after they joined the Confederate army in Madrid. In contrast to the case of the infantry there were no, or at least few, units of cavalry left in Portugal, while the units that remained with the main Confederate army and continued to fight with them remained relatively strong. Like the infantry the numbers of cavalry with the army based in eastern Spain dwindled over time but much slowly and with a lot less disbandment or combining of units. The Portuguese cavalry units also had little tradition compared to the infantry and so there was no need to maintain the unit.

All this seems to have meant that the 20 regiments reorganised in 1707 were units in both Portugal and Spain. Sometime after Almansa in 1707 the Portuguese cavalry was reorganised into 21 squadrons and so, in theory, perhaps 7 regiments. Therefore possibly the other 13 regiments were in, or at least being hastily raised in, Portugal. It proved to be very difficult to find good quality or sufficient horses for these units. The situation changed over time as the forces in Portugal were strengthened and those in Spain declined. For example, in 1710 there were 22 or 23 Portuguese cavalry regiments – six in Spain and 16 or 17 in Portugal. It seems from the information we have that the reorganization of the cavalry was not followed strictly. Many units do not seem to have had the 'official' number of squadrons, for example. It does seem that the Portuguese cavalry after 1707 in Portugal fielded similar numbers as before. The 16 or 17 regiments in Portugal in 1710 totalled 38 squadrons, very similar to the 39 that they had in 1706. The quality of these new regiments was very suspect and not comparable to that achieved by the older units.

Portuguese Uniforms

Details of the uniforms of the Portuguese army at this time are very difficult to obtain and remain largely unknown. A few general principles are known and we have a few specific examples for individual units.

Infantry

The infantry had formerly been dressed mainly in blue coats but with some other colours in use as well. By this period they were supposed to be in white grey coats, these seem to have been nearly white. Some units had retained their older uniforms and because they were unusual they are known about. For other units we only have two examples of what they wore and one of these is from after this period and so may not be reliable. Condray advances the theory that the bulk of the army wore white grey coats with facings and lace in the colours of the regimental colonel's livery. The livery of the colonel of the Chaves in 1707 was red and gold (yellow) and his unit had red facing and the officers, at least, had gold lace and decorations. Less reliably, a picture from 1720 of a soldier from the Porto regiment shows him with red facings and again the colonel of this unit has a red livery.

The following are the known uniforms of regiments during this period. Some date to after the war and so may be incorrect for the period of the conflict:

Unit	Date	Coat	Facing	Waistcoat & Breeches	Button & Hat Lace
Armada	1715	Green	Yellow	Yellow	Yellow
Campo Maoir		Blue	Red	Red	White
Chaves	1707	White	Red	White	Yellow
Lisboa	1717	Light Blue	White	White	White
Porto	1720	White	Red	White	White

It is possible that the Junta da Commercio also had blue coats as they had a similar background as the Campo Maoir.

For the remaining units of the army we have, at best, the liveries of the regimental colonels to guide us. If this theory is correct then many of the units would have uniforms similar to the Chaves and Porto ones noted above.

The same as Chaves: Moura and Nova de Moura

The same as Porto: Almeida, Braganza, Bras da Silveira, Caminha, Castelo de Vide, Corte Real, Lagos and Olivencia

In addition, here are some other colour schemes suggested by the theory.

Unit	Coat	Facing	Waistcoat & Breeches	Button & Hat Lace
Castel Braco	White	Blue	White	Yellow
Conde de Areiras and Siva da Portalegre	White	Purple	White	White
Conde de Cascais (Castro)	White	Blue	White	White
Pinhel (Pinheiro?)	White	Green	White	White
Serpa	White	Green	White	Yellow
Vasconcelles	White	Black	White	White

Cavalry

Even compared to the lack of information on the Portuguese infantry the information on the cavalry is sparse. Francis[10] claims that before the 1707 reforms the Portuguese cavalry had no uniform at all. Instead, each soldier just wore whatever he wished and that they looked like "a band of vagabonds rather than trained troops".

From 1707 the cavalry uniform became standardised. The coats were to be white grey, like the infantry, and they were to wear the tricorne. Some of the dragoons, possible all of them, wore a hat similar to the French dragoon bonnet of the period. The known example was red with a light blue lining that was turned up and edged with white fur. Probably the dragoons would also have worn tricorne hats as well, as this was usual practice. It also seems that some of the Portuguese cavalry fighting with the Confederate army wore red coats. This was possibly as part of an attempt at deception and may not reflect the usual uniform of the troop.[11]

Condray speculates that, as with the infantry, the cavalry may have used the livery of the regiment's colonel for the colour of the facings and lace. This may be the case but we have no examples that this was so. Using this theory here is what the uniforms would have looked like, where the livery of the colonel is known:

Unit	Coat	Facing	Waistcoat and Breeches	Buttons & Hat Lace
Conde de Prado and Guardias das Minas	White	Blue	White	White
Joao Dantas da Cunha and Sousa Carvelho Dragoons	White	Blue	White	Yellow
Conde de Arcos, Pedro Machado Brito Dragoons, Praca de Bragenza and Olivencia	White	Red	White	White
Mello de Silva Dragoons, Praca de Moura and De Moura	White	Red	White	Yellow

---

10 D. Francis, *The First Peninsular War: 1702–1713*, p.52.

11 N. Dorrell, *Marlborough's Last Chance in Spain: The 1710 Spanish Campaign* (Sweden: Arnfelts, 2011), p.85.

5

The 1704 Campaign: Portugal Invaded and Gibraltar Captured

The 1704 campaign was to be the first full campaign of the war in Iberia for the Confederate force. As the forces gathered it became clear that the situation in Portugal would force the army there to stand on the defensive. The Portuguese army was in a deplorable state. The infantry units were very understrength, disorganised, short of equipment and in no state for an offensive. Even worse, the cavalry was in the same kind of condition and was desperately short of horses. The French had secretly bought as many Portuguese horses as they could before Portugal joined the war, possibly in anticipation of this event. This meant that horses generally and good quality horses in particular were in desperately short supply in Portugal as the campaign opened. The Portuguese had agreed to provide their British and Dutch allies with horses as well. so the British and Dutch sent the personnel for their cavalry units but no horses. This, of course, made the horse shortage even worse as for Portugal very large numbers of horses were required. Because of this only a fraction of the Confederate cavalry actually took the field in 1704. Many remained in the rear waiting for horses to ride, although the numbers available in the field did increase over time.

Without large numbers of cavalry it was impossible to contemplate an offensive by the forces in Portugal. Even more so as there was growing evidence that the French and their Spanish allies were gathering at the border for their own offensive. The Portuguese forces and their allies decided to concentrate on defending the Portuguese border against the expected attack. Meanwhile the Confederate offensive action would take place at sea. The British and Dutch would launch another expedition similar to the one they organised in 1702, and this time the target would be Barcelona, capital of Catalonia. Catalonia was thought to be sympathetic to the Confederate cause. In addition Catalonia had its own language and traditions, considered itself as separate to the rest of Spain and had ambitions of independence, a view that persists to this day. Thus, it was potentially an area that might – and as we will see, did – support the Confederate cause.

The Army in Portugal

The army formed in Portugal consisted of units from the British, Dutch and Portuguese armies.

The British Contingent

Meinhardt Schomberg, 3rd Duke of Schomberg, was commander of the British contingent. He was the son of the more famous Duke of Schomberg from the 17th century. The British contribution to this army Schomberg led was two cavalry regiments (six squadrons) and eight infantry regiments, perhaps 8,000 men at full strength. The British also sent five 'saker' guns, probably 5-pounders, for the field train and also five 24-pounder siege guns. One of the cavalry regiments and two of the infantry regiments were drawn from the garrison of Ireland. The rest of the force was composed of veterans of Marlborough's army withdrawn from Flanders.

6 Meinhardt Schomberg, 3rd Duke of Schomberg

From Ireland:
Harvey's Horse (two squadrons), later the 3rd Horse
Brudenell's, later disbanded
Montjoy's, later disbanded

From Flanders:
Royal Dragoons (4 squadrons), later the 1st Dragoons
Lord Portmore's, later the 2nd Foot
Stuart's or Stewart's, later the 9th Foot
Stanhope's, later the 11th Foot
Barrymore's, later the 13th Foot
Blood's, later the 17th Foot
Duncanson's, later the 33rd Foot

The cavalry units did not have any horses; they were to be provided with horses by the Portuguese. But in the event the shortage of horses in Portugal meant that at first only a detachment from Harvey's regiment was mounted and operating with the army. Later on during the campaign more mounts were found and the numbers actually with the army grew. But it would not be until the end of the campaign that all had acquired a horse and could join the army.

It seems likely that at least some of the battalions sent to Portugal in 1704 did not have pikes. It was still the case that officially, and in general, British battalions continued to have a sizeable proportion of their men armed with pikes, but it is likely that from this time on the units sent to Iberia went without them. Records concerning the replacement of pikes in British units are rare and fragmented but we do have some for the forces sent to Portugal in 1704. The Calendar of State Papers records that the forces sent to Portugal should not have pikes; it seems likely that this was at the specific request of Schomberg. There is, for example, a specific request in another record from Schomberg that Stewart's (Stuart's) regiment be allowed to swap its pikes for muskets. Finally, there is an order that three of the infantry regiments from Holland were ordered to hand in their 582 pikes and to draw extra muskets to replace these. These units were Stuart's, Blood's and Duncanson's regiments, and give an idea of numbers of pikes involved.

The Dutch Contingent

Lieutenant General Fagel was in command of the Dutch contingent. The Dutch sent six infantry regiments each of a single battalion, a horse regiment with two squadrons and two dragoon regiments with a total of three squadrons; five cavalry squadrons in total. These amounted to 3,960 infantry and 852 cavalry from the following units.

Cavalry:

Rhoo's Horse (NLC 15)	2 squadrons
Schlippenbach Dragoons (NLD 2)	1 squadron
Mattha Dragoons (4th Dragoons)	2 squadrons

Infantry:

Welderen (NL 3)
Fagel (NL 42)
Holstein-Norburg (NL 13)
Friesheim (NL 51)
Vicouse (NL 53)
Noyelles en Falais (NL 17)

Like the British cavalry, the Dutch cavalry travelled without horses to Portugal. They too then found that there was a big shortage of horses and so it was difficult to mount the units. It was not until late in the campaign that some units were able to take the field because of this. Also like the British, the Dutch infantry seem to still be using pikes in their units at this time. It is not known if, like the British units sent to Portugal, the Dutch units also left their pikes at home and took muskets instead. But as the Dutch sent their cavalry to Portugal without horses in the same way as the British did it must be a strong possibility that they also followed the British lead on pikes.

The Portuguese Contingent

The Portuguese contribution to the campaign was the whole of their army but the problem is that it is not clear *what* their army actually consisted of at this time. In Chapter 4 this is discussed more fully. From this it seems likely that the army consisted of 20 tercios of infantry from the old army and 33 tercios of new units of auxiliaries. The tercios of the new auxiliary units were

Map 2
The campaigns in Portugal
1704–05

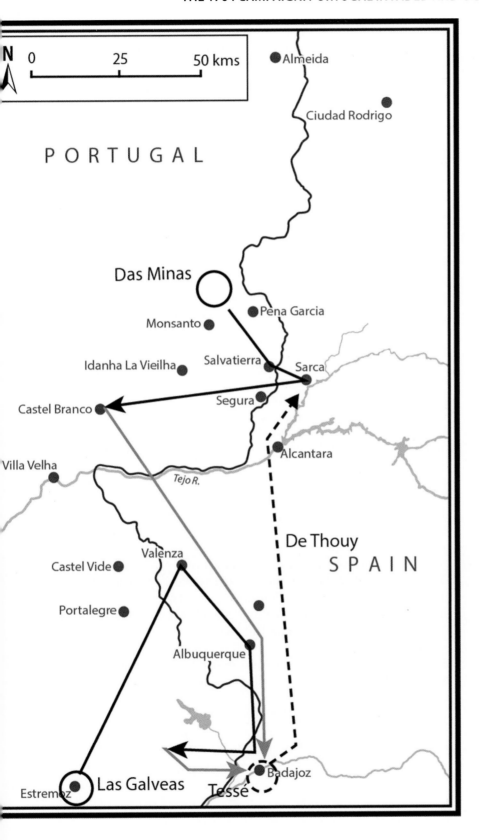

still in the process of being raised and were generally very understrength, especially early in the year. They were probably not capable, generally, of taking the field. The 20 tercios of the old army were also understrength and in disarray, but still were capable of active campaigning. It seems likely that the infantry units in the field were largely the old army tercios and that the new auxiliaries only did garrison duty.

The Portuguese cavalry was all from the old army but, like their British and Dutch allies, they were also short of horses, while the condition of those they had was appalling. The Portuguese had agreed to provide the British and Dutch cavalry with horses and loyally provide horses to them first. This meant that the Portuguese cavalry was at first largely without mounts and unable to take the field, while even the horses they did get tended to be poor. The cavalry probably mustered around 80 squads in theory, most likely these were organised into about 40 companies/squadrons. But it was not until the end of the campaign that most of these could take the field mounted.

There were 15 Portuguese guns with the largest field army. None are recorded with the other army but it is possible that there were some there also.

These forces were supposed to total around 28,000 men. Parnell claims that at the start of the campaign the Portuguese troops actually numbered around 20,000.[1]

The Invasion of Portugal

As the campaigning season approached superior Bourbon forces started to mass near the Portuguese border around the River Tajo (in Spanish)/Tejo (in Portuguese). In response to this the border garrisons were strengthened and two groups of field troops formed to cover the threatened sectors of Beira and Alentejo – one north of the Tejo and one south. The cavalry were desperately short of horses and perhaps only 700 were actually mounted. The remainder stayed in the rear while they attempted to obtain enough horses to take the field. In this they were perhaps lucky as the poor logistics of the Portuguese soon broke down causing shortages at the front. This in turn soon led to disease and desertion as the conditions in the camps deteriorated. The British and Dutch, who were not in any case used to conditions in Portugal, suffered especially badly and their units shrank. Because of this only 20,300 infantry could be mustered in the two groups.

Southern Group, in Alentejo Province based around Estremoz
About 12,000 men under the overall command of Portuguese Count De Las Galveas.
- Portuguese – about 5,000 men.
- British under Schomberg – about 4,200 men: detachment of Harvey's Horse (100 men?) plus 6 infantry battalions (Barrymore's, Blood's, Brudenell's, Montjoy's, Portmore's and Duncanson's).

---

1   A. Parnell, *The War of Succession in Spain: 1702–1711*, p.68.

- Dutch under Fagel – about 2,000 men: detachment of about 100 cavalry (probably 1 squadron) plus 4 battalions (Fagel's and Holstein-Norburg's along with probably Friesheim's and Welderen's)
- Artillery – 15 Portuguese 5, 6 and 7 pounders (Sakers), 5 British Sakers, 5 British 24 pounder siege guns.

Note: Stuart's/Stewart's regiment was part of the garrison of Castel Vide and Stanhope's was part of the garrison of Portalegre.

Northern Group, in Beira Province based around Almeida

About 9,000 men under the overall command of Portuguese Marquis Das Minas.

- Portuguese – 18 cavalry squadrons (companies) and 16 tercios, probably around 8,000 men.
- Dutch – 2 infantry battalions (probably Noyelles en Falais' and Vicouse's), probably around 1,000 men. Francis says there were also 400 cavalry, probably 4 squadrons.[2]
- Artillery – none known but possibly 5 to 10 guns may have been present based on usual practice.

Pitted against these forces were about 28,000 French and Spanish troops, including perhaps 8,000 cavalry. These were in three groups under the overall control of the French general the Duke of Berwick. Berwick was in fact British, the son of James II. He was also a relative of the Duke of Marlborough and would feature heavily in the story of the war in Iberia. Berwick commanded the largest group of 14,000 men, while the Spanish generals Tzerclaes de Tilly and Ronquillo commanded the other two groupings with 5,000 and 9,000 men respectively. Berwick had a significantly larger army than the Confederates and a decisive advantage in cavalry. His troops were also well supplied and organised compared to their opponents, who were clearly in disarray.

Berwick decided to strike across the border. The plan was that Ronquillo would advance towards Almeida in the north and guard the flank of Berwick's advance. Berwick would advance north of the River Tejo and along the line of the river, and in the south Tilly would support Berwick's advance by advancing along the southern bank of the Tejo. On 4 May the invasion started and soon Portuguese fortresses, mainly small, were falling to Berwick's troops. Salvatierra, Segura, Rosmarinos, Cabreros, Pena Garcia and the stronger fortress of Monsanto surrendered quickly. Only the fortress Idanha-la-Vieilha offered much resistance but even this was quickly taken by storm. The next target for Berwick was the larger fortress of Castel Branco. Up until this point there had been no significant opposition to Berwick's advance but approaching the area was Fagel and the Dutch contingent from the forces around Estremoz. Berwick detached 4,000 men under De Thouy to attack Fagel while he led the rest of his army to lay siege to Castel Branco. This Berwick quickly achieved after a four day siege.

---

2   *Ibid.*, p.91.

7. François-Nicolas Fagel

Fagel's move was not part of some planned counter-attack but instead was a product of what was to be a major problem for the Confederates efforts – internal disagreements. Fagel had been at Estremoz as part of the forces there but had quickly fallen out with Schomberg. This rapidly escalated and so in early May, before news of the Bourbon attack had arrived, Fagel decided that he could not stay in the same location as Schomberg and so left with the Dutch troops under his command. He was in command of around 100 Dutch cavalry: Fagel's, Holstein-Norburg's and two other Dutch regiments – four battalions in total. Francis also claims that some Portuguese forces were involved in this action but gives few details.[3] These other two regiments were probably Friesheim's and Welderen's, as both of these officers were with the force. Fagel marched north aiming for Idanha-la-Vieilha, not knowing that this location would shortly be assaulted by the enemy. Fagel had crossed over the river into Beira Province and was marching towards Castel Branco on the way to Idanha-la-Vieilha when he learnt about Berwick's offensive. Even worse, he realised that De Thouy and a superior enemy force was moving to attack him. Fagel therefore sent the cavalry off to join Minas at Almeida and withdrew with the infantry. On 27 May at Zarcedas De Thouy's forces caught two of the Dutch regiments, Fagel's and Holstein-Norburg's, and they surrendered after offering only token resistance. This was a big setback but did allow Fagel and the two remaining regiments to escape to the west. Francis states that a Portuguese marine regiment joined Fagel at this point.

South of the river little had been happening. Both sides seemed to be happy to leave the other alone and wait to see what would happen. Yet Berwick was growing discontent with this situation and so moved to Villa Velha to cross to the southern side of the river. Once across Berwick moved to Portalegre and was joined there by Tilly and his troops. This fortress was garrisoned by Stanhope's British battalion, two Portuguese battalions and some militia. It was also a reasonably strong fortress and should have offered considerable resistance. Yet the Portuguese were dispirited by events and the Portuguese commander surrendered almost immediately. More Confederate troops entered captivity.

In the north Ronquillo had not felt strong enough to confront Minas' troops. Instead he contented himself with progressing around Beira province destroying all he could. In response Minas was moving towards Spain to cross the border and give the area around Ciudad Rodrigo the

---

3   D. Francis, *The First Peninsular War: 1702–1713*, p.96.

same treatment as Ronquillo was giving Beira. When Berwick moved south Minas was ordered to instead move and confront Ronquillo, who was now unsupported in Beira. On 11 June Minas' troops made contact with Ronquillo's at Montsanto. Ronquillo knew that Minas was coming, he had captured a small Spanish occupied town shortly before, and had decided to pull back as he was unsupported. When Minas' troops, the cavalry, arrived near Montsanto they were confronted by 21 mainly French squadrons who had come to reconnoitre. The French promptly attacked and after initially doing well the action broke down into a swirling cavalry melee. Ronquillo did not have his infantry but during the action the Portuguese infantry arrived. At this point Ronquillo pulled back his cavalry and fell back towards his infantry. As Ronquillo withdrew he discovered that his infantry had pulled back even further and so the French cavalry pulled away from the area in some disorder. Seizing his chance Minas promptly recaptured the fortress of Monsanto which Berwick had captured earlier in the campaign.

In response to the events around Monsanto Berwick again moved north to stabilise the situation there. He had hoped to regain Monsanto or bring Minas to battle and so create other opportunities. At this time an extra 4,000 Spanish Bourbon troops arrived in the south under Villadarias. With these extra troops D'Asfeld, who had been left in command by Berwick, proceeded to invest another fortress in the area, Castel Vide. There were three battalions defending this fortress, two Portuguese and Stuart's/Stewart's British. The siege opened on 21 June and after a breach was made the garrison surrendered on the 26th.

By this time the Iberian summer was at its height and campaigning traditionally paused at this point. All of the armies were tired or disorganised and so campaigning died down. For example Stanhope states that the French cavalry had lost two thirds of their horses already in the short campaign.[4] Four or more Portuguese battalions along with two British and two Dutch battalions – Stuart/Stewart's, Stanhope's, Fagel's and Holstein-Norburg's – had been captured. This represented a considerable portion of the available manpower of the army. So it was that both sides had reasons to settle back into camps to wait for the heat of the summer to die away. Meanwhile, events at Gibraltar were unfolding.

Gibraltar and the Portuguese Counter-Offensive

While the forces in Portugal stood on the defensive the Confederates planned to use the sea to launch an offensive. It was hoped that a combined naval and land force could strike at the major Confederate targets – Barcelona, Cadiz or Mahon in Minorca. A large naval force was assembled under Admiral Rooke at Lisbon. Prince George of Hesse-Darmstadt was to command the land forces. He had famously defended Barcelona in 1697 when it was besieged by the French so had useful experience. Unfortunately because of the confusion the Portuguese army was in they could not supply the troops

---

4   P. Stanhope, *History of the War of the Succession in Spain*, p.94.

GIBRALTAR
Sampt dem Hafen, und negst
angelegener Gegend.

Alt Gibraltar

Mont de Singe

Castiel

GIBRALTAR

Baja de Gibraltar

8. A contemporary engraving of the Bay of Gibraltar

that they had promised and neither could the British and Dutch troops in Portugal be spared. Hesse-Darmstadt was supposed to command 5,000 troops but instead he had to make do with a force scraped together from various marines. This consisted of four British marine regiments totalling 1,900 men, 400 Dutch marines and about 70 Spanish/Catalan volunteers.

Hesse-Darmstadt's Force (2,400 men):
Seymour's Marines (later 4th Foot)
Saunderson's Marines (later 30th Foot)
Villiers' Marines (later 31st Foot)
Fox's Marines (later 32nd Foot)   1,900 British marines
Dutch marines from the Dutch ships   400 men
Catalan volunteers from Barcelona   70 men

At first this lack of land troops did not seem to be crucial. Lisbon was full of

rumours of French attempts to besiege fortresses in Italy with naval assistance. If the rumours proved true the fleet would sail to the threatened fortress and drive the French naval support away. This operation had priority over the attempt to seize a Spanish port but there was no hard news about whether it was actually happening or not. A letter suggesting that the French were preparing to move on the port of Nizza arrived and Rooke decided that he had to act. On 8 May the fleet left for Italy expecting to be engaged in naval action and therefore the lack of land forces would not be important. Once on the journey Hesse-Darmstadt suggested that they could stop at Barcelona, scene of his triumph of 1697 and on the route the fleet was taking, to see if anything could be achieved there. Rooke agreed to this as long as the conditions were favourable and there was only a short delay. On 29 May the fleet arrived at Barcelona. The Confederates knew that there was discontent in Barcelona and that some of the leaders of the area favoured the Confederate cause. Hesse Darmsatdt hoped that the large fleet could overawe the defenders and gain some kind of advantage. The marines landed and the fleet lightly bombarded the defences to back up Hesse-Darmstadt's demands, but the Spanish were not impressed. So on 1 June the fleet departed Barcelona to continue to Nizza. A few days later, on 4 June, a dispatch ship caught up with the fleet with the news that Nizza was not being attacked and so the fleet did not need to continue. This also meant that the French fleet, the one that was supposed to be attacking Nizza, was still at large. Rooke was reluctant to commit the fleet to any action until the French fleet was neutralised. So for nearly two months Rooke waited for the French fleet to do something. Meanwhile Hesse-Darmstadt and others were getting increasingly annoyed with Rooke's attitude and tried to get him to undertake various schemes that they suggested, primarily to attempt to take

9. The Battle of Malaga, 24 August 1704, by Isaac Sailmaker

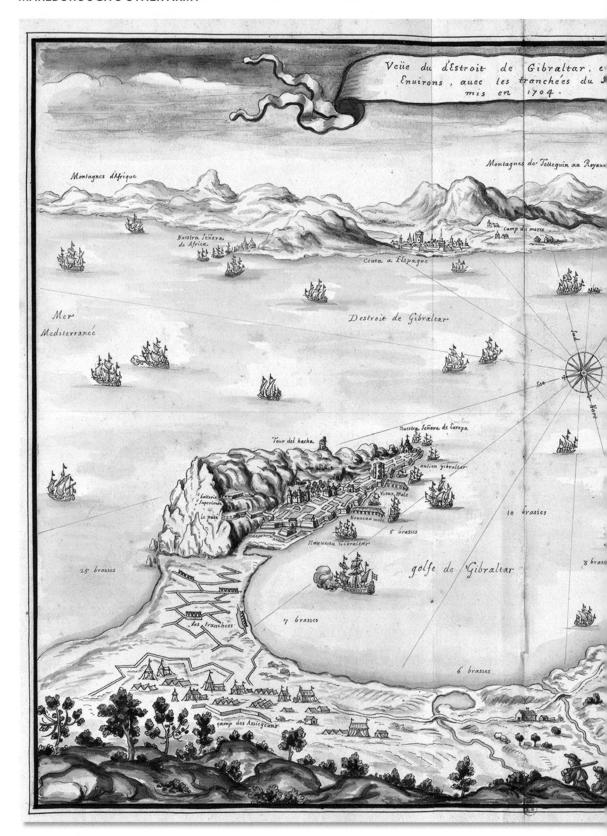

10. A contemporary view of the taking of Gibraltar, 1704

11. (above): Prince George of Hesse-Darmstadt

12. (below): Admiral Sir George Rooke, by Michael Dahl

Cadiz. Rooke was reluctant, believing that he and Hesse-Darmstadt did not have enough forces to achieve the objectives. The deadlock was finally broken on 28 July when Hesse-Darmstadt persuaded Rooke that they did have the resources to take Gibraltar. Gibraltar was at the time a relatively minor fortress and many troops from the area had been sent to Portugal; Villadarias' troops mentioned above had come from this area, for example. It was hoped that it could be easily taken and provide some kind of success for the expedition. It was also an important strategic position despite its' relatively small size.

From July 31 the Confederate forces assembled at Gibraltar and commenced operations. The fortress was defended by 80 regular soldiers, 390 militia and volunteers. Hesse-Darmstadt had 2,400 men along with numerous sailors taken from the fleet in support. Crucially he also had access to nearly 1,500 heavy guns mounted on the various ships in the fleet. By 3 August preparations were complete and the attack started with an enormous bombardment by the fleet. After five hours of this part of the defences were flattened and the decision was made to send the troops in to capture them. Shortly afterwards these defences were occupied without resistance and it was clear that the garrison was not capable of resisting much further. After negotiations it was agreed that the garrison would surrender in three days if relief had not arrived, a common face-saving formula of the time. So, on 6 August the Spanish marched out of Gibraltar and Hesse-Darmstadt's forces took possession of the fortress.

The initial garrison of Gibraltar consisted of the attacking forces with the addition of 72 British sailors left by the fleet. The fleet then departed to eventually fight the French navy at the drawn Battle of Malaga. Hesse-Darmstadt was in command of the garrison. It was clear that the Bourbon forces would react to the capture of the fortress and so he immediately set to repairing the damaged parts of the fortress and improving the defences. By 24 August the first Spanish forces had arrived in the area and started to blockade the fortress. At first the number of forces was small but over time the number of besiegers grew. In early October a French naval squadron arrived off Gibraltar. This cut off the beleaguered garrison completely and also brought substantial land troops to aid the besiegers. By this time the besiegers numbered 12,000 men, 4,000 French and 8,000 Spanish. It was now that the siege started in earnest and by the end of October serious attacks on the fortress started. These attacks mounted over time.

The arrival of a relieving naval squadron in early November enabled the French naval squadron to be driven off. This squadron brought fresh supplies and some of the sailors disembarked and participated in the subsequent land actions. Both the supplies and extra manpower were sorely needed as the Bourbon bombardment and attacks continued, but without success. By December the garrison of Gibraltar had dwindled to around 1,000 men and despair was setting in, there were even some attempts at mutiny to force surrender. Yet the enemy still pursued the siege and pressed the attack. It was therefore decided by the Confederate high command to send more troops to bolster the depleted defenders. Luckily by this time reinforcements had arrived in the theatre and the campaigning on the Portuguese border had died down.

During the invasion of Portugal four British and Dutch regiments had been captured and also many other loses had been sustained from normal campaign wastage. There was also growing dissatisfaction with Schomberg, who had been ineffective as a commander, and also been the centre of much disagreement. Therefore it was decided to send a replacement British commander and additional troops to strengthen the army. The new British commander was Henri de Massue, originally Marquis de Ruvigny but now Earl of Galway. Galway was a French Huguenot who had fought with distinction for his homeland until forced by his religious convictions to change sides. He was an experienced soldier who was to be a key to events in the war. The new commander brought new troops with him, although they did not arrive until November. The reinforcements consisted of a new cavalry regiment, four infantry battalions and 2,230 replacements.

Reinforcements
British:
Cunningham's Dragoons (four squadrons – 443 men) later the 8th Dragoons
Guards detachment from the 1st and Coldstream Guards (700 men)
Lord Donegal's (876 men) later the 35th Foot
1,500 British replacements
Dutch:
Bruhese's (NL 4)
Waes' (NL 33)
1,320 men in the two above battalions.
730 Dutch replacements.

In early August news of the capture of Gibraltar arrived in Portugal. Soon it was clear that many of the enemy troops in the border area had left the area to join the attempt to recapture Gibraltar. This meant that the Confederates could attempt an offensive on land. It was decided to strike towards, and

Des Barons de Pointis Flotte wird in der Bay von Gibraltar geschlagen den 20 Mart: 1705

13 Pointis' fleet is repelled in the Bay of Gibraltar, March 1705

hopefully capture, Ciudad Rodrigo. To do this an army of 20,000 men (3,000 cavalry and 17,000 infantry) was assembled at Almeida. In theory these were under the command of the Portuguese king and the Confederate candidate for the Spanish throne. In reality, command was with Das Minas, the Portuguese general, and Galway. In 26 September the army started to advance towards the River Aqueda. They needed to cross this river to continue but Berwick had assembled his forces on the opposite bank to block their advance. On 2 October Das Minas' army reached the Aqueda and the fragile Portuguese supply arrangements collapsed. Because of this it took five days before Berwick's defences could be probed. It soon became clear that Berwick had taken up a strong position. This was enough to persuade Minas to abandon the attack and retire to Portugal. Both Minas and Berwick were then content to end the campaign and reorganise for the following year.

The end of the campaign on the border meant that reinforcements could be sent to Gibraltar. These consisted of three British battalions, a Dutch battalion and possibly a Portuguese battalion. These forces, arriving on 23 December, were as follows:

December Reinforcements for Gibraltar

British:
Guards detachment (1st and Coldstream Guards) – around 700 men.
Lord Donegal's (35th Foot) – around 876 men.
Barrymore's (13th Foot) – probably round 600 men

Others:
Waes' Dutch regiment – around 400 men
A Portuguese regiment?

Notes: Barrymore's regiment was probably around 600 strong as these units seemed to have totalled about 2,180 initially. It seems that 1,900 landed at Gibraltar and 280 were captured while attempting to land. This seems to be confirmed by an entry in the Calendar of State Papers.[5] This states that the Guards, Donegal's and Barrymore's regiments totalled 108 sergeants, 108 corporals, 72 drummers, 1,900 'effective' privates plus a complete complement of officers, about 120 to 130 in total. This gives a total of about 2,320 men. The Portuguese regiment is not mentioned by all sources and so may not have been present. Yet as information on the Portuguese is scarce it may be that their participation has just been missed. It is also possible that this unit has been misidentified and confused with the Catalan volunteers who were with the initial assault force. There was a unit of Catalan exiles in Portugal which was called the Tercio del Almirante de Castilla or sometimes Tercio de Enríquez de Cabrera y Toledo. Some sources record that three companies, or possibly more, of this unit served at Gibraltar but there is no mention of them elsewhere. It seems likely that this unit is the 'Portuguese' regiment that was in Gibraltar. Because it was actually Catalan other sources may have confused it with the Catalan volunteers from Barcelona. They may also have dismissed it and failed to list it after confusing it with the volunteers, probably because they assumed it was the relatively small number of volunteers rather than the approximately 500 men the tercio could muster. Francis suggests that the 500-man Portuguese unit was under the command of Montandre, a Huguenot proposed by Galway.[6] This could mean that the unit was a more of an ad hoc group, perhaps a new unit formed out of available personnel or a detachment from other unknown units. The number given for the Waes regiment may be without officers, NCOs, etc. The entry in the Calendar of State Papers mentioned above says that this unit was 500 strong.

By the time the December reinforcements arrived at Gibraltar the French navy was back in the area and so the reinforcements had a little trouble getting to Gibraltar. Four companies of the 13th and 35th regiments were captured in their boats as they tried to land. 280 men were captured and so only 1,900 British troops arrived. The reinforcements were soon in the thick of the continuing Bourbon attacks. The end of campaigning on the Portuguese border had also released enemy forces to reinforce the attackers

---

5   C.S. Knighton (ed.), *Calendar of State Papers, Domestic Series, of the Reign of Queen Anne*, vol. 2 1704–05, entry 1198.
6   D. Francis, *The First Peninsular War: 1702–1713*, p.137.

at Gibraltar. At this time Berwick was replaced by Marshal de Tessé. Berwick did not agree with the concentration on retaking Gibraltar and refused to go there in person to achieve it. He was thus replaced by someone who would prosecute the attack more vigorously. With fresh troops and a fresh commander the assaults continued and even grew in strength.

Over the following months the Bourbon forces bombarded, assaulted and tried everything they could think of to dislodge the defenders but without success. By March 1705, with the garrison again getting dangerously small, further Confederate reinforcements were prepared.

March 1705 Reinforcement
Bruhese's Dutch regiment (NL 4)
Montjoy's British regiment
Total 1,200 men
Another two Portuguese battalions were put on stand by to go but were not committed.

The uneventful transporting of these troops showed that the end of the siege was near as it was clear that the enemy's resolve was weakening. The arrival of these troops convinced Tessé that it was not possible to take Gibraltar. By the beginning of April he had decided to abandon the effort and started to disengage his forces from the complicated positions they found themselves in. From 20–28 April the besieging forces slipped away largely without interference and the siege ended, as did the 1704 campaign.

The Confederates had managed to secure the important fortress of Gibraltar to use as a base in the future. They had the worst of the fighting on the border but given the state of the army their losses could have been a lot greater.

6

The 1705 Campaign: Frustration at Badajoz and Triumph at Barcelona

During the 1705 campaign there were three main areas of activity. At the start of 1705 the siege of Gibraltar was still in full swing and would continue to be an active front until the end of April. The Portuguese army, along with allied units attached to it, were still stationed along the border with Spain and would campaign there during the coming campaign season. Finally, in the summer, another expeditionary force would arrive from Britain and Holland. This force under the Earl of Peterborough would sail to Barcelona and form the basis of the Confederate army in Catalonia.

In January 1705 there were a number of reports, recorded in the Calendar of State Papers,[1] which give details of the strengths of British units at this time.

- Harvey's Horse: 18 sergeants/corporals, 13 drummers, 174 rank and file. 32 men short of establishment. 205 men in total, which with officers would be around 220 men.
- Royal Dragoons: 40 sergeants/corporals, 32 drummers, 276 rank and file. 132 short of establishment. 348 men in total, which with officers would be around 370 men.
- Cunningham's Dragoons: 30 sergeants/corporals, 24 drummers, 168 rank and file. 138 short of establishment. 222 men in total, which with officers would be around 240 men.
- Portmore's Foot: 78 sergeants/corporals, 26 drummers, 593 rank and file. 57 short of establishment. 697 men in total, which with officers would be around 740 men.
- Blood's Foot: 78 sergeants/corporals, 26 drummers, 627 rank and file. 23 short of establishment. 731 men in total, which with officers would be around 775 men.

---

1   C.S. Knighton (ed.), *Calendar of State Papers, Domestic Series, of the Reign of Queen Anne*, vol. 2 1704–05.

- Duncanson's Foot: 78 sergeants/corporals, 26 drummers, 602 rank and file. 48 short of establishment. 706 men in total, which with officers would be around 750 men.
- Brundenell's Foot: 78 sergeants/corporals, 26 drummers, 586 rank and file. 64 short of establishment. 690 men in total, which with officers would be around 730 men.
- Montjoy's Foot: 78 sergeants/corporals, 26 drummers, 583 rank and file. 67 short of establishment. 687 men in total, which with officers would be around 730 men.

Another entry, number 1198, gives a similar picture. This has an overall total for the three cavalry regiments and five infantry regiments listed above. According to this entry these units had 223 sergeants, 255 corporal, 199 drummers, 3,709 effective privates. They were 561 short of establishment. This gives 4,386 men in total, which with officers would be around 4,650 men. 750 British recruits and replacements would arrive later in the year. Clearly the aim was to make good the short fall although of course by the time the recruits arrived the short fall would be greater.

Interestingly this entry also states that Stuart's/Stewart's and Stanhope's regiments had a total of about 300 altogether. These two units had been captured during the 1704 campaign. Arrangements had been made to exchange 640 men from these regiments and they would later return to Portugal. They were used to rebuild Stuart/Stewart's regiment which then joined the field army again. The remnants of Stanhope's regiment were then sent back to Britain to recruit the unit back to strength. Stanhope stayed in Portugal and so the unit became Hill's.

Gibraltar

Up until the end of April the siege of Gibraltar continued, see chapter 5 for details. The following units were at Gibraltar in April when campaigning elsewhere commenced:

British:
4 Marine battalions: Seymour's (4th Foot), Saunderson's (30th Foot), Villiers' (31st Foot), Fox's (32nd Foot)
4 Infantry battalions: Guards detachment, Barrymore's (13th Foot), Donegal's (35th Foot), Montjoy's

Others:
Three non-British battalions: Bruhese's (NL 4), Waes' (NL 33), and an unknown Portuguese tercio (battalion)

Frustration at Badajoz

The continuing siege of Gibraltar meant that considerable amounts of the enemy's troops were tied down. This in turn meant that the forces in Portugal had an opportunity to strike across the border into Spain. As in 1704 there were initially two concentrations of Confederate forces in 1705. In Beira province, north of the River Tejo, was Das Minas, while to the south of the river in Alentejo Province based around Estremoz was the larger army under the nominal command of Las Galveas. Las Galveas was in his eighties and not up to active campaigning so the actual command was shared by the Portuguese general Corzana, the British general Galway and the Dutch general Fagel. Each commander would take it in turns to be in overall command for a week at a time.

The plan was to field an army of 25,000 infantry, 6,000 cavalry and 32 guns – 31,000 men in total. There were to be 10,000 in Das Minas' command and the other 21,000 in Las Galveas'.[2] These numbers were clearly theoretical sizes and in reality the numbers would be smaller. The combined forces, according to the *Österreichische militärische Zeitschrift*[3] came to 22,200 infantry and 5,000 cavalry. These were divided into 39 infantry battalions and 50 cavalry squadrons. The infantry consisted of 30 Portuguese battalions (tercios), five British battalions and four Dutch battalions. seven of the Portuguese battalions were 'militia', presumably auxiliary units. The cavalry consisted of 40 Portuguese squadrons and 10 British and Dutch squadrons. It is known that two of the three British cavalry regiments still did not have enough horses to take the field at this time. It seems likely that the situation was the same with the Dutch cavalry. It seems unlikely that the British and Dutch could actually field 10 squadrons, at least at anything like full strength, because of the continuing shortage of horses. It is also possibly that the numbers of Portuguese cavalry were similarly over stated.

Parnell details the forces as follows:[4]

Southern Group, in Alentejo Province: about 26 battalions and 33 or 34 squadrons, although probably the squadrons were very small or less squadrons were really available as not all had horses. About 17,000 men under the nominal command of Portuguese Count De Las Galveas. The contingent commanders took it in turn to be the actual commander.

14. Charles Mordaunt, 3rd Earl of Peterborough, by Sir Godfrey Kneller. (National Portrait Gallery, London)

---

2   *Österreichische militärische Zeitschrift*, Band 1 1838, p.164.
3   *Österreichische militärische Zeitschrift*, Band 2 1838, p.241.
4   A. Parnell, *The War of Succession in Spain: 1702–1711*, p.123.

Portuguese contingent under Corzana – about 12,000 men
Cavalry: about 24 squadrons
Infantry: about 17 battalions (tercios)

British contingent under Galway – about 2,700 men
Cavalry: Harvey's Horse (200 men)
Infantry: five battalions – Blood's, Brudenell's, Portmore's, Stuart's/ Stewart's and Duncanson's.

Dutch contingent under Fagel – about 2,300 men
Cavalry: Up to five squadrons drawn from Rhoo's Horse (two squadrons), Schlippenbach's (one squadron) and Mattha's Dragoon (two squadrons). It is likely that not all of these had horses and were active.
Infantry: four battalions – Friesheim's, Noyelles en Falais', Vicouse's and Welderen's.
Artillery: 24 Portuguese field guns, five British Sakers (5-pounders), 20 heavy siege guns, 80 Coehorn mortars, seven other mortars.

Unavailable: The British Royal and Cunningham Dragoons were not available for active service, they were left in Lisbon as they were short of horses.

Northern Group, in Beira Province: about 13 battalions and 16 or 17 squadrons. About 8,000 to 9,000 men under the overall command of Portuguese Marquis Das Minas.
All of the units were Portuguese in this command.
It is not known how many battalions and squadrons were with the two groups but the northern group was about half the size of the southern group. Therefore it is likely that given the total numbers of battalions and squadrons the numbers given are approximately correct in theory. As the British, and probably the Dutch, might not have actually fielded all their cavalry units the number of squadrons in the south was probably less. Similarly there is no indication about the size of Das Minas' command. It would have numbered around 8 to 9,000 men based on the suggestion that this command was about half the size of Las Galveas'.
In the Calendar of State Papers there is a breakdown of the strengths of the British foot regiments in Portugal in January 1705:[5]

Blood's:	495 well, 137 sick, 66 men short. Total 698 men.
Brudenell's	499 well, 65 sick, 134 men short. Total 698 men.
Portmore's	593 well, 43 sick, 62 men short. Total 698 men.
Stuart's/Stewart's	647 well, 25 sick, 26 men short. Total 698 men.
Duncanson's	538 well, 49 sick, 111 men short. Total 698 men.
Total:	2,772 well, 319 sick, 399 men short.

---

5   C.S. Knighton (ed.), *Calendar of State Papers, Domestic Series, of the Reign of Queen Anne*, vol 4, 1705–06, p.46.

The figures are for 'effective men, including corporals' and clearly do not include officers and others normally part of a unit.

Duncan states that during this year the British sent six 3-pounder mountain guns, often called grasshopper guns, but there is not any other evidence for these being used.[6]

It was decided that Das Minas would attack towards Ciudad Rodrigo in the north. In the south the army would strike into the Spanish province of Extramadura. Galway wished to go straight to the principal fortress of the area, Badajoz. The other Confederate commanders were more cautious and wished to tackle some smaller targets first. So it was decided that the first target would be the fortress of Valenza. The army marched on 24 April and arrived at Valenza on 2 May. By 8 May a practical breach had been made in the defences. An assault was made and forced the garrison back into the castle where they then surrendered. The next target was another small fortress, Albuquerque. The attack on Albuquerque started on 16 May and by 20 May this fortress had also been taken.

Meanwhile Das Minas had also advanced. He moved to Salvatierra, which he took and then he did the same with Sarca. Previous to this time there had been no enemy field forces in the area but as the fighting at Gibraltar had now stopped the enemy forces from that place started to arrive. Berwick had been replaced by Tessé and during May Tessé arrived in the area, closely followed by some of his troops. Tessé did not have enough troops to confront Las Galveas' command but he could attempt to curb Das Minas' activities. He therefore detached 6,000 to 7,000 troops under Thouy to confront Minas' command. The approach of Thouy's troops was enough to convince Das Minas to end his activities and to pull back. Both sides in the north now lapsed into inactivity as they went into summer quarters.

Having taken Albuquerque the decision was finally made for the southern group to advance to Badajoz, but Tessé was now active in the area. He did not have a large army but he manoeuvred his force to slow down Las Galveas' advance. By 4 June the Confederates were within four miles of Badajoz but doubts were growing about the feasibility of the project. The Portuguese were no longer in favour of the project and also the heat of the summer was approaching. With the joint commanders unable to agree the army dithered.

LE MAL DE TESSÉ.

15. René de Froulay, Comte de Tessé, by Rigaud

---

6 F. Duncan, *History of the Royal Regiment of Artillery*, vol. 1 (London: John Murray, 1879, 3rd ed., p.66).

On 13 June orders arrived to break the deadlock and the army was ordered to withdraw back to Portugal and go into summer quarters.

During the summer the situation in Iberia was transformed by Peterborough's expedition to Barcelona and the aftermath of this. The success of this expedition meant that the frontier region had not been greatly reinforced by Bourbon troops. Once again an attempt to take Badajoz would be made when campaigning resumed after the summer break, although Fagel was not in favour of this. Das Minas was now in overall command but still with Corzana, Fagel and Galway taking it in turn to be in actual command. The forces to be used were the two forces from earlier in the campaign. They were to combined and now operated together. On 30 September the two groups met at Caya. The combined army was about 21,000 strong and consisted of 16,400 Portuguese, 2,500 British and 2,100 Dutch troops. Details are not known but were probably generally the same as earlier in the campaign. The two British dragoon regiments were now with the forces in Catalonia, but they had not actually been with the army earlier. It is also possible that some of the Portuguese forces were left in garrison, most likely the auxiliaries formerly with the army.

The French general Tessé was again tasked with trying to stop the attempt to capture Badajoz. Tessé only had about 4,000 troops and so he was at first only able to watch from a distance. The invaders reached Badajoz on 2 October and by 11 October they were ready to start bombarding the fortress. Soon a breach had been made and preparations were made to assault the fortress. Meanwhile Tessé had received 7,000 reinforcements and decided he must act before this could happen. On the night of 13 October Tessé moved with the bulk of his troops to relieve the garrison of Badajoz. Tessé attacked the outposts first thing in the morning and caused some panic, Fagel in particular did not perform well. During the confusion Tessé managed to reinforce the garrison with 1,000 fresh troops. Having stabilised the situation Tessé once again pulled back. Now his force was larger Tessé could take up a threatening position near Badajoz. Realising that this force would have to be dislodged for the siege to continue Fagel, the commander at the time, led the army to confront Tessé. Tessé was in a very strong position and so Fagel was reluctant to attack. Fagel instead bombarded Tessé's position but with little effect. Having made half-hearted attempts to change the situation Fagel recommended withdrawal and Das Minas agreed. So on 16 October the army started to retrace its steps and within a few days was back in Portugal. Shortly afterwards the army returned to quarters and finished campaigning for 1705.

Fagel was disillusioned with the constant arguments and had earlier in the campaign expressed the desire to return to Holland. So with the disappointments of the autumn campaign he decided to leave and return home. The Confederates in Portugal had achieved some successes but given the weakness of their opponents they had missed a great opportunity. It was clear to all that the division amongst the commanders had robbed them of the chance to make a big impact on the war. This lacklustre campaign was a contrast to the major events of the 1705 campaign in Iberia which were being played out in Catalonia and surrounding areas.

The Barcelona Expedition

Following the success of the capture of Gibraltar in 1704 the high command decided to attempt another amphibious attack in 1705. Barcelona, the capital of Catalonia, was an attractive target for such an attack. Rumours and intelligence suggested that the Catalans were discontented and inclined to support the Confederate cause. To lead this new expedition the Earl of Peterborough was appointed, also becoming the senior British commander in Iberia. Peterborough had a little military experience but was a politician. He was also a politician with a history of causing problems, even to his friends, and controversy. His appointment was at least partially motivated by the desire to get him out of the way.

Peterborough had the services of a strong naval force and initially a force of 11 battalions.

Peterborough's Initial Force
    British: six regiments
        From England:
        Rivers' (formerly Columbine's, later 6th foot)
        H. Hamilton's (later 34th Foot)
        Elliot's (later disbanded)
        From Ireland:
        Charlemont's (later 36th Foot)
        Gorge's (later disbanded)
        J. Caulfield's (later disbanded)
    Dutch: 2 Marine regiments with two battalions each.
        St. Amant's (NL 5)
        Palm's, formerly Swansbel's (NL 24)
    Catalans: Ahumada regiment (formerly Tercio del Almirante de Castilla and sometimes called 1st Spanish regiment) – one battalion of about 470–500 men.

Note: It is not known if most of these units still contained pikes. Elliot's regiment had replaced their pikes but we have no information about the other units. It is likely that as Elliot's unit was pikeless they all were.

These units arrived at Lisbon during June – by this time the campaign on the border had wound down for the summer. Similarly the Bourbon siege of Gibraltar had finished. This meant that the potential existed to reinforce the attacking force. A conference of senior commander was called on 11 July when it was decided that the experienced Hesse-Darmstadt would accompany the expedition. Archduke Charles, the Confederate candidate for the Spanish throne, would also accompany the expedition. In addition the expedition would take troops from the other forces in Iberia. The two British dragoon regiments which were in Lisbon were to accompany the expedition. They had so far taken little part in the war due to lack of horses but now had enough to take the field. It was also agreed that the expedition would stop at Gibraltar before launching their attack. They would leave two of the inexperienced British units with the expedition at this time to garrison

Gibraltar. As the threat to Gibraltar had receded the expedition would take the eight experienced British marine and infantry regiments in exchange for the two new units.

Units left at Gibraltar: Elliot's and J. Caulfield's regiments.

Final Composition of Expedition
  British: eight squadrons and 12 battalions
    Initial Forces:
    Charlemont's (36th Foot), Gorge's, H. Hamilton's (34th Foot) and Rivers' (6th Foot)
    From Lisbon:
    Royal (1st Dragoons) and Cunningham's Dragoons (8th Dragoons)
    From Gibraltar:
    Marine regiments: Seymour's (4th Foot), Saunderson's (30th Foot), Villiers' (31st Foot), Fox's (32nd Foot)

Infantry regiments: Guards detachment, Barrymore's (13th Foot), Donegal's (35th Foot), Montjoy's

Dutch: 4 battalions
St. Amant's (NL 5) and Palm's (NL 24)

Catalans: 1 battalion
Ahumada regiment.

On 5 August the fleet left Gibraltar and sailed towards Barcelona. Five days later the expedition paused on its journey to get water near the fortress of Denia in Valencia. The locals soon heard that Archduke Charles was with the expedition and indicated their support of his cause. This included the garrison of Denia, who left the fortress, which was promptly occupied by the Confederates. After a few days the expedition continued on to Barcelona and they arrived there on 22 August. Over the next few days the troops started to land and moved close to Barcelona but did not actually attack it. The problem was that Peterborough was not convinced that the expedition was capable of taking Barcelona and instead he favoured sailing to Italy. Peterborough held a series of conferences designed to convince the leaders of the expedition to go to Italy or possible move to Valencia and campaign there. This idea was not popular and Sir Cloudesley Shovell, the commander of the fleet, and Hesse-Darmstadt were in favour of at least attempting to take Barcelona before going somewhere else. Archduke Charles was initially neutral but also came to be in favour of some kind of attempt on Barcelona over time.

The impasse in the high command took three weeks to resolve, during which the Spanish defenders of Barcelona strengthened their defences. After much confusion the Confederate high command finally reached a decision. Hesse-Darmstadt undertook to attack and attempt to take an important outlying position of Montjuic. The supporters of an attack on Barcelona hoped that by taking it the Earl of Peterborough, and the other opponents of an attack, would be encouraged to sanction the attack on Barcelona. Peterborough and the opponents in turn thought that a failure to capture the Montjuic fort would lead to the expedition moving on to try something else.

For this attack Hesse-Darmstadt assembled a selected assault force. The spearhead of the attack was to be 400 British grenadiers and they were supported by 600 infantry (400 British, 100 Dutch and 100 Spanish) under Charlemont. In reserve were 300 dragoons and 1,000 more infantry under Stanhope. Hesse-Darmstadt would accompany the attack and direct it personally. During the night of 13–14 September this force moved into position and on the 14th the assault started. The initial attack was quickly brought to a halt by the defenders. Hesse-Darmstadt then decided to attack again and personally led the troops forward. Barely had this attack started when he was hit and died shortly afterwards. The death of the greatly respected German commander initially halted the attacks but soon they were renewed as various groups resolved to continue the job that the valiant commander had lost his life trying to do. These subsequent attacks succeeded in pushing the defenders back and allowed the capture of the outer works of the fort. This gave the Confederates the space to bring up artillery and soon these guns started to bombard the remaining defences. On 17 September the guns hit the powder store and soon afterwards the garrison of Montjuic surrendered.

The fall of Montjuic meant that the attack on Barcelona could now commence. Sir Cloudesley Shovell disembarked 2,500 British and 680 Dutch sailors who were formed into ad hoc units for their land based duties. About 3,000 miquelets were also available to prosecute the siege along with numerous ordinary local people. Miquelets were irregular troops who supported the Confederate cause. The navy also commenced a bombardment and sent some of the heavy guns from their ships to do duty as land-based siege artillery. While the navy and Spanish irregulars continued with the siege the various regular troops largely watched. The loss of their energetic leader Hesse-Darmstadt seems to have led to a period of inactivity. By 24 September some of the siege guns were in place and the bombardment of the defences started in earnest. Over the following days more guns were added to the effort. On 3 October the Confederate guns opened a large breach in the defence which could be assaulted. The garrison had not been very active during the siege and when summoned to surrender with honour on 4 October they readily agreed, and it was agreed that they would march out on the 14th. The angry citizens of Barcelona took matters into their own hands and started to attack the Spanish garrison and they had to seek the protection of the Confederates earlier than schedule. Around 2,500 of the garrison were so disaffected that they decided to join the Confederate cause rather than travel away with the remainder of the Spanish troops.

The capture of Barcelona, a major city and second only to Madrid in Spain, was a major achievement for the Confederates. It had been captured relatively cheaply and this alone justified the decision to send the expedition to this area. Yet the situation was to get even better. With the Confederate forces gaining success around Barcelona the pro-Confederate sympathisers in Catalonia rose in support. This resulted in the miquelets arriving at Barcelona, as mentioned above, to aid in the taking of the city. Meanwhile across Catalonia other irregular forces moved to secure the other fortresses in the province. Catalonia was quickly secured and became the heart of the Confederate effort in Spain for the rest of the war. To the south of Catalonia was the province of Valencia and this too was rising in revolt. With the help of a Spanish dragoon regiment, under Don Rafeal Nebot, which switched sides, local irregular forces managed to win over most of this province as well. Only the fortress of Alicante remained loyal to Philip and his French allies in Valencia.

The capture of Barcelona, Catalonia and Valencia also brought the forces in the area some welcome additional units. These units were the true start of the Carolean Spanish army that would feature in the rest of the war, and indeed in some cases they fought to the bitter end of the war in Spain. By the end of 1705 the Carolean army consisted of eight regular infantry and seven regular cavalry units, along with numerous irregular formations. One of the infantry units was the Ahumada regiment, sometimes identified as the 1st regiment; this may have recruited an extra battalion at this time. This unit had formerly been counted as part of the Portuguese army but now transferred to Charles' army. The second unit was a small regiment of Aragon rebels raised by Ferrer, this unit is sometimes identified as the 2nd regiment. This numbered less than 200 men and was lost when Spanish forces moved to secure Aragon in late December 1705 and early 1706. The other six regiments all came from Barcelona. Five of them were former units of the Spanish army, one was a Neapolitan unit in the service of the Spanish. The final regiment was composed of Germans living in Barcelona, primarily former members of a German unit commanded by Hesse-Darmstadt in 1697 and disbanded in the city at the end of the conflict. These units are sometimes identified as regiments three to six. The cavalry was similarly a mixed bag of units. Three of them were former Spanish units. One was from Barcelona, one from Valencia and the last probably a collection of individuals. The other four units were raised by sympathetic Catalans, two in November and two in December.

These were the units of the Carolean Spanish army by the end of 1705:

Infantry:
- 1st Regiment: Ahumada – two battalions: former unit of exiles in the Portuguese army
- 2nd Regiment: Ferrer's – about 170 men: Aragon rebels destroyed when the Spanish advanced to Barcelona.
- 3rd Regiment: Don Antonio Paguera's – one battalion: Later the 'Reials Guàrdies Catalanes', the Catalonian Guards.
- 4th Regiment: Don Joseph Paguera's – one battalion: Later the 'Reina Anna' or Noyelles.
- 5th Regiment: Colbatch's or Kaulbars' – one battalion: German regiment.
- 6th Regiment: Castiglioni's or Castillione's – two battalions: Neapolitan unit, formerly Tercio de Recco in the Spanish army.
- 7th Regiment: Generalitat de Catalunya or Diputació del General (La Deputacion) – one battalion: Former Spanish unit.
- 8th Regiment: Ciutat de Barcelona or El Rei (La Cuidad or City) –

two battalions: former Spanish unit.
- 10th Regiment: Diputació del Regne de València – a few companies at first but raised to one battalion within a few months.

Cavalry:
- 1st Cavalry: Zinzendorff's Dragoons or El Rei or Dragons del Rei: 500 former Spanish dragoons from the Barcelona garrison.
- 2nd Cavalry: Morras' Horse: Probably formed from 150 mixed recruits from various garrison – a Castellan/Navarrese unit. But possible a new regiment raised in November 1705.
- 3rd Cavalry: Subies or Sobie's Horse: Probably a new Catalan unit raised in November 1705 but possibly the mixed recruits mentioned above.
- 4th Cavalry: Don Rafeal Nebot's Horse: 500 former Spanish cavalry from the garrison of Valencia.
- 5th Cavalry: Joan Nebot's Horse: Raised in Catalonia, December 1705.
- 6th Cavalry: Josep Nebot's Dragoons: Raised in Catalonia, December 1705.
- 7th Cavalry: Josep Moragues Horse: Raised in Catalonia, November 1705.

In December the Confederates dispersed some of their forces around the area they controlled:
- To Lérida on the Aragon border: Cunningham's Dragoons, 'the English Marines' (probably two units only, including Saunderson's now commanded by Wills), two Dutch battalions (probably Palm's regiment), Castiglioni's Neapolitans (two battalions) and the Ahumada regiment. Total 3,700 men.
- To Gerona near the French border: Charlemont's Foot, two Dutch battalions (probably St. Amant's regiment), one Carolean Spanish regiment (probably Don Joseph Paguera's 4th Regiment). Total 2,000 men.
- To Tortosa on the Valencia border (this province was not secure at the time): Royal Dragoons, Barrymore's, Donegal's and Montjoy's Foot.

7

The Carolean Spanish Army

The Spanish fought on both sides during this war. Some supported the French candidate Philip as Spanish king and others supporting the Confederate candidate Charles. Although there were some early armed Spanish supporters of Charles the Carolean army only became a reality following the arrival of the expedition to Barcelona in 1705. Barcelona is the capital of Catalonia and its capture sparked the formation of a significant Carolean party in Spain. Catalonia was the core area of support for Charles and indeed continued the fight even after Charles had given up the struggle. Catalonia provided the largest contingent of troops to Charles' forces. However, a significant number of units were recruited from other parts of Spain and elsewhere.

After the events of 1705 the Carolean Spanish army was a significant numerical part of the Confederate forces in Iberia. Yet the number of units that feature in the field army was generally smaller. This was because much of the army was normally tied up garrisoning Catalonia and nearby areas.

Carolean Spanish Organisation and Tactics

Infantry

Initially the organisation of the Carolean infantry was confused. It seems likely that the Ahumada regiment used Portuguese organisation as it was formed in Portugal. The units of the army which had formerly been part of the Bourbon Spanish army probably retained the organisation of that army. Unfortunately the organisation of this army was in the process of changing at the time and so it is not clear which organisation these units actually had. Finally the units which were raised in the initial stages of the conflict in Catalonia, and surrounding areas, are totally unknown. But it is likely that they would use the Spanish army organisation as this would be familiar. In 1706 to clear up the confusion Charles issued regulations fixing the organisation to be used by units in his army. This organisation, with minor changes, was used during the remainder of the war.

Organisation up to 1706[1]

Ahumada Regiment: Probably Portuguese organisation – see above for details of Portuguese organisation.

Spanish Organisation: Probably used by the existing units and newly raised units in the early stages of the conflict. Up until 1704 Spanish infantry were in 'tercios'. In late 1704 the organisation changed and units became regiments of a single battalion.

Tercios (up to 1704): Staff of seven men, one company of 59 grenadiers, 12 companies of 59 men (including 10 pikemen). Total 773 men.

Regiment (from September 1704): Staff of seven men, one company of 64 grenadiers, 11 companies of 64 men. Total 775 men.

It is not known which of these organisations was used. The units seem to have been called 'regiments' rather than tercios and so may have followed the regimental organisation.

Later Organisation from 1706[2]

Following the ordinances issued in 1706 the organisation of an infantry battalion was set as follows. In theory some units were supposed to muster a second battalion. But often this was on paper only and the units actually only had a single battalion.

Reials Guàrdies (Royal Guard) Organisation: Staff of 11 men, later increased to 16 men. 1,085 men in 12 companies. Total 1,096 (later 1,101) men.

Standard Infantry Organisation: Staff of 11 men, later increased to 16 men. One company of 90 grenadiers. 10 companies of 100 men. Total 1,101 (later 1,106) men.

Bourbon Spanish units at the start of the war retained pikes within their units – 10 pikes to 37 muskets in the early organisation. The pikes were supposed to be replaced in later organisations but it is probable that this took some time to achieve in practice, while newly-raised units in the Carolean army would probably have to make use of available weaponry, possibly including pikes. It is therefore likely that some Carolean units had pikes at the start of their involvement in the Confederate forces. How many did so and how long they kept them is not known.

At the start of the war the various units of the army would have used conventional rank firing tactics of the period. They could have continued using these tactics during the rest of the war, as indeed many armies did. Yet as they fought in conjunction with British and Dutch units it may be that they changed to using the platoon firing that these nations favoured. There is no evidence for this but it was common for other units that operated with the British and Dutch to do this and so it is possible the units of this army did the same.

---

1   C.A. Sapherson, *Armies of Spain 1701–1715* (Leigh-on-Sea: Partizan Press, 1997), pp.3–4.
2   <http://www.11setembre1714.org/Unitats/b-infanteria-frame.html>

Cavalry

As with the infantry it is likely that the Carolean cavalry used the organisation of the Bourbon Spanish forces at least initially and in the early stages of their activity. In 1706 the new regulations issued by Charles also covered the organisation of the mounted troops.

Organisation up to 1706[3]

Spanish organisation used by the existing units and probably by newly raised units in the early stages of the conflict.

Horse regiments: up to four squadrons each of four companies of 40 men.

Dragoon regiments: one horse grenadier company and 11 line companies of 59 men, organised into three squadrons. Total 714 men.

Later Organisation from 1706[4]

Following the regulations of 1706 the Carolean Spanish units changed to the following organisation.

Cavalry Regiments: Staff of 11 men. 10 companies of 57 men. Total 581 men.

The number of staff in the unit was later raised to 18 men.

It is not known what tactics the Carolean Spanish cavalry used. The former units of Philip's army must have used the tactics of the Bourbon Spanish army. These seem to have been similar to the French cavalry tactics of the period but even more aggressive. French cavalry tactics of the period consisted of a charge at the gallop but with little order, sometimes preceded by a volley of pistols before the charge started. The Carolean cavalry probably continued to use the tactics of the Spanish cavalry. As with the infantry it is possible that as the cavalry operated with the British and Dutch cavalry they may have adopted their tactics. It was not as common for this to be the case as with infantry, however.

Artillery

There is little information about Carolean Spanish artillery. It appears to have been standard artillery of the period and as with the other armies involved in these campaigns there is no evidence of 'regimental' or 'battalion' guns.

Miquelets and Militia

The Carolean Spanish army also deployed large numbers of miquelets and militia. Both of these were irregular forces whose organisation varied greatly. They often appeared, or were raised, during times of crisis and then faded away when the situation stabilised. It was rare for these forces to take part in formal battles but they did participate more regularly in irregular actions and skirmishes. Miquelets were mainly Catalans and were renowned for their skills in irregular mountain warfare. Militia were raised more generally but more commonly in non-Catalan areas. Both Miquelets and militia were

---

3   C.A. Sapherson, *Armies of Spain 1701–1715*, pp.13, 21.
4   <http://www.11setembre1714.org/Unitats/b-cavalleria-frame.html>

commonly used as labour in siege operations. Due to their relative numerical strength they often provided 'bulk' to flesh out the small numbers of regular forces available. Francis says of the Miquelets that "They could live on little and were excellent in the kind of fighting they knew, they knew no drill and needed to be handled and employed in a very different way from professional troops."[5] But they would not do anything unless paid regularly and this was often a problem.

The Miquelets were not uniformed but instead wore the common dress of the native villagers. Francis says this was "a loose short overcoat of dark cloth and of a flesh-colour shirt of light wool sometimes with silver buttons". In addition they had "wool breeches, boots of cloth or leather, or sandals, and oilcloth stockings". Equipment consisted of a small pouch slung on a strap, a gourd and some spare clothes and a few simple supplies. Conch shells were used for signalling.

Spanish Uniforms

Not all of the uniforms of the units involved in the campaign are known to us. The following are the known uniforms of the units from this campaign

Cavalry

Unit	Coat	Facing	Waistcoat	Breeches	Buttons & Hat Lace	Saddle Cloth
Zinzendorff's (1st)*	Red	Red	Straw	Straw	Yellow Buttons	Red edged Yellow
Morras (2nd)**	White	Red	Red	Straw	Yellow	Red edged Yellow
R. Nebot (4th)	White	Blue	Blue	Straw	White Buttons, no lace	Blue edged White
Aragon (12th)**	White	Red	White	Straw	Yellow	Red edged Yellow

* The cuffs were edged yellow. The unit wore a brown cap with red front shield edged yellow

** The unit wore visible black back- and breastplates. The Aragon unit may also have worn helmets.

5   D. Francis, *The First Peninsular War: 1702–1713*, p.182.

Infantry

Unit	Coat	Facing	Waistcoat	Breeches	Stockings	Buttons & Hat Lace
Ahumada (1st)	Grey	Red	Red	White	White	White
Catalonian Guards (3rd)	Yellow	Red	Red	Red	Red	White. No hat lace
Castiglioni (6th)	Grey	Blue	Grey	Grey	Grey	Yellow
La Deputacion (7th)	White	Red	Red	Red	Red	White. No hat lace
La Cuidad (8th)	Red	Yellow	Yellow	Yellow	Yellow	Yellow, no hat lace
Cuidad de Cartagena (11th)	Grey	Grey	Grey	Grey	Red	White
Cuidad de Zaragoza (13th)	Grey	Grey Green	Grey	Grey	Red	White
Taafe (23rd)	Light Grey	Yellow	Light Grey	Light Grey	White	Yellow
Buol (25th)	Dark Grey	Red	Yellow	Yellow	Red	Yellow buttons, White lace
Faber (26th)	White	White	Red	Red	Red	Yellow buttons

British Infantry

(Illustration by Mark Allen, © Helion & Company)

See Colour Plate Commentaries for further information.

British Cavalry and Dragoons

(Illustration by Mark Allen, © Helion & Company)

See Colour Plate Commentaries for further information.

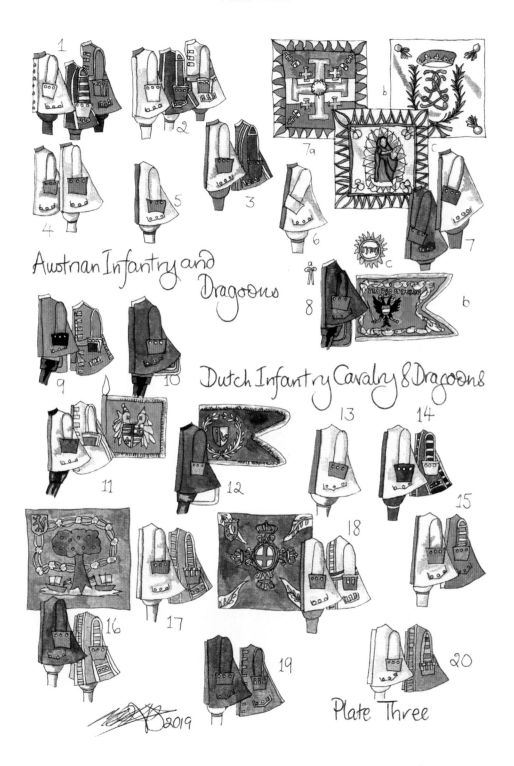

Austrian Infantry and Dragoons; Dutch Infantry, Cavalry and Dragoons

(Illustration by Mark Allen, © Helion & Company)

See Colour Plate Commentaries for further information.

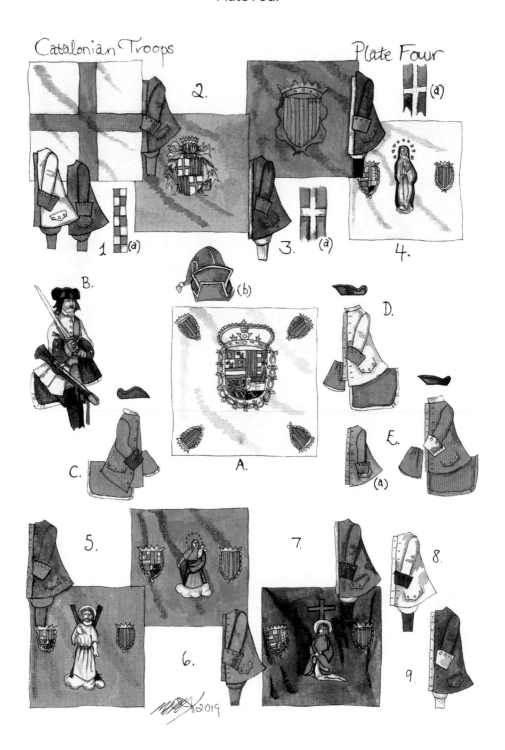

Catalonian Troops

(Illustration by Mark Allen, © Helion & Company)

See Colour Plate Commentaries for further information.

French Infantry

(Illustration by Mark Allen, © Helion & Company)

See Colour Plate Commentaries for further information.

Plate Six — French Cavalry and Dragoons

Anjou · Thury Marcillac · La Ferronays · Villiers/Croi

A · Trumpet VILLIERS/CROI · C

Trooper DE FLESCHE

B

Trooper NOAILLES · Regt. LANGUEDOC

D.

Regt. SAUMERY · Regt. ASFELD

2019

French Cavalry and Dragoons

(Illustration by Mark Allen, © Helion & Company)

See Colour Plate Commentaries for further information.

Spanish (Bourbon) Army Infantry

(Illustration by Mark Allen, © Helion & Company)

See Colour Plate Commentaries for further information.

Spanish (Bourbon) Dragoons and Cavalry; Portuguese Army

(Illustration by Mark Allen, © Helion & Company)

See Colour Plate Commentaries for further information.

8

The 1706 Campaign: Barcelona Besieged, Madrid Gained and Lost

Valencia

At the end of 1705 the Bourbon forces in Iberia started to react to events in Catalonia, Valenica and surrounding areas. In mid December 2,500 troops from Aragon under Torres moved into Valencia province to try to regain some lost ground. This force moved into the vital Monroyo pass area to hamper movement between Catalonia and Valencia. They captured a few villages but at San Mateo they were brought to a halt. San Mateo was a walled town and a small Confederate garrison was there under Lieutenant Colonel Jones. This consisted of 30 British Royal Dragoons, 300 Catalan miquelets and 700 Valencian militia. Some citizens also took up arms when Torres approached. In the absence of artillery San Mateo was difficult to attack. Jones had managed to get word to Tortosa, about 28 miles away, of the attack and so he could expect relief. Having to resort just to musketry the last few days of December 1705 and the early part of January 1706 were full of attacks and sallies by the attackers and defenders of the town. Torres received some reinforcements and by 9 January the garrison were short of food and ammunition. On that day Torres' force suddenly stopped attacking and marched away from the town. The following day the reason for this became clear as around 2,000 Confederate troops under Killigrew approached. These consisted of the following units:

Zinzendorff's Dragoons (1st Spanish): about 300 men
Royal Dragoons (1st British): about 170 men
Barrymore's (13th), Donegal's (35th) and Montjoy's British Foot: about 1,100 men in total
500 Valencian Militia
Four guns

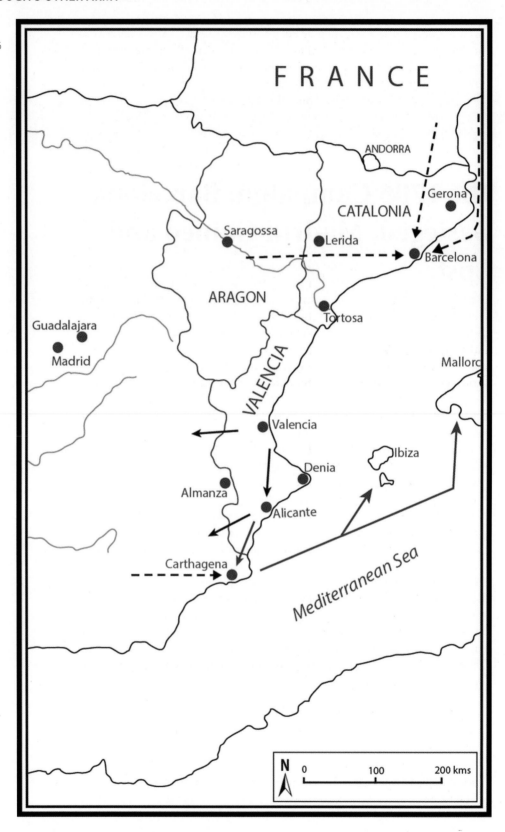

Map 3
Catalonia, 1706

This force was also accompanied by Peterborough. He had been in Barcelona and had been the centre of various arguments there about the war and what to do. Peterborough's time in Spain was shrouded in arguments and controversy, some of which became bitter disputes over time that carried on for years after these events. Opinion is divided about who was at fault in this but one thing is clear and that is that during his time the Confederate high command was very divided and constantly bickering. This was to be a constant problem in Iberia generally but perhaps reached its lowest point during Peterborough's time. Peterborough went to Valencia to get away from the infighting at Barcelona and was reluctant to return.

Meanwhile, Torres continued to wreak havoc in Valencia and was joined by 2,300 Spanish troops and militia under Arcos. These forces caused much destruction but were unable to achieve something more concrete and so the remaining 3,800 men withdrew to the west and observed events in Valencia. Peterborough had meanwhile been building his forces in Valencia into what was a considerable force, for this theatre and time. About 100 Spanish cavalry (Morras' Horse (2nd Spanish)) and 1,200 infantry (Colbatch's (5th Spanish), Gorge's, and Rivers' (6th) British Foot) came from Catalonia, in addition to around 200 men of Nebot's Horse (4th Spanish) from Valencia and a further 3,000 or so Valencian militia. In addition Barrymore's (13th) foot were converted to a dragoon regiment of around 300 men, these were known as Pearce's Dragoons and they were disbanded at the end of the war.

Cavalry: about 1,100 cavalry
Zinzendorff's Dragoons (1st Spanish): about 300 men
Morras' Horse (2nd Spanish): about 100 men
Nebot's Horse (4th Spanish): about 200 men
Royal Dragoons (1st British): about 170 men, possibly 200 men if Jones' detachment also joined the army.
Pearce's Dragoons: about 300 men

Infantry: about 5,500 infantry, 2,000 regulars and 3,500 militia
Rivers' (6th), Donegal's (35th), Montjoy's and Gorge's British Foot: about 400 men per unit
Colbatch's (5th) Spanish Foot: about 400 men
3,500 Valencian Militia
Four guns

This force cleared the remaining enemy troops from the area and marched into the city of Valencia. For the time being Valencia was quiet and the action shifted to Aragon.

Barcelona Besieged

The fall of Barcelona and subsequent events had been greeted with dismay by the French and their Spanish supporters. Tessé was ordered to move from the Portuguese border with as many troops as possible to Aragon. A French force under Legal was assembled north of the Franco-Spanish border along with a supporting fleet. By 21 January 1706 the advanced parties of Tessé's forces started to clash with the Confederate forces in the Aragon area under Cunningham. Over the next few days the Bourbon vanguard under D'Asfeld, nine battalions and nine squadrons in total, clashed with Cunningham's force. This force consisted of 800 British troops and 400 Dutch troops. The British troops were probably Cunningham's Dragoons (about 200 men), Will's and another Marine battalion (about 300 men each). The Dutch troops were a battalion, or possibly both battalions, of Palm's regiment. On 26 January Cunningham's and D'Asfeld's troops fought an all-day action in which the outnumbered Confederates in a strong position beat off the Bourbon attacks. Cunningham was wounded in the action and after his troops had withdrawn to Balaguer he died; Killigrew took over command of his unit.

The Bourbon forces aimed to recover Barcelona and Tessé favoured a cautious approach involving systematically clearing the area of Confederate troops before moving to tackle Barcelona itself. But he was ordered to march straight to Barcelona where he would be joined by the French fleet and Legal's troops. The key was to act quickly before Confederate reinforcements could arrive and to rely on the French navy to keep him supplied. Tessé, accompanied by Phillip, the French candidate for the Spanish throne, had about 12,000 men and in March he started moving towards Barcelona. At around the same time Legal led about 9,000 French troops over the border into Spain and started marching to join Tessé, around the same time as the French fleet sailed. Tessé was harassed by large numbers of miquelets during his march but no regular force moved to block his path for the simple reason that none capable of doing this was in the area. By 3 April all of these forces had arrived at Barcelona, completely wrongfooting the Confederates' plans.

The situation at Barcelona was dire. Peterborough was determined to build up the forces under his command in Valencia and so he had moved more units to that province before the Bourbon advance. From Lérida he ordered Castiglioni's Neapolitans (two battalions) and the Ahumada regiment to march to Valencia and he also sent some detachments of Carolean Spanish cavalry from Tortosa. These totalled about 2,400 men according to Parnell.[1] To replace these units some units from the garrison of Barcelona were sent to Lérida and Tortosa. Hamilton's (34th Foot), a 'Neapolitan' battalion (possibly the Spanish 7th regiment misidentified) and some 'newly raised Catalan' units were sent. Hamilton's regiment went to Tortosa and the 'Neapolitan' battalion probably went to Lérida but the other units are not known. This left only about 1,400 regular soldiers in Barcelona – about 400 Carolean Spanish cavalry, 700 infantry from Don Antonio Paguera's 3rd Spanish infantry, 300 British Guards and a small number of British gunners from the train.

As the Bourbon forces approached Archduke Charles sent urgent messages for reinforcements. The initial response to this came in the form of 1,500 miquelets who rushed into the city before the enemy forces arrived. Hamilton's (34th) Regiment (about 400 strong) also managed to return.

---

1   A. Parnell, *The War of Succession in Spain: 1702–1711*, p.151.

They used mules to rush back to Barcelona just before the city was sealed off. Meanwhile 5,000 militia were raised by the city itself. Tessé had around 21,000 men but knew that time was short. He was relying on the French navy for supplies and support but it was only a matter of time before the Confederate navy intervened or some other relief arrived. Therefore Tessé decided to press on as quickly as possible. On 4 April Tessé launched a surprise attack on the Montjuic fort, a key position in the defences, before all of his army had arrived. This attack was beaten off and the Bourbon army started the process of establishing a formal siege.

Meanwhile the Catalan miquelets outside Barcelona started harassing attacks on the enemy camp; these would continue during the rest of the siege. Other welcome aid arrived on 5 April from Gerona as Donegal, the commander of the garrison of Gerona, responded to the call for aid. With Charlemont's Foot (36th), two Dutch battalions (probably St. Amant's) and one Carolean Spanish regiment (identified as 'Neapolitan' but probably Don Joseph Paguera's 4th Regiment). Donegal embarked on boats and sneaked past the French fleet down the coast into Barcelona. 1,800 regular troops were a very welcome addition to the available forces. On 6 April a detachment of dismounted dragoons from Cunningham's regiment arrived by boat from Lérida.

By 12 April Tessé's forces had batteries in position to start bombarding Montjuic fort and Barcelona itself. After a few days' bombardment a second assault on Montjuic fort was attempted on the 15th. This attack had some partial success but was eventually repulsed. The bombardment continued and by 21 April practical breaches were made in the defences of Montjuic fort. In the evening another assault was made. This assault, led by French grenadiers, was successful and eventually drove the British, Dutch and Spanish defenders from the fort with heavy losses on both sides. Donegal was killed in the fighting. The Bourbon forces now concentrated on Barcelona itself but time was running out for them. Peterborough had been in Valencia at the time the siege started and was reluctant to come to Barcelona's aid. The reason for this was and still is controversial but it is clear that he did not possess the military strength to directly confront the Bourbon forces besieging Barcelona. By 21 April Peterborough had arrived at the headquarters of the miquelets outside Barcelona with 600 British and Carolean Spanish cavalry from Valencia. Once in the area Peterborough could do little practically to aid the defence. More practical help arrived on 23 April when more reinforcements arrived for the Confederates in Barcelona. 400 men from a 'Neapolitan battalion', possibly the Spanish 7th regiment misidentified, again managed to slip into Barcelona by boat.

These events just increased the sense of urgency in the Bourbon camp and Tessé intensified his efforts to take Barcelona. The number of guns bombarding the wilting defences of Barcelona mounted steadily and from 3 May a mine was started. The defences and defenders of Barcelona were stretched to the limit but the end of the siege was in sight. On 7 May the French fleet departed and the following day the Confederate relief fleet from Lisbon arrived. The Bourbon forces were still more numerous than the Confederate forces in the area but they were now without a supply line. They lingered in the area for a few more days and then slipped away, ending the siege.

Reinforcements to Barcelona (May 1706)
From Britain: Royal Fusiliers (7th Foot), Breton's Foot (later disbanded)
From Ireland: Mohun's, T. Caulfield's and Dungannon's Foot (all later disbanded)
These five battalions had an official strength of 4,170 men

Replacements: 300 recruits for the Foot Guards, although some sources give 338 including officers and servants. 940 replacements for the rest of the army. 1,300 horses

New Carolean Spanish Units (1706)
Infantry
- 9th Regiment: Ciutat de València – 1 battalion
- 11th Regiment: Ciudad de Cartagena – 1 battalion raised in Carthagena after that was captured. Later the 'Alcantarilla'.
- 12th Regiment: Ciutat d'Alacant – 1 battalion raised in Alicante after that was captured. Later Richards'.
- 13th Regiment: Ciudad de Zaragoza – 1 battalion raised in Saragossa when that was captured: Later the 'Alcaudete'.
- 14th Regiment: F. Ferrer's – 1 battalion (?) raised in Lisbon from Spanish prisoners of war.
- 15th Regiment: Claret's – raised in Aragon but never fully recruited. About three companies (150 men) strong when captured in 1707.
- Cavalry
- 8th Cavalry: Antoni de Clariana Horse: Later was the Guàrdies Reials de Cavalleria Catalana (Catalonian Guard cavalry)
- 9th Cavalry: Antoni Mas' Horse: Raised in Valencia, January 1706. Never fully raised and lost at Carthagena in November.
- 10th Cavalry:Jaume Rosell's Horse: Raised in Valencia, January 1706. Never fully raised and lost at Origuela in October 1706 with a strength of 113 men.
- 11th Cavalry: Joan Tàrrega's Horse: Raised in Valencia, January 1706. Garrisoned Gerona in 1706 with a strength of 300 men.
- 12th Cavalry: Aragón Cuirassiers: Raised in Saragossa, Aragon after Saragossa was captured. Later was the Córdoba. The unit was a cuirassier regiment.

Madrid Gained

While the crisis in eastern Spain was unfolding dramatic events were occurring in Portugal. The army there was under the overall command of Das Minas with the British under Galway. Galway was an experienced commander and could see that the Bourbons would have to respond to the loss of Barcelona. They would probably strip down the forces facing the Portuguese army to deal with this loss. Because of this he was in favour of an aggressive campaign by the army in Portugal, possibly even marching for Madrid. Galway was increasingly acting as the de facto army commander but he did not have

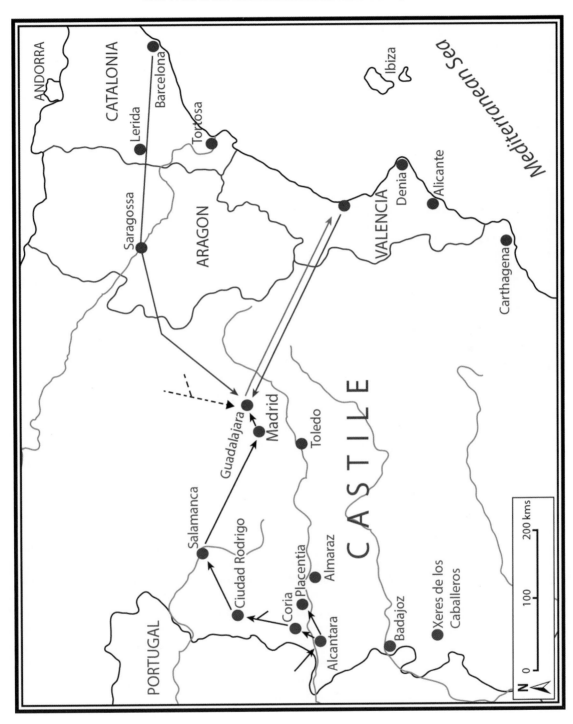

Map 4
The Madrid campaign,
1706

Henri de Ruvigny.
Earl of Galway.

16. Henri de Massue, Marquis de Ruvigny, 1st Earl of Galway, attributed to Michael Dahl

the actual command and so could not make this decision. The Portuguese and the official army commander Das Minas were not so certain that Galway was correct and were reluctant to commit themselves to anything so adventurous. After much persuasion the Portuguese high command agreed on a limited offensive into the Spanish province of Extramadura. The attack aimed to capture the fortress of Alcantara initially. To do this an army of 19,000 to 20,000 men was assembled at Elvas.

Galway[2] states that this army had 42 cavalry squadrons, 35 infantry battalions, 18 field guns and a siege train of 24 heavy guns. The British contingent to this force was two squadrons, five battalions and 10 field guns. These numbered about 200 cavalry and 2,000 infantry, according to Parnell.[3] The Dutch force is said to have consisted of four squadrons and four battalions and was commanded by General Friesheim. Parnell states these numbered about 2,000 men, presumably about 400 cavalry and 1,600 infantry. The bulk of the army was Portuguese; Parnell gives 3,600 cavalry, 11,100 infantry, eight field guns and 24 heavy guns. Galway records this was 36 Portuguese squadrons and 26 Portuguese battalions. Unfortunately there are some problems with this breakdown of forces. The first concerns the Dutch contingent, which should have five cavalry squadrons. The Dutch often seem to have disbanded some units to add the personnel to other units and thus bring them up to strength. It seems likely that this is what has happened in this case and that the single squadron from Schlippenbach's Dragoons had been disbanded in this way, if only temporarily. A more difficult problem is with the Portuguese. Borges[4] and later army sizes suggest that the army had fewer infantry units, probably 20 battalions, and more cavalry squadrons, at least 39 and maybe as many as 46 squadrons. It seems likely that the reason for the difference between the two is that represent different stages in the campaign and that some units had joined or left the army. Borges provides a breakdown of the Portuguese units in the army according to some correspondence of the period but which probably dates to later in the campaign. This list is given below but it is probably lacking six Portuguese battalions which started the campaign with the army. Also, it probably contained 10 extra Portuguese squadrons to the earlier army.

---

2   Earl of Galway, *An Account of the Earl of Galway's Conduct in Spain and Portugal* (London: J. Baker, 1711, 2nd ed.), p.31.

3   A. Parnell, *The War of Succession in Spain: 1702–1711*, p.172.

4   J.V. Borges, *Conquista De Madrid 1706*, pp.93–96.

Das Minas' Army 1706

British: Under the command of Galway, 200 cavalry and 2,000 infantry.
Cavalry
Harvey's Horse (3rd Horse – two squadrons)

Infantry
Five battalions – Blood's (17th), Brudenell's, Portmore's (2nd), Stuart's/
Stewart's (9th) and Wade's (33rd, formerly Duncanson's)

Artillery: 10 field guns.

Dutch: Under the command of Friesheim, 400 cavalry and 1,600 infantry.
Cavalry
Drimborn's Horse (NLC 15 – two squadrons), Mattha's Dragooons (4th
Dragoons – two squadrons)[5]

Infantry
Four battalions – Welderen's (NL 3), Friesheim's (NL 51), Vicouse's (NL
53) and Noyelles en Falais' (NL 17) regiments

Portuguese
Cavalry
The list in Borges contains 46 squadrons but not all of the regiments and
the numbers of squadrons in them are noted. It seems likely that 10 of
these squadrons were not with the army at the start of the campaign.
Between four and seven squadrons seem to have been left in the garrisons
of captured areas during the march to Madrid. Most likely seven squadrons
from the Tras os Montes Troops were left behind.

1st Line: 12 squadrons: General de la Cavaleria (one sqn), Guardias de
Minas (one sqn), Noronha (two sqns), Massa (? sqns – possibly Amasa/
Almansa with three squadrons), Prado (? Sqns), Machado de Britto (?
Sqns)
2nd Line: 10 squadrons: Galveyas (three sqns), Vidigueira (two sqns),
Mendonca (two sqns), Algarve (one sqn), Lisbon (two sqns)
Cavalaria: 24 squadrons: Beira (six squadrons), Minho Troops (seven
squadrons – a group of units), Tras os Montes Troops (11 squadrons – a
group of units)

Infantry
The 20 tercios (battalions) below marched to Madrid. Another six units were
with the army at the start of the campaign and were left in garrisons during
the march. The identity of these six units is not known.

---

5   Probably Schlippenbach's (NLD 2) single dragoon squadron has been disbanded and incorporated
     into the other units. Alterntively it may have still existed and have been overlooked.

Aveyras	Ilha
Silveyra	Sousa
Vasconcelos	Mello
Azevedo	Freire
Couto	Tomar
Carvalho	Oliveira
Henriques	Castelo
S. Payo	Branco
Machado	Gama
Castro	Pereira
Camara	Gale

Artillery:
Eight field guns and 24 heavy guns.

Opposing this force was a new French commander, the English Duke of Berwick. He was to prove a gifted commander, although not as much as his more famous relative, the Duke of Marlborough. Berwick was outnumbered and so was forced on the defensive. At first it looked like he would be able to hold the Portuguese army in check. Yet as events around Barcelona unfolded it became increasingly clear that an opportunity for the Portuguese army existed to take advantage of their immediate opponent's weakness.

It was agreed that the Portuguese would cautiously advance across the border and attempt to take Alcantara. Alcantara was a fortification but perhaps not the most important in the area. It was a safe target to aim for which Das Minas and the reluctant high command would agree to. On 31 March the Portuguese advanced towards the frontier to confront Berwick's forces. There was a brief engagement at Brocas on 8 April between the Confederate advance guard and Bourbon rearguard. By 10 April the Confederates had arrived at Alcantara and opened their attack on the strongly garrisoned fortress. A breach was soon made in the defences and on the 14th the approximately 4,000 strong garrison surrendered. In addition to the loss of a considerable number of troops a large quantity of weapons, supplies and equipment was also found in the fortress. These two losses considerably weakened the Bourbon position.

The Confederates now moved to take a number of other important locations in the area. By 28 April they had captured Coria and Placentia, amongst other lesser places. By this time Das Minas and the Portuguese were starting to worry that they had advanced far enough from home, especially as the outcome of the siege of Barcelona was still in doubt. Berwick had been unable to seriously contest the Confederate advance but his army shadowed the Portuguese advance. A fortified position at Massagona was constructed to block further Confederate advances. He had also moved to try to secure the vital bridge on the road to Madrid at Almarez further to the rear. Berwick clearly understood the opportunity the Portuguese army had.

After some discussion and persuasion by Galway the Portuguese agreed to advance to Almarez. The army captured this vital position on 4 May after some brisk but small-scale actions. The road to Madrid was now open but

Das Minas and the Portuguese could not be persuaded to take it. It was, in their view, far too risky to continue the advance away from Portugal while the outcome of the Barcelona siege was in the balance. With further persuasion it was agreed to attack Ciudad Rodrigo. This was a step sideways, a compromise between the Portuguese desire to move closer to their border and Galway's desire to continue the advance. Facing little opposition the Confederates had captured Ciudad Rodrigo by 26 May.

By this time the success of the campaign so far, patient diplomatic work at court and the good news from Barcelona, it was now known that the siege has been broken, had given the Portuguese high command encouragement. Buoyed up by these factors orders were sent for the advance on Madrid to be attempted. After quickly collecting supplies the Confederates started their advance on 3 June and four days later they had reached the important city of Salamanca, which immediately surrendered. Berwick was by now retreating back towards Madrid and trying, without success, to form an army capable of stopping the Portuguese

17. James FitzStuart, Duke of Berwick

advance. During this period news of the crushing French defeat at Ramillies in Flanders had arrived in Spain. It seemed that nothing could stop the Confederate progress on all fronts. The Portuguese army reached the outskirts of Madrid on 27 June and a formal entrance into the city was conducted. The Portuguese army had left six battalions and somewhere between four and seven squadrons behind as garrisons of the places they had captured during the campaign. This, combined with the effects of the long march of around 400 miles, had reduced the Portuguese to around 14,000 men. Das Minas was always reluctant to continue further east and at each stage Galway had to persuade him to continue the advance. Yet they had captured a large part of Spain and the Spanish capital. They had presented the Confederates with the chance to secure total victory in Iberia. It just now remained for the position obtained to be secured, although this would prove to be more difficult to achieve.

As soon as Madrid was captured urgent messages were sent to Barcelona asking for King Charles, Peterborough and the Confederate army to march for Madrid as soon as possible. At that time Peterborough had marched off to Valencia with most of the infantry as the first part of a supposed march to Madrid. This left King Charles in Barcelona but without a suitable force to attempt a march through territory still under enemy control. No further news arrived so Galway sent more messages and after a few weeks marched east to Guadalajara, about 60 kilometres north-east of Madrid. In effect Galway was reaching out towards the east in the hope that despite the lack of news the Confederate forces in that area were moving towards Madrid. Unfortunately it also meant that the bulk of the Portuguese were now to the east of Madrid at the end of a long and vulnerable supply route.

This would not have been a problem if the situation in the east had been better. Peterborough had taken all the British troops from Barcelona except the marines and Royal Fusiliers; the fusiliers went to Lérida, and marched to Valencia. These gave a field force of around 8,000 men, 14 field guns, four heavy guns and two mortars in Valencia. These were supposed to be the force that would advance to link up with the Portuguese army in Madrid. Yet it soon became clear that no preparations had been made for this move. Peterborough was once again away from the rest of the high command and the constant arguments and disagreements he had with them. Peterborough was not keen on returning to Barcelona or marching for Madrid, either of which would result in his loss of independence. So instead he undertook a number of local offensives in the Valencia area. In theory this was to usefully use the time until the advance to Madrid could be started but inevitably led to delays and reflected Peterborough's reluctance to go to Madrid.

Peterborough sent a force of three infantry battalions (the Foot Guards, T. Caulfield's and Dungannon's) and one dragoon regiment (Pearce's former infantry regiment) under Wyndham to besiege two small fortresses in New Castile. Gorges, with four infantry battalions (Gorges (formerly Donegal's, later 35th), Allen's (formerly Gorges), Montjoy's and Mohun's) and one horse regiment (probably a Spanish unit) were sent to operate against Alicante, the only remaining fortress in Valencia in enemy hands. A small force of one infantry battalion (Alnutt's (formerly Charlemont's), later 36th), and a dragoon detachment from Killigrew's regiment (formerly Cunningham's 8th) under Alnutt invaded Murcia. This left just three infantry battalions (Southwell's (formerly Rivers', later 6th), Hamilton's (later 34th Foot) and Breton's) and two dragoon regiments (the Royal Dragoons and the rest of Killigrew's) under Killigrew in reserve in Valencia. On 26 July Peteborough finally received a direct order to join Charles and so he proceeded to meet up with Charles and Galway but only with 400 dragoons with him. These dragoons seem to have been the newly-raised British Peterborough's dragoon regiment; it was actually commanded by Nassau. This unit seems to have been raised in July in Valencia by mounting soldiers from various regiments and sources.

With the forces in Valencia doing little to link up with the Portuguese it was left to the forces in Catalonia to do something. The mainly Carolean Spanish and Dutch forces in Catalonia had been pressing into Aragon, the province to the west of Catalonia, with some success. Noyelles, the new commander of the Carolean Spanish army, advanced on Saragossa, the capital of Aragon, with 500 Spanish horse and 2,500 Spanish and Dutch infantry. Saragossa quickly surrendered and this was followed by the majority of the rest of the province being won over. News of Galway's success arrived at this point and it was understood that it was vital to link up as soon as possible. It became clear that contact with the Portuguese could not be made via Valencia and so Saragossa became the chosen route to link up. On 24 July Charles and Noyelles left Saragossa escorted by two Spanish horse regiments, a troop of Spanish dragoons and three infantry battalions (two Dutch and one

Neapolitan), about 2,000 men. These travelled through enemy-controlled territory and joined Galway's on 6 August. Shortly after this the Ahumada and Colbatch's Spanish battalions arrived as well, about 800 men. Later these were joined by Peterborough, who finally arrived with his 400 dragoons and these brought Galway's forces to around 15,000 men.

The two pro-Confederate armies had joined up, if only tentatively, and at least in theory had divided Spain's pro-French areas into two halves. The Confederates controlled the capital city, the second major city within Spain and a considerable portion of the mainland territory, but all was not as good as it appeared. The high command was very divided and often acting at cross-purposes. The link between Portugal and Madrid was very fragile. Similarly the line of communication from Madrid to Catalonia and other Confederate-controlled territory in eastern Spain was very exposed. These links from Madrid essentially consisted of narrow corridors of territory barely under Confederate control. Nor was Madrid securely held and crucially the Spanish population in the city, and surrounding area, were not enthusiastic supporters of the Confederate cause. Around Barcelona the Carolean Spanish regular forces now numbered more than 7,000 men and in addition there were 8 to 10,000 miquelets, visible evidence of the area's support of the Confederate cause. In contrast the inhabitants on Madrid and surrounding area were wary of the Confederates and maintained a neutral stance until events unfolded. Only 370 recruits for the Carolean army were available in Madrid in early August.

Madrid Lost

While the Confederates were attempting to link up the French and Spanish had not been idle. Berwick had received reinforcements and gathered a strong force that was capable of acting directly against Galway's force. Seizing the opportunity presented by the Confederate movement to Guadalajara Berwick dispatched a force to seize Alcala, located roughly half way between Guadalajara and Madrid. This move cut off the Portuguese army, and other forces at Guadalajara, from Madrid and indeed from Portugal. This was followed shortly after by the Bourbon army retaking Madrid, despite spirit resistance from the 370 Confederate recruits mentioned above. By swift decisive action Berwick exploiting the divisions within the Confederate high command and had undermined the recent Confederate successes, with minimal losses.

Lacking the strength and supplies to confront Berwick Galway had little option than to retreat back to Valencia. The troops there could be added to his forces and the fleet was operating in that area which would open up communications with Portugal. The Portuguese were understandably extremely worried about developments. The bulk of their army was now cut off from Portugal and only weak forces remained in Portugal. A Bourbon offensive into Portugal now would meet little opposition from the remaining troops there. On August 11 Galway started the necessary move to Valencia and Berwick shadowed this move. Berwick's army by this time outnumbered their opponents but Berwick concentrated on blocking any possible move to the west and so reopening communications with Portugal. By September 28 Galway had reached Valencia province.

While events were unfolding elsewhere the troops in the Valencia area had been busy. The combined Confederate fleet had arrived at Carthagena and using marines had captured this port. Following this the fleet moved to Alicante. Here it joined 2,000 miquelets and Gorges' force mentioned above. Around 1,300 marines and sailors were landed, along with artillery and a regular siege was started. Another 1,300 British infantry and 200 Spanish cavalry arrived shortly after to join the attack. With the assistance of the navy's guns the attack on Alicante fortress continued slowly in the face of stiff resistance from the Bourbon Spanish garrison led by General Mahony, an Irish general in the service of Spain. By 2 September the garrison's position was worn away and terms were sought. Having secured Alicante the Confederate fleet now sailed off to capture the Spanish islands of Ivica and Majorca. These swiftly fell and rounded off a successful series of actions, but perhaps at the cost of the failures around Madrid.

In early October Berwick's troops reached the area and started to pick off isolated groups of Confederate troops. The minor fortress of Cuenca which was defended by four battalions (Colbatch's, Ahumada's, a 'Neapolitan' and a Dutch) fell on 10 October. A small force of 300 British infantry, 150 dragoons from Killigrew's regiment (8th) and 900 irregulars at Elche were surprised on 23 October and overwhelmed. This was shortly followed by the loss of the nearby Origuela fortress which was defended by Valencian irregulars and also Rosell's Spanish horse (10th). The climax to this minor offensive was directed at regaining the recently lost Carthegena. Carthegena was defended by a few Carolean Spanish horse from Mas' (9th Spanish) Horse, 800 Valencian miquelets and about 2,000 townsmen. Berwick's army arrived at Carthegena on 11 November, and after about a week they had breached the defences and recaptured this fortress.

Berwick then entered winter quarters and ended the campaign. The Confederates had also suffered minor loses in Aragon and the Portuguese front as local Bourbon forces counter-attacked, Alcantara was recaptured on December 15, but the 1706 campaign was over. The Confederates had made great advances but they had been unable to fully take advantage of these and indeed had then made potentially decisive losses. The capture of Madrid was potentially a decisive move but had been wasted by the subsequent loss. The balance in Iberia had been tipped more in their favour but not yet decisively.

9

The 1707 Campaign: Disaster at Almansa

The Confederate cause had had great success in the campaigning of 1706. In Iberia some of the gains made had been lost but they were still in a lot stronger position than previously in the war. But in other areas even greater success had been achieved. In Flanders Marlborough's great victory had allowed the capture of a string of enemy fortresses. Meanwhile the Imperial commander Eugene of Savoy had won a great victory at Turin and this had cleared Italy of opposing forces. Over the winter of 1706–07 there was much discussion amongst the Confederate leaders about how to further capitalise on the successes of 1706. It was agreed that the major effort in 1707 would be Italy/southern France. Eugene would lead an invasion of southern France and try to take Toulon, a vital French position. To support his effort the other fronts, including Spain, would try to keep the pressure on the enemy to avoid reinforcements being sent to Toulon. In addition an expedition was planned to south-western France led by Earl Rivers. This area of France near the Spanish border was the stronghold of the Protestant Huguenots. These had suffered persecution and were a source of support for the Confederates. A large number of the troops in the expedition were recruited from discontent Huguenots and it was hoped that the local population would rise in support of the expedition. Before the expedition could leave Britain intelligence was received that meant that the landing in south-western France was doomed to failure. So instead it was decided that the troops would be used in Spain to make another attempt to capture Cadiz, and the expedition therefore travelled to Lisbon in late 1706. Once it arrived there the Portuguese were reluctant to let it leave. The Portuguese king had died, and with the bulk of the Portuguese army campaigning in Spain they wanted the expedition's troops to protect Portugal. This delay meant that the Cadiz operation also had to be cancelled and so it was decided that instead the troops would join Galway's forces in Valencia.

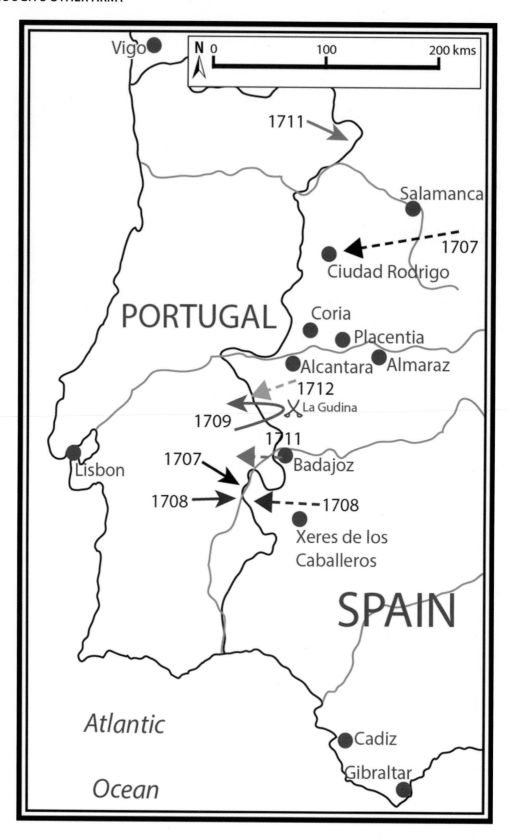

Map 5
Campaigns
in Portugal,
1707–12

Earl Rivers' Expedition – Lisbon late 1706/early 1707

British Contingent
From Britain:
Cavalry: eight squadrons
Carpenter's Dragoons (later 3rd Dragoons) – two squadrons,
Essex's Dragoons (later 4th Dragoons) – two squadrons,
Guiscard's Dragoons (Huguenot unit, later disbanded) – four squadrons

Infantry: (seven battalions)
Blosset (Huguenot)
Hill's (later the 11th Foot)
Hotham's
Mark Kerr's
Nassau's (German)
Sybourg's (Huguenot)
Watkins'

All units except Hill's were disbanded before the end of the war.

From Flanders (three infantry battalions):
Mordaunt's (later the 28th Foot),
Farringdon's (later the 29th Foot),
Macartney (disbanded in 1713)
Total 8,152 men (this may be without officers, musicians, etc.)

Two Marine battalions totalling 1,200 men (this may be without officers, musicians, etc.):
Wills (later the 30th Foot),
Borr (later the 32nd Foot)

Dutch Contingent: 4,000 men
Cavalry: five squadrons
Schlippenbach Dragoons (NLD two to three squadrons),
Mattha Dragoons (4th Dragoons – two squadrons)
Infantry: four battalions
Torsay (NL 46), Lislemarais (Huguenot – NL 54) Belcastel (Huguenot), and Caliver (Huguenot regiment jointly funded by Britain – disbanded in 1708)

Artillery Train (British):
20 24 pounders
6 Culverins
4 12 pounders
4 Demi-culverins
6 Mortars
60 Coehorn mortars
6 Sakers (5-pounders) – these were the only field pieces.

Joined at Lisbon:

Francisco Ferrer's Spanish regiment (Spanish 14th) – a 648-strong unit raised from Spanish prisoners of war in Portugal.

Gibraltar:

Watkins' Regiment was left at Gibraltar as part of the garrison. J. Caufield's and Keppelfox's (formerly Waes' NL 33) Dutch regiment were taken from the garrison and accompanied the expedition to Valencia.

The expedition therefore consisted of 13 cavalry squadrons (eight British and five Dutch), 18 infantry battalions (12 British, five Dutch and one Spanish) and 40 guns by the time it arrived at Alicante on 8 February 1707. This was a total of about 14,000 men at full strength. Galway claims that these troops amounted to no more than 7,000 effectives after their voyage and delay in Portugal.[1] He further claims that the British troops were reduced to around 4,500 men shortly after arriving in Valencia.

This, in the context of this campaign, was a major reinforcement and prompted a debate amongst the Confederate high command about what to do in the upcoming campaign. One faction led by Galway wanted to honour the general Confederate plan and launch an attack, preferably a renewed attempt to secure Madrid launched from Valencia. This would aid the campaign in Spain and in addition could divert forces away from the Toulon area. At a minimum it should mean that no enemy troops could be dispatched from Spain to aid the forces defending Toulon. Unfortunately Noyelles, the commander of the Carolean Spanish army, and a number of other senior figures were not in favour of this course of events. Instead this group wanted to disperse the army to secure the area already controlled and counter a potential threat to Catalonia from a small enemy force in Rousillon. At the heart of the problem were the personal differences, strife and hostility within the Confederate high command that would plague the campaign in Iberia. Archduke Charles, faced by growing division, decided on a compromise and chose to return to Catalonia with Noyelles, the Carolean Spanish and a few other units, leaving Galway and the remaining forces in Valencia.

In mid-March Charles, Noyelles and their forces left Valencia for Catalonia. These consisted of all the Carolean Spanish units, Winterfeldt's Dragoons and the Dutch Noyelles en Falais' (NL 17) regiment. Winterfeldt's Dragoons are a mysterious unit as there is no other evidence concerning it. It appears not to be Spanish as it is listed separately to them and seems to have had four squadrons, see below. At this time there were 10 Dutch cavalry squadrons in the area but only six of these are listed with Galway's forces. It therefore seems likely that Winterfeldt's Dragoons were an ad hoc unit consisting of the four 'missing' Dutch squadrons. If so this unit would consist of two squadrons each from the Schlippenbach (NLD 2) and Mattha Dragoons (4th).

---

1   Anonymous, *An Account of the Earl of Galway's Conduct in Spain and Portugal*, p.81.

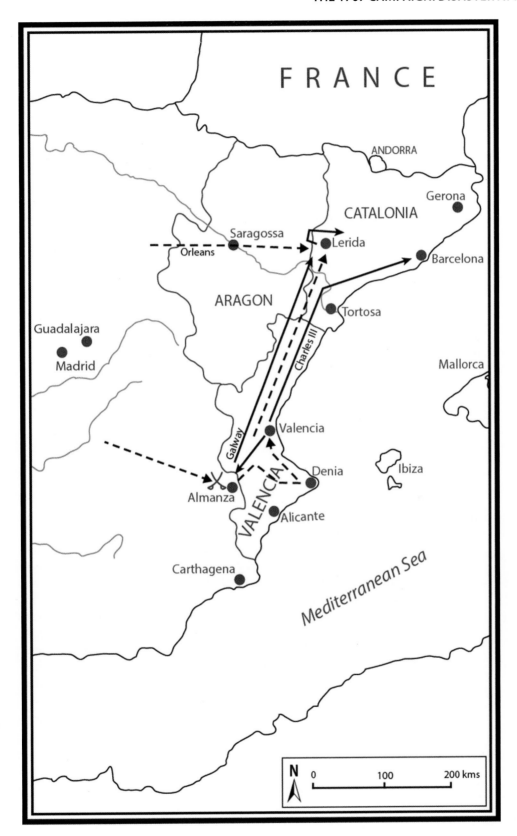

Map 5
Catalonia,
1707.

FRANCE

ANDORRA

Gerona

CATALONIA

Saragossa

Orleans

Lerida

Barcelona

ARAGON

Tortosa

Charles III

Guadalajara

Madrid

Mallorca

Valencia

Galway

Ibiza

Denia

Almanza

VALENCIA

Alicante

Carthagena

Mediterranean Sea

N

0   100   200 kms

These troops, along with those already in Catalonia, and potentially available for field services, at least according to Galway,[2] consisted of 29 squadrons and 14 battalions. These could have amounted to 10,000 men and were the following units:[3]

Cavalry: 29 squadrons
Zinzendorf's Dragoons (1st Spanish) – five squadrons
Morras' Horse (2nd Spanish) – five squadrons
Sobias' Horse (3rd Spanish) – five squadrons
Nebot's Horse (4th Spanish) – five squadrons
Aragon Horse (12th Spanish) – five squadrons
Winterfeldt's Dragoons – four squadrons, probably two squadrons each from the Dutch Schlippenbach (NLD 2) and Mattha Dragoons (4th)

Infantry: 14 battalions
St. Amant's (NL 5 – two battalions)
Palm's (NL 24 – two battalions)
Noyelles en Falais' (NL 17)
Two British Marine regiments - probably Wills (30th) and Borr (32nd)
Royal Fusiliers (7th British)
Catalonian Guards (3rd Spanish)
Noyelles (4th Spanish)
La Deputacion (7th Spanish)
La Cuidad (8th Spanish)
Ciudad de Zaragoza (13th Spanish)
Don Juan Taraga (An unknown unit, probably Spanish)

The Royal Dragoons (1st) were also detached from the available forces and retired to Culera. This unit was totally exhausted from the previous campaigns and from outpost duty over the winter. This had a strength of 302 men according to the weekly return of 22 April 1707.

One of the 20 Portuguese battalions also seems to have left the available field army at this time but it is not clear why. It is most likely that it was placed into a garrison in Valencia but it may also have marched to Catalonia. It is also possible that Friesheim's regiment (NL 51) was also detached for some unknown reason. As will be discussed below, there is some doubt about whether this unit was with Galway's army. To complete the losses from the field force, on 22 March Montandre's regiment (formerly Dungannon's) was ambushed near Alicante by Spanish dragoons. 32 of Montandre's men were killed and the other 322 men within the unit were captured – another battalion would be unavailable to Galway in the upcoming campaign.

The various garrisons also took potential manpower for the army away from the coming action:

---

2   *Ibid.*, p.81.
3   Anonymous, *The Present State of Europe*, vol. 18 (London: H. Rhodes, 1707), p.237.

At Gerona: Royal Fusiliers (7th Foot) and two Marine battalions – probably Wills' Marines (30th) and Borr's Marines (32nd): About 1,200 men.

At Alicante: Hotham's, Sybourg's (Huguenot), Blosset (Huguenot) and one Marine battalion. Seymour's (4th Foot) and Churchill's (ex Villiers') (31st Foot) were both marine units at this time and seem to have rotated between garrison and maritime service. About 1,200 men.

At Gibraltar: Elliot's and Watkins': About 800 men.

At Denia: a detachment of 200 men.

In theory there were also another six British battalions available for service.

Brudenell's
T. Caulfield's
Donegal's (35th Foot)
Farringdon's (later the 29th Foot)
H. Hamilton's (later 34th Foot)
Mohun's

These units had been 'reduced' and so were not capable of taking the field. 'Reduced' meant that the rank and file of the units had been taken and used to build up other units. Some of the officers, non-commissioned and others would also join other units. Only a skeleton staff of these units remained and they could not take the field. These units would return to Britain to be rebuilt when transport was available. The sum of all these actions meant that despite the arrival of Rivers' troops Galway's army was no stronger.

The division, dispersion and losses of the Confederates would be a problem as Galway was determined to at least try to act offensively against Berwick's opposing forces. Galway would have liked to march to Madrid but he knew that Berwick was being reinforced by 8,000 French troops under Orléans. This would give Berwick a comfortable numerical advantage and would make a Confederate advance on Madrid impossible. Instead of a march on Madrid Galway planned to steal a march on his rival. Galway would strike at some isolated Bourbon positions and magazines before Berwick could assemble his still dispersed forces and take the field. On 10 April Galway led his forces to attack Yelcha, where the principal enemy magazine was located. Berwick reacted by recoiling away as he had been caught by surprise and needed to collect his forces. This enabled Galway to follow up his initial success by attacking a number of other smaller magazines and locations. While doing this Galway learnt that Berwick had collected together all the available troops in the area and on 22 April had marched forward to Almansa, about 25 miles away from Galway's position at the time. Galway also learned that Orléans had not yet joined Berwick's army. In short Berwick's forces were in striking range and also relatively weak.

18. The Battle of Almansa, by Balaca

The Battle of Almansa, 25 April

For Galway it was too good an opportunity to miss and might be the only chance he would get to fight a decisive battle when the two armies were reasonably balanced. On April 24 Galway consulted the army's leaders and it was decided to march quickly to Almansa. The army left immediately and were eight miles away from Almansa by 25 April. That morning the Confederate army set out for Almansa and by noon had arrived on a plain outside it. The army paused to rest as it was a hot day and had been an exhausting march, and then deployed for battle. Meanwhile Galway needed to consider what to do against Berwick's army, which was deployed under the walls of Almansa on the plain opposite. The problem was that Berwick's army was clearly a lot stronger than Galway's, contrary to expectations. What Galway did not know was that his intelligence was at fault. It was true that Orléans personally had not yet arrived in the area but unfortunately for the Confederates the 8,000 reinforcements Orléans led had arrived. With them Berwick's army amounted to 52 or 54 battalions and 76 squadrons, a total of 25 to 26,000 men. Galway was not facing an enemy approximately the same strength as his forces but one with a significant numerical advantage.

The details of Galway's army are not certain, although the general picture is clear. The army is usually given as 42 infantry battalions, between 53 and 60 cavalry squadrons (depending on source) and 30 guns. Unfortunately each of these numbers is slightly problematic and need to be looked at. Neither is it certain how many men were in Galway's army at the time of battle. Despite these uncertainties it is clear that the Confederate were significantly outnumbered in the battle.

First of all, if we look at the infantry one would expect the army to have 43 battalions and not 42. There were at the time 44 British, Dutch and Portuguese battalions that one would expect to be with the army. All of the orders of battle available agree that only 19 of the 20 available Portuguese battalions were at the battle, giving 43 battalions. The Portuguese battalion might have been used to garrison the recent conquests or guard the army's baggage or the army's supply lines or some other task. Whatever it was doing its role does not seem to have been recorded but it also does not seem to have been at the battle.

In addition to this all sources (including, crucially, Galway, who you would expect to be well informed about the units he commanded), agree that a further battalion was not at the battle. In short that there were 42 battalions present. Unfortunately it is not clear which unit might not have been present although the most likely is Friesheim's regiment (NL 51). A number of orders of battle do not feature this unit and so this makes this a possibility. All the other Dutch infantry units at the battle were destroyed, although some were rebuilt later in the war, and were no longer listed in records of this army. Yet the Friesheim regiment was still intact and in Spain in the following year. It therefore seems likely that it was not at the battle. If it was detached on some other duty there is no record of it or what it was doing. Yet like the Portuguese battalion that was certainly absent perhaps it was on some unspecified task. The colonel of the regiment Friesheim was certainly at the battle, where he was one of the senior commanders. It is possible that this has caused confusion amongst the sources that mention the presence of the regiment. On balance it seems likely that Friesheim's regiment was not present.

The number of cavalry squadrons with the army varies considerably in the various sources. The number is given as 53, 55 or 60 squadrons. On the face of it this is a problem but seems to be related to problems with the British cavalry. When the numbers of squadrons per nation are given there is agreement about the number of Dutch and Portuguese squadrons. In the case of the Portuguese there is not agreement on the names of the units or the numbers of squadrons per unit. Yet they all agree on the total number of Dutch and Portuguese squadrons and the only variation is in the number of British squadrons. This seems to be because some sources are using the full theoretical number of squadrons. Others use a number of squadrons based on the actual number men in the unit at the time or the usual notional number of squadrons at the time. So for example the unit that would later be the 8th Dragoons, Killigrew's at this time, seems to have officially sent four squadrons to Spain but more usually it was counted as two squadrons. Yet by this time, see below, it had 51 men or less and this was less than the official size of a troop. It therefore could be counted as just a single squadron or even not included in the squadron total in some sources. In short this unit could be counted as anything from zero to four squadrons by different sources. This accounts for the different number of squadrons quoted by various sources. Yet while the numbers of British squadrons vary the number, type and identity of regiments involved are consistent over all the sources. In addition we have data concerning the number of men within these units at around this time. Therefore it is not important that the notional number of squadrons these units were organised into is unknown because the overall picture is clear. The British units were organised into eight, 10 or 15 squadrons but the total number of actual soldiers was the same whatever number of squadrons they were organised into.

Finally, the artillery is often stated to have numbered 30 guns with no details of their type or source. Yet other sources state that the army had 20 Portuguese guns and six British guns. Probably this means that 20 of the guns were from the original Portuguese army and so would include British guns. The six other guns, the British guns mentioned, are probably the six guns that accompanied Rivers' expedition. It is possible that there were four other guns, to make the total of 30 guns specified in other sources. These could have come from an unknown third source, probably the original forces in the area or one of the fortresses. It is not known if the four extra guns were with the army but it seems likely that they were and that this is the reason for the total of 30 guns given elsewhere.

Infantry: 42 (or 43) battalions
   British: 16 battalions[4]

Combined Foot Guards	400 men	Macartney's	484 men
Alnutt's (36th Foot)	412 men	Montjoy's	508 men
Blood's (17th Foot)	461 men	Mordaunt's (28th Foot)	532 men
Breton's	428 men	Nassau's (German)	422 men
J. Caulfield's	470 men	Portmore's (2nd Foot)	462 men
Gorge's (35th Foot)	616 men	Southwell's (6th Foot)	505 men
Hill's (11th Foot)	472 men	Stewart's (9th Foot)	467 men
Mark Kerr's	429 men	Wade's (33rd Foot)	458 men

   Dutch: seven (or eight) battalions

Belcastel (Huguenot)	Torsay (NL 46)
Cavalier (Huguenot)	Vicouse's (NL 53)
Keppelfox's (NL 33)	Welderen's (NL 3)
Lislemarais (Huguenot – NL 54)	Friesheim's (NL 51)

   Friesheim's regiment was probably not at the battle.

   Portuguese: 19 battalions
These 14 battalions from the original Portuguese were present and had the same name as previously.

Aveyas	Henriques	S. Payo
Azevedo Couto	Ilha	Silveyra **
Camara	Machado	Tomar
Carvalho	Mello	Vasconcelos
Castro	Pereira	

** The Silveyra regiment is either the Galba or Iberia unit from below. The other was also present but was using a different name by this time.

In addition to the above units five other regiments were present. These units would have been from the original Portuguese are but they were using a different name.

Delgardo	Golle	Zamora
Galba or Iberia **	Lopez	

4 The numbers of men each unit comes from Galway, who gives their strength "some few days before the battle" in a weekly return of 22 April. Anonymous, *An Impartial Enquiry into the Management of the War in Spain by the Ministry at Home* (London: J. Morphew, 1712), Appendix p.6.

The six regiments who were part of the original Portuguese army and are missing from the list of units at the battle are below. One of these was detached at the time of the battle. The other five were present at the battle but using another name.

Castelo Branco	Gale	Oliveira
Freire	Gama	Sousa

Cavalry: 53, 55 or 60 squadrons
 British: eight, ten, or 15 squadrons[5]
 Harvey's Horse (3rd Horse) – 227 men
 Killigrew's (8th Dragoons) – 51 men
 Pearce's Dragoons – 273 men
 Peterborough's Dragoons – 303 men
 Guiscard's Dragoons (Huguenots) - 228 men
 Combined Carpenter's (3rd Dragoons) and Essex's (4th Dragoons) – 292 men

 Dutch: six squadrons
 Drimborn's (NLC 15 – two squadrons)
 Schlippenbach's (NLD 2 – two squadrons)
 Mattha (4th Dragoons – two squadrons)
 Portuguese: 39 squadrons.

These seven regiments with 22 squadrons from the original Portuguese were present and had the same name as previously.

 Algarve (one sqn)
 Beira (six sqns)
 General de la Cavaleria (one sqn)
 Guardias de Minas (one sqn)
 Minho Troops (seven squadrons – divided into Do Minho (three sqns) & Dominche (four sqns)
 Noronha (two sqns)
 Tras os Montes Troops (four sqns)

A further six regiments are listed with the remaining 17 squadrons but these have names or numbers of squadrons that are different to previously.
 Almansa (three sqns)
 Campo Mayor (three sqns)
 Lisboa (three sqns)
 Moura (three sqns)
 Olivenca (three sqns)
 Villaviciosa (two sqns)

---

5 The numbers of men each unit has comes from Galway, who gives their strength "some few days before the battle". They were organised into eight, 10 or 15 squadrons.

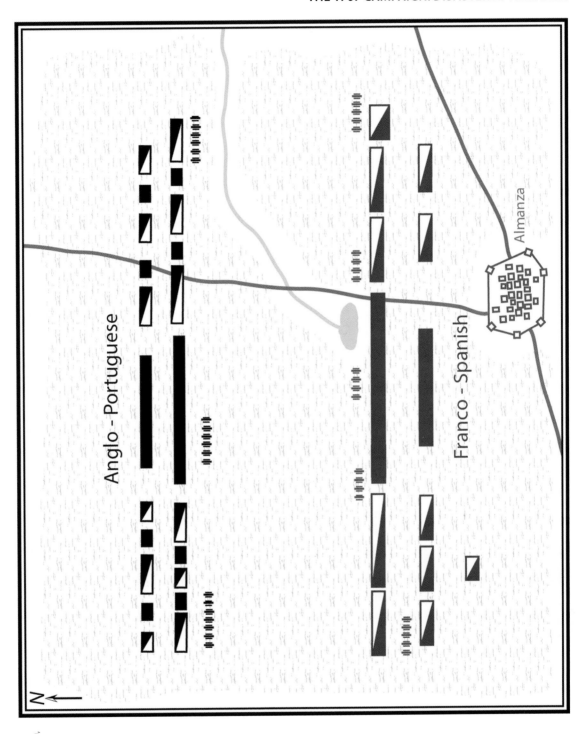

Anglo - Portuguese

Franco - Spanish

Almanza

N

Map 6
The Battle of Almansa,
April 25 1707

The original list of units gave seven other regiments in the army. So it would seem that one of the original regiments has been combined with one or more of the regiments above. Further evidence of this might be that the Lisboa regiment does appear in both lists but at this time has an extra squadron when compared to previously.

These are the seven regiments from the former list which are almost certainly the six other regiments above, although probably in a different format.

Galveyas (three sqns)
Lisboa (two sqns)
Machado de Britto (? sqns)
Massa (? Sqns – possibly this is the Almansa regiment)
Mendonca (two sqns)
Prado (? sqns)
Vidigueira (two sqns)

Artillery: 26 or 30 guns

This army amounted to about 4,500 horse and 11,000 foot effective on the day of the battle.[6] This is a surprisingly low figure, especially in the light of the British unit sizes from a few days before the battle. These figures for the British units who comprised about one-third of the army total 8,900 men and would suggest a much larger army. The figures for the British infantry give an average of about 470 men per battalion; whereas the average based on the figure given for effective strength at the battle works out as about 260 men per battalion. This is about 55 percent of the strength given for the British units a few days before. To lose about 45 percent of a unit's strength in 'a few days' seems to be excessive, even given the difficult conditions in Spain. It seems possible that the effective strength given does not include officer, drummers and non-commissioned officers. These were often omitted in period sources which frequently only given the number of ordinary soldiers. It therefore seems likely these would have added perhaps as 2,000 to 2,500 men to the total for the army. It may be that the figures have also been distorted or misrepresented in some other ways. If British units were stronger than average this could have distorted the figures and created a false impression of the overall loses of the army before the battle. Another possibility is that Galway as the British commander would naturally have reasonably full details of the state and losses of the British units. Yet it is unlikely that he would as reliable information as this about the Dutch and Portuguese troops. The conditions of the march were tough and many of the British units were new to the theatre and so relatively unused to the campaigning conditions. If this was the case then perhaps the British units suffered more than the other units that also would have distorted the figures. Maybe it was just the case that Galway deliberately understated the number of men he had to help explain why he suffered such a great defeat.

---

6   Anonymous, *An Account of the Earl of Galway's Conduct in Spain and Portugal*, p.81.

It is therefore possible that the army was bigger than the 15,500 men claimed or that the figures have been distorted. It is possible that the army actually numbered at least 18,000 men and possibly more. There is no evidence the above but a figure of 18,000 or more would provide a more probable figure for the army size at the time of the battle. Whatever was the case it was clear that Galway's army was considerably outnumbered by Berwick's army. Berwick probably commanded around 18,000 infantry and 7,000 cavalry. Galway would have around 12,000 to 13,000 infantry and 5,000 to 5,500 cavalry, if his army was around 18,000 strong.

The Confederate army deployed matching the frontage of Berwick's forces in a relatively thin line. The imbalance in cavalry was particularly concerning given the generally open plain the battle was to be fought on. To counter this Galway posted some of his infantry with the cavalry to even the odds a little. A council of war was then held to decide what to do and this decided to launch an attack in the hope that this might catch their enemy off guard and defeat them. The only alternative to the council seemed to be to abandon Valencia and fall back to Catalonia. Consequently, the Confederate army advanced and their opponents moved forward to meet them. At first the attack seemed to go well for the Confederates. The left half of the army which contained the British and Dutch units attacked first and did well. They made some headway against their opponents but did not make a decisive breakthrough. Ferocious attacks by the Spanish cavalry and the use of Bourbon reserves meant they did not secure victory and the attack stalled. The Confederate right had been told to hang back and to attack after the left had engaged. This they did but perhaps not as vigorously as the other half of the army. Many sources, mostly British, suggest that the Portuguese cavalry on the right collapsed almost immediately. Yet from other sources it is clear the Portuguese on the right fought well for a considerable period until the Bourbon forces managed to work around the open flank of this wing. Attacked from the front and flank the Portuguese cavalry pulled back in good order. Unfortunately this exposed the Portuguese foot in the centre, which had pushed forward in support of the rest of the infantry.

The Portuguese infantry of the centre were engaged in the front by the Bourbon infantry and were now caught in the flank by enemy cavalry and dispersed. This in turn exposed the mainly British and Dutch left half of the army. The Combined Foot Guards, a 'Marine' battalion, Mordaunt's, J. Caulfield's, Nassau's and Welderen's foot battalions all seem to have been destroyed or captured at this point in the battle.[7] It seems likely that the 'Marine' battalion destroyed at this time was probably Montjoy's. The Combined Foot Guards and Montjoy's were captured but it is not certain if it was at this time or later on as part of the group of 15 captured the next morning. With the army collapsing the Cavalier regiment formed square, a rarity on the battlefield at the time, to buy some time for the rest of the army. They paid for this by being wiped out by combined arms attacks, but did partially succeed. The Confederate cavalry of the right wing made

7   J.A.C. Hughill, *No Peace without Spain*, p.260.

some counter attacks and some of the remaining infantry made a stand. Yet nothing could save the situation, losses were heavy and the remainder of the Confederate army withdrew in disorder.

The Confederate army had lost about 4,000 killed and wounded along with about 1,000 prisoners on the battlefield, but more pain would follow. A group of 13 or 15 battalions from the centre managed to pull off the battlefield together and withdrew to a hill about eight miles from the battlefield by nightfall. By the following morning these troops, numbering about 2,000 men, were surrounded by Bourbon forces and forced to surrender. All sources list the following 13 units in this group.

British:
   Breton's
   Gorge's (35th Foot)
   Hill's (11th Foot)
   Macartney's
   Portmore's (2nd Foot)

Dutch:
   Belcastel
   Keppelfox's (NL 33)
   Lislemarais (NL 54)
   Torsay (NL 46)
   Vicouse's (NL 53)

Portuguese:
Three unknown regiments

Some sources include one or both the Combined Foot Guards and Montjoy's among those captured. Indeed, both of these units were captured but it is not certain if it was during the battle or as part of the group of 15 captured the next morning. Both units had a large number of unwounded officers captured, which strongly suggests that they could have been present, or at least a significant proportion of the units. This brought the total of casualties to 4,000 casualties and 3,000 prisoners. The cavalry had suffered during the battle but had been able to withdraw easily and avoid further loses. For the infantry it was different matter; they had suffered greatly in the battle and the withdrawal. The 20 'Portuguese' guns were also lost, along with various other items of equipment. Even those units that made it off the battlefield were scattered across the countryside and would take time to reassemble. Galway's army was in effect destroyed and Valencia lay exposed to attack.

The Aftermath

Immediately after the battle Galway pulled the forces he retained 50 miles from Almansa into Valencia province. Once a breathing space had been achieved Galway started to organise the defences of the province and collect the stragglers from the battle. At this stage about 5,000 of the remaining troops were dispersed around the area. Most of these eventually returned to the army, about 1,500 to Galway's army and the rest to Catalonia. Because of their mobility the cavalry were relatively intact, but the infantry had been shattered as a body. The Dutch battalions at the battle were destroyed and disappeared from the order of battle of the Confederate army in Spain, although some were later rebuilt elsewhere. The surviving personnel from these units were probably eventually incorporated into the remaining Dutch units. The surviving British and Portuguese infantry would later be reorganised but for the moment they, along with the Dutch, were temporarily organised into ad hoc groups under surviving officers. 2,800 replacements and recruits, 1,600 Dutch, 800 Portuguese and 200 Spanish, had recently arrived in Valencia from Lisbon and this helped with the desperate situation.

Despite these welcome reinforcements it was clear that there was no hope of remaining in Valencia province and that the army had to retire to Catalonia. Galway sent ad hoc groups of survivors of the battle to strengthen some of the garrisons of the province. These were intended to merely delay the Bourbon advance rather than seriously frustrate it. Word was sent for distant units to meet him at Tortosa and the battered army started marching for Tortosa and Catalonia. Tortosa was reached by 19 May and shortly after moved to defend the line of the River Cinca, the Catalonian border. Meanwhile Orléans had arrived at the front and taken charge of the Bourbon forces. He directed Berwick to pursue the defeated Confederates into Valencia province and secure that province. Orléans returned north to organise a similar advance into Aragon. Both groups of Bourbon forces would move to the Catalonian frontier, which was clearly the destination of Galway's force. Berwick quickly captured the city of Valencia and a number of smaller fortresses without serious opposition. More serious opposition was provided by Alcira, captured 1 June, and Xativa, captured 12 June. Both of these locations had received reinforcements of ad hoc survivors of the battle and put up a reasonable resistance. The loss of most of the province was accompanied by the loss of five pro-Confederate units. The Ciutat de València (9th Foot), Diputació del Regne de València (10th Foot), Claret's (15th Foot), Joan Nebot's Horse (5th Cavalry) and Josep Nebot's Dragoons (6th Cavalry) were all lost at this time and disappeared from the order of battle. The remnants of the infantry units were put into, or reduced into, the Ciutat d'Alacant (12th Foot). Joan Tàrrega's Horse (11th) was raised in Valencia but stationed in Catalonia during this period, but this unit was also reduced and the personnel added to the other cavalry units. It seems likely that any survivors of the 5th and 6th cavalry were similarly added to other units, although this is not recorded.

The capture of these locations brought Berwick's command to the major fortress of Denia. On 15 June the siege of Denia started but was vigorously opposed by the garrison. Denia was defended by 360 Spanish regulars from the Ciudad de Cartagena (11th Foot) and Ciutat d'Alacant (12th Foot) regiments, 185 British regulars from Montandre's and Hotham's regiments and about 2,500 miquelets and armed citizens. Over the following weeks four determined and bloody assaults were made by Berwick on Denia

19. Philippe, Duke of Orléans, by Santerre

without success. On 11 July Berwick left forces to cover the defiant fortress and continued his march towards Catalonia.

Orléans had by this time led other forces into Aragon against minimal resistance. On 25 June Saragossa fell and the rest of Aragon quickly followed. Valencia province was also largely in Bourbon hands but Alicante, Denia and a number of smaller fortresses still remained under Confederate control. Yet the majority of two provinces had been lost to the Confederate cause, a heavy blow and the Bourbon forces were closing on Catalonia. By late June both Orléans' and Berwick's forces had arrived at the River Cinca, on the route to Catalonia. The situation on the Confederate side was now desperate as the high command remained divided and Galway was receiving minimal assistance from the Catalonian forces. To buy some time Galway used his relatively intact cavalry, about 4,000 men by this time,[8] to frustrate Orléans attempts to cross the Cinca. This they did for a time but on 1 July the Bourbons managed to get a force across the river. Unable to contest this Galway again moved away, this time back to the major fortress of Lérida. By 13 July both armies were in the Lérida area and the period of excessive heat had started. Because of this both armies entered quarters and Galway finally had time to rest and reorganise.

Galway organised the surviving British infantry into five battalions by reforming the five most senior units. One of the Spanish units of Charles' army was taken into British pay and strengthened, while four new Catalan battalions were raised for British service and the Portuguese troops were reorganised. By early September the Bourbons were once again ready to continue campaigning and it was clear that when they did so they would lay siege to Lérida. Therefore Galway drew his forces together about 20 miles east of Lérida to attempt to contest this move. Parnell states that these forces amounted to 4,800 cavalry, 7,600 regular infantry, 2,200 miquelets and 20 guns.[9] Of these about 5,000 were Portuguese, 3,300 British, 4,900 Spanish (2,700 in English pay and 2,200 miquelets) and 1,400 Dutch. They would have included the following units:

---

8   A. Parnell, *The War of Succession in Spain: 1702–1711*, p.233.
9   *Ibid.*, pp.235–236

British:
Cavalry:
Harvey's Horse (3rd), Royal Dragoons (1st), Carpenter's Dragoons (3rd), Essex's Dragoons (4th), Pepper's formely Killigrew's Dragoons (8th), Pearce's Dragoons, Nassau's formerly Peterborough's Dragoons and Guiscard's Dragoons.

Infantry (all reformed from survivors of the battle):
Portmore's (2nd), Southwell's (6th), Stewart's (9th), Hill's (11th) and Blood's (17th).

Dutch:
Cavalry: Drimborn's (NLC 15), Schlippenbach's (NLD 2) and Mattha (4th Dragoons).

Infantry: Friesheim's (NL 51) and possibly another unit.[10]

Spanish:
Infantry: Saragossa regiment (formerly of Charles' army), Blosset's Catalan regiment (newly raised with two battalions) and Galway's Catalan regiment (newly raised with two battalions).

Portuguese:
Unknown. Based on the forces existing in early 1708 at least 22 squadrons and five battalions, possibly more.

Garrison of Lérida (1,800 regulars and 800 miquelets):
British: three battalions: Royal Fusiliers (7th), Wills' Marines (30th) and probably Borr's Marines (32nd).

Dutch: two 'corps': probably Leefdael's (formerly Palm's NL 24) regiment and possibly another unit.[10]

Portuguese: Unknown (one battalion).
Miquelets: 800 men

By late August Orléans was ready to continue the campaign and by mid-September the Bourbon forces had sealed off Lérida. Yet Orléans lacked siege guns and was also awaiting the outcome of events at Toulon in France. The Confederates had launched a major attack on this important position which

---

10   The exact composition of the Dutch contingents are not clear. There were three unaccounted for regiments in Catalonia at the time with five battalions – St. Amant's (NL 5 – two battalions), Leefdael's formerly Palm's (NL 24 – two battalions) and Noyelles en Falais' (NL 17). Given the size of the contingent with Galway it seems likely that at least one more battalion was with that force and possibly more. Another two 'corps' were in Lérida and it seems likely Leefdael's regiment was one of these. As this regiment had two battalions it is not clear if this was the only unit or if another unit was also involved.

had drawn some of Orléans' troops away. By the beginning of October heavy guns had arrived and so had good news from Toulon. Orléans at this time commanded about 23,000 men, considerably more than Galway's forces, and the siege could now proceed. After a few days the bombardment of Lérida started but the defence was vigorous and well-led. The defenders mounted sorties on the besiegers' lines and delayed the process. Once a breach in the outer defences was made the defenders also threw back the initial assaults and only after hard fighting were thrown back themselves. The stubborn resistance continued as renewed Bourbon effort took each line of defence.

Despite this spirited defence the Bourbons continued to make progress but with great losses. It was clear that Galway needed to act to assist the defenders of Lérida. On 29 October Galway therefore advanced towards Lérida and Orléans countered by detaching a force under Berwick to confront this move. Blocked by Berwick, Galway did not feel strong enough to attempt to force the issue and after lingering in the area without halting the siege for a week he withdrew again. The garrison held out until 14 November when the remaining 600 men of the garrison were given the honours of war by the besiegers and handed over the parts of the fortress they still controlled. Following the loss of Lérida the Bourbons secured some other smaller locations with some detachments but generally both sides entered winter quarters.

In late 1707 and early 1708 a number of changes were made. In November 1707 when the army entered winter quarters the following British and British paid troops were with the army in Catalonia:[11]

A List of the Effective Number of the Queen's Forces in Catalonia.

Cavalry

Harvey's Horse (3rd)	148
Royal Dragoon (1st)	320
Carpenter's Dragoon (3rd)	95
Essex's Dragoon (4th)	120
Pepper's Dragoon (8th)	81
Pearce's Dragoon	192
Guiscard's Dragoon	287
Nassau's Dragoon	223
Total cavalry	1,466

Infantry[12]

Portmore's (2nd)	410
Southwell's (6th)	411
Stewart's (9th)	386
Hill's (11th)	437

---

11 Anonymous, *An Impartial Enquiry into the Management of the War in Spain by the Ministry at Home*, p.12.

12 The number is brackets are the strength of the unit in October.

Blood's (17th)	266
Blosset's 1st Catalan	407 (382)
Blosset's 2nd Catalan	508 (506)
Galway's 1st Catalan	491 (530)
Galway's 2nd Catalan	502 (439)
Saragossa (Spanish)	424
Total infantry	4,242

At the same time five battalions were raised in Catalonia to help guard the frontier during the troubled time. These were the following regiments:

de Rubí's
Desvalls'
Sagarriga's
Reart's
Xammar's

These units were supposed to be 1,000-strong but never achieved anything like that number. They never received uniforms either and were disbanded after a short life in early 1708.

Shortly after this time further changes were made. Stewart's regiment was reduced and the men used to increase the size of the other four British units. One of Galway's Catalan battalions seems to have been sent to Portugal with Galway early in 1708. The remaining battalion was renamed the Whiters battalion. Essex's and Pearce's Dragoons were also both reduced and the personnel used to strengthen the other mounted units. Moragues' Horse (7th Spanish) was reduced and the personnel used to build up the strength of the Clariana Horse (8th). This unit was also renamed the Guàrdies Reials de Cavalleria Catalana (Catalonian Guard cavalry). Finally the remaining Portuguese troops in the army were reorganised and taken into British pay. Only 3,708 cavalry and 3,330 infantry remained at this point and they clearly could not return to Portugal at this time. Meanwhile a new Portuguese army was being raised in Portugal to replace the forces that had marched away and been lost.

The Portuguese Front 1707

The departure of the Portuguese field army earlier in 1706 had left Portugal very thinly defended. Few units of the original regular army remained and so the defence of Portugal rested with the newly raised 'auxiliary' units, these had been raised at the start of the war. These units were inexperienced and poorly trained. Initially it was hoped that the original field army would return to Portugal. By 1707 it was clear that the original field army would not return and that additional forces would be needed to defend Portugal and to re-open the Portuguese front. The remnants of the original army would now be paid directly by the British. In Portugal the auxiliary units would be upgraded and new units would be raised to rebuild the lost field army. This would obviously take time and meanwhile Portugal was very vulnerable to attack.

At the start of the campaign the Portuguese could only muster 9,500 men, after garrisons were detached, to defend the frontier. This army under the Duke of Cadaval amounted to 14 battalion and 15 squadrons. The Spanish were also relatively weak initially but the Spanish soon received reinforcements and started to recapture minor Portuguese held positions. In June four British battalions arrived in Portugal to strengthen the defence.

Reinforcements to Portugal
Pearce's (later the 5th Foot)
Newton's (later the 20th Foot)
Sankey's (later the 39th Foot)
Stanwix's (later disbanded)

The arrival of these four battalions was off set by the losses and detachments the Portuguese had suffered or made in the earlier part of the campaign. By September the army was still only 15 battalions strong, including the four British battalions, and 15 squadrons strong, about 8,500 men, when the Spanish moved on the major Portuguese held fortress of Cuidad Rodrigo. The garrison of this fortress consisted of 1,300 Portuguese regulars, 400 British and several hundred militia. After a siege of 15 days the Spanish launched a surprise assault and managed to catch the garrison by surprise, possibly because of some duplicity on the part of the Spanish. After minimal resistance the Spanish secured the fortress. Stung by this unexpected turn of events the Portuguese tried to besiege Moura. Yet when a relief force approached the Portuguese lifted this siege on 14 October. Both sides were happy to withdraw into quarters bringing the 1707 campaign to an end.

The 1707 campaign had been a disaster for the Confederates and they had lost many of the gains made the previous campaigns. It marked a turning point in the course of the war in Spain and Portugal. The Confederates were now very much on the defensive. In addition the following years would see an increasing number of Imperial troops coming to the area and a change of officials taking a leading role in events. These would change the dynamics within the Confederate high command.

10

The 1708 Campaign: Tortosa and Denia Lost, Menorca Gained

The events of the two previous campaigns clearly called for changes in the Confederate camp. Galway and Das Minas left Spain to return to command in Portugal, although in Das Minas' case this was largely a nominal appointment as he no longer took active command. They took with them about 1,800 of the Portuguese troops and a Catalan regiment, probably the 1st battalion of Galway's regiment. To replace them came two prominent personalities in the next phase of the war. Taking over from Galway in charge of the British forces was Stanhope. Stanhope had local contacts and had lived in Spain before the war. He had been in the peninsula for some time at this point but acting mainly in a political role. Stanhope was gifted and destined for a senior position in the future and indeed eventually became virtual Prime Minster of Britain after the war. This was his first senior military command. The other important arrival was the Austrian general Starhemberg. Starhemberg was an experienced general who had fought in Italy and Hungary during the present war. He was a reliable commander but not an overly gifted one. Despite this he was generally considered the second best Imperialist commander and so his appointment showed a serious intent to achieve something in this theatre. Starhemberg was appointed head of the Confederate forces and was in direct command of the Spanish, Austrian and Palatine troops. Stanhope had direct control of the British and Portuguese troops, along with de facto control of the Dutch. More importantly Britain provided most of the money for the Confederate cause and so became a rival centre of power in the Confederate camp. This situation would continue the divisions which had plagued the Confederate cause so far.

More troops from out of the theatre were urgently needed to stabilise the situation and continue the fight. The situation in Flanders meant that the number of British and Dutch reinforcements would be limited and also would take some time to arrive. The failure of the Confederate attack on Toulon and the situation in Italy, where there were now no French troops, meant that there were Imperial troops stationed there that were surplus to the area's needs. Italy was also relatively close and so troops from there could quickly arrive. So it was that Austrian units and Palatine units arrived in the theatre accompanied by a new Austrian supreme commander of the Confederate forces in Spain. These two factors would change the balance of power within the Confederate high command and complicated matters.

In early 1708 we have two breakdowns of the forces in Catalonia, Valencia and Majorca. The first is from March,[1] the second April,[2] they are as follows:

British
Infantry, March
'Marines'[3]	664 (500)
Southwell's (6th)	674 (500)
Blood's (17th)	674 (500)
Mordaunt's (28th)	693 (938[4])
Blosset's 1st Battalion[5]	398 (-)

Infantry, April[6]
Portmore's (2nd)	- (500)
Hill's (11th)	- (500)
Wade's (33rd)	- (938[4])

Cavalry, March
Harvey's Horse (3rd)	306 (260)
Royal Dragoon (1st)	345, 26 without horses (330)
Pepper's Dragoon (8th)	232, 38 without horses (150)
Guiscard's Dragoons[7]	316, 47 without horses (330)
Nassau's Dragoon	345 (330)

Cavalry, April
Carpenter's Dragoons (3rd)[8]	- (150)

Dutch
Infantry
St. Amant's (NL 5)	598 (607)
Leefdael's (NL 24)	524 (444)
Friesheim's (NL 51)	475 (482)
Noyelles en Falais' (NL 17)	379 (410)

---

1 *Feldzüge des Prinzen Eugen von Savoyen*, 10. Band (1708) (Vienna: K.K. Kriegs-Archiv, 1885), p.520.

2 *Österreichische militärische Zeitschrift*, 1840 Band 2, pp.292–295.

3 The marines are probably either Wills'(30th) or Borr's (32nd) Marines or a combined unit of both of these units.

4 Mordaunt's and Wade's units were formed from returning stragglers and wounded, survivors of Almansa and others. They had a combined strength of 938 men in April.

5 This unit is listed as British although it was initially composed of Spanish personnel. It was disbanded by April and probably the personnel were added to other units.

6 Portmore's and Hill's existed in March but it is not clear if Wade's did.

7 Guiscard's Dragoons were reduced at the end of the year and the men added to Pepper's unit.

8 This unit was reduced or sent home soon after this time.

Cavalry

Drimborn's (NLC 15)	247 (247)
Schlippenbach's (NLD 2)	364 (364)
Mattha (4th Dragoons)	349 (349)

Portuguese

Infantry, March

F. Dabren	350
S. de Bollions	350
P. Gayetana	350
Vadt	350

Infantry, April

Suazer	300
Sottomayor	300
Cataneo	300
De Saa	400
Ares	300

Probably the four units in March are the same as four of the April units, most likely those not in Denia, but with different names.

Cavalry, March

Tavor	464, one dismounted
De Prado	464, 38 dismounted
Naronha	476, 11 dismounted
Susa	479
Almeida	409, 50 dismounted
Mello	442, 22 dismounted
Gamma	388, 18 dismounted
Uzares	130
Comp. des Profossen	27

Cavalry, April

Almedia
Meria
O'Kelly
Castro
Miranda
Cunea
Sottomayor

These units totalled 2,402 men in April.

The Almeida regiment features in both lists. The other six units in the April list are probably the same as other the six listed in March, possibly with the Gamma, Uzares and Comp. des Profossen combined into a single unit.

Spanish

Infantry, March

Catalonian Guards (3rd)	327 (330)
Noyelles (4th)	230 (741 – 367 in 2nd battalion in Majorca)
Shover (5th)	423 (477)
'Castilian Guards' (Castiglioni 6th)	761 (814)[9]
La Deputacion (7th)	366 (347)
La Ciudad (8th)	425 (353)
Ciudad de Zaragoza (13th)[10]	186 (252, 84 in Denia)
Ferrer's (14th)	534 (502)
Whiters' (21st)[10]	483 (801 – included Blosset's 22nd in April)
Blosset's 2nd Btn (22nd)[10]	293 (merged with 21st by April)

Infantry, April

Ciudad de Cartagena (11th)	161 (in Denia)
Ciutat d'Alacant (12th)	593 (66 in Denia)
Taafe (23rd)[11]	950
Various Garrisons	236

Cavalry, March

Zinzendorf's (1st)	346 plus 60 dismounted.
Morras' (2nd) officers[12]	421 plus four dismounted and 28 reformed
Sobias' (3rd)	300
Nebot's (4th) officers	389 plus 51 dismounted & 33 reformed
Catalonian Gds (8th)	500 all dismounted
Aragon (12th)	281 plus nine reformed officers[12]

Cavalry, April

Zinzendorf's (1st)	322 plus 111 dismounted
Morras' (2nd)	286 plus 131 dismounted
Sobias' (3rd)	306 plus 92 dismounted
Nebot's (4th)	324 plus 121 dismounted
Catalonian Gds (8th)	552 all dismounted.
Aragon (12th)	218 plus 81 dismounted
Detachments in Majorca	95 plus 6 dismounted
Various Garrisons	63 plus 59 dismounted

---

9   Many sources identify a Spanish unit as the Castilian Guards but the identity of this unit is not clear. It seems to be an alternative name for Castiglioni's (6th) unit as this unit is not identified elsewhere.

10   In British pay.

11   This unit was formerly raised in Italy in the Bourbon Spanish army. It was captured in Italy and taken over by the Imperialist army. In early 1708 it was shipped from Italy and transferred to the Spanish Catalan army. It had two battalions.

12   Reformed officers are the officers of units that have been disbanded and are awaiting a command.

Imperialist
Infantry, April
Reventlau   1,200 in three battalions

This unit was the first of a larger Imperialist contingent that would arrive in this year and the following years.

Palatine
Infantry, April

Leibregiment zu fuss	656
Barbo	632
Coppe	565
Bentheim	676
Efferen	691
Schonberg	372

These units nominally had two battalions each. The exception was Schonberg's which was only a single battalion. This contingent was formerly employed by the Imperialists in Italy. In 1708 it transferred, along with some cavalry which had not arrived at this point, to Spain. In Spain it was mainly paid for by the Dutch but also in part by the British.

The Confederate forces were clearly not in any shape to directly confront the superior Bourbon forces at this point. By July the enemy forces were preparing for the upcoming campaign. Orléans with the main Bourbon army of around 22,000 men would clearly aim to complete the conquest of Valencia by taking Alicante and Denia. To do this they would also have to take Tortosa, the gateway to Valencia, in Catalonia. A second force of around 10,000 men under Noailles was being prepared in France and would attempt to intervene in the north. To counter these threats the Confederates prepared the threatened garrisons as much as was possible and formed into groups to attempt to counter their opponents. In the north a group of around 4,000 men under Prince Henry of Hesse-Darmstadt would attempt to block Noailles, while in the south the main army of about 10,200 under Starhemberg would attempt to frustrate the planed operations against Tortosa, Denia and Alicante.

Full details of the forces involved are not available but the following details are known:[13]

Starhemberg's Main Army Near Tortosa
10,200 men – 3,000 Germans, 3,000 Spanish, 2,000 British, 1,200 Dutch, 1,000 Portuguese.

The Dutch contingent probably includes Drimborn's Dutch cavalry regiments.

---

13   A. Parnell, *The War of Succession in Spain: 1702–1711*, pp.246–247.

The British contingent was Harvey's Horse, the Royal Dragoons, Pepper's, Nassau's and part of Guiscard's (about 1,000 men). In addition there was Southwell's and Wade's infantry (about 800 men). Many of the other British units were recruiting in Britain.

Prince Henry of Hesse-Darmstadt's Army at Ampurdan
10 battalions and 12 squadrons, about 4,000 men.

The Spanish contingent was six battalions and eight cavalry squadrons from these units.

Infantry: Noyelles (4th), La Deputacion (7th), La Ciudad (8th), Ferrer's (14th) and Taafe (two battalions – 23rd).

Cavalry: Morras' Cavalry (2nd) and Nebot's Cavalry (4th).
The Dutch had two battalions in this army – probably the St. Amant or Noyelles en Falais' units. The Schlippenbach's and Mattha's Dragoons with four squadrons were with the group.

There were two unknown Portuguese battalions present.

Garrison of Tortosa
3,200 regulars and 1,000 miquelets – three Dutch battalions, three German battalions, two battalions of Spanish and Portuguese. The Dutch Leefdael's and Friesheim's may have been in this group. The German battalions were one each from the Barbo, Bentheim and Efferen Palatine regiments. The Spanish Whiters' infantry and Aragon cavalry units were also present.

Garrison of Denia
About 1,000 regulars and an unknown number of irregulars

227 British. Mainly marine detachments from Borr's, Churchill's, Seymour's and Wills' regiments. The Spanish Ciudad de Cartagena infantry regiment and various other detachments and fragmented units, probably 500 to 600 men. Plus an unknown number of miquelets and armed citizens. Approximately 300 men of the Ares Portuguese regiment.

Garrison of Alicante
About 2,000 men

The Ciutat d'Alacant Spanish infantry regiment of about 400 men and about 800 miquelets. About 800 British regulars from Hotham's and Syburg's Huguenot regiments.

Tortosa, Denia and Alicante

With preparations completed Orléans moved on Tortosa and arrived at this gateway between Valencia and Catalonia on 11 June. The next day D'Asfeld, Orléans' second in command, also arrived at the fortress and the siege could begin. The defences of Tortosa had been strengthened but as Orléans army was about 22,000 strong the Confederates could not directly confront it. The defenders of Tortosa were active and had plentiful ammunition but they could only hope to slow down the progress of the siege and not stop it. By 10 July the Bourbon forces had made a breach in the defences, Confederate supplies were starting to get short and there was no sign of relief. It was time for the garrison to seek terms. On 15 July the remnants of the garrison handed over the fortress and marched out with full honours after a creditable defence. The three Palatine battalions from Barbo, Bentheim and Efferen regiments were effective destroyed by their participation in the siege, mainly by desertion rather than casualties.

20. Guido Wald Rüdiger, Count Starhemberg.

At this point in the campaign there was a lull as events in Flanders caused the Bourbon army to be weakened. Some of the troops from Orléans' army moved north in the aftermath of the French defeat at Oudernarde. At the end of July more Confederate troops arrived from Italy and Starhemburg felt strong enough to advance. This move was only half-hearted and was quickly blocked as the remaining Bourbon troops took up a strong blocking position. The Confederate forces were still outnumbered by their opponents. For three months the two main armies faced each other but neither made any significant moves.

Reinforcements from Italy, July 1708

Palatine Cavalry
Four horse regiments (1,083 men, 1,078 horses)
Stolzenberg's (237 men, 227 horses)
Spee's (267 men, 267 horses)
Frankenberg's (291 men, 292 horses)
Schellard's (288 men, 291 horses)

The unit strengths are from December 1707, when the units were in Italy.

Imperial Cavalry
Jorger's Dragoons (about 1,000 men at full strength)

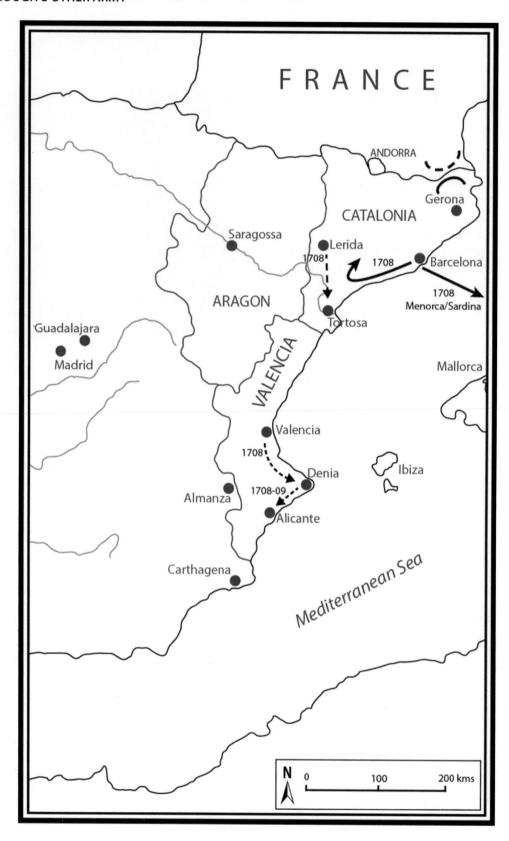

Map 7
Catalonia,
1708–09

Hussars (one company of 50 to 100 men, probably from Ebergenyi's regiment)

Imperial Infantry
Two regiments of three battalions each: Guido Starhemberg's and the Osnabruck regiments. About 3,600 men.
Approximately 2,200 cavalry and 3,600 infantry.

By this time the campaign in Flanders had also brought the activity in northern Catalonia to a halt. Noailles had moved south from Perpignan in France during May with the intention of joining Orléans main Bourbon force. The Prince of Hesse-Darmstadt countered by occupying a strong position on the River Ter to block this move. Over the following weeks the Confederate forces foiled all attempts to advance by Noailles' troops. By the end of June news arrived of the events in Flanders, notably the Battle of Oudernarde, and much of Noailles' army marched north as a result of this. Noailles and the rest of the army also pulled back and ending the threat from the north.

The lull in campaigning further south had given the Confederates a chance to press the enemy in an area where they had superiority, at sea. The plan was to use the naval superiority of the Confederates to capture further isolated Mediterranean garrisons. The first target was Cagliari in Sardinia, control of this fortress effectively gave control of the island. In August about 1,000 Spanish troops and 600 British marines, detachments drawn from the four regiments in the theatre, set sail. On 11 August the expedition arrived at Cagliari. After a short bombardment by the naval guns the Confederate troops started to land and the fortress quickly surrendered. Some of the Spanish troops were left as a garrison for the newly acquired fortress and the expedition set sail for Minorca.

A new Spanish regiment (24th) was raised in Sardinia. This was the Carles Llorach or Sardenya regiment.

Minorca had a number of fortified positions and would require a more serious effort to capture. Stanhope, the British commander in Catalonia, had assembled reinforcements for the 600 British marines which remained with the fleet. These rendezvoused with the fleet returning from Sardinia at Minorca on 13 September. The additional troops were about 800 Spanish troops, 600 British troops (Southwell's regiment), 600 Portuguese and 10 guns plus some mortars according to Parnell.[14] Another source lists the following units being involved in this phase of the operation:[15]

British
Detachments from the Royal (1st) and Pepper's (8th) Dragoon regiments.
Detachments from Borr's, Churchill's, Seymour's and Wills' Marine regiments
Southwell's (6th) infantry regiment

---

14 *Ibid.*, p.254.
15 <http://www.11setembre1714.org/batalles/batalla-1708-09-29-menorca-frame.html>

Imperial
Gschwind infantry regiment (probably detachments only)

Spanish
Mallorca Militia Battalion – about 300 men raised in Majorca
Castiglioni (6th) – probably detachments only
Ciudad de Cartagena (11th) – probably detachments only
Faber (26th) – This unit was formerly a unit raised in Italy in the Bourbon Spanish army. It was captured in Italy and taken over by the Imperialist army and then transferred to the Spanish army.

The understrength Aragon Spanish cavalry regiment was also sent from Tortosa but this unit seems to have arrived later.

Portuguese
G. Albuquerque infantry regiment, about 200 men
This was a total of about 2,500 men

Under the command of Stanhope these forces quickly moved to capture the island. Various minor positions were quickly captured and by 19 September the Confederates were ready to tackle St. Philip, the major fortress on the island. They would do this with the assistance of 32 additional guns landed from the fleet. After a short but brisk siege the Bourbon forces had no choice but to capitulate and so on 2 October they handed over the fortress. Southwell's regiment and about 200 British marines were left as garrison of the island. The Aragon Spanish cavalry also seem to have remained as a garrison. The remainder of the expedition returned to the mainland after a very successful time. The capture of Sardinia and Minorca were great successes but could do little to influence the campaign on the mainland.

D'Asfeld, the Bourbon commander in Valencia, had by this time decided to complete the capture of Valencia province by attempting to take Denia and Alicante. Having collected about 12,000 troops D'Asfeld arrived at Denia on 1 November. Soon after this the siege began and the garrison sought relief. The garrison commander had sent to Catalonia for help before the siege began but had not had a reply by the time the siege started. Alicante was also asked for help and on 11 November 200 Spanish regulars and 150 miquelets arrived by sea from Alicante. This was far too little to change the situation and already by this time a partial breach had been made by D'Asfeld's forces. This allowed part of the defensive positions to be taken by assault. Following this the Bourbon troops could attempt to breach the main defences. By 18 November a major breach in the remaining defences had been achieved and the defenders of the fortress had little choice but surrender.

This left only Alicante still in Confederate hands. Having received additional forces D'Asfeld with about 14,000 men now moved on Alicante. The advance guard of the army arrived at Alicante on 28 November and the main body a few days later. By 1 December the fortress was put under siege. The outer defences were held by the Spanish and were weak. So quickly some of these were taken and the rest abandoned. Yet the castle remained and this was in an exceptionally strong position. It was nearly impossible to bombard and so the walls would have to be mined instead, a time-consuming operation which meant that a relief force would have time to arrive.

Once again the garrison commander of Alicante had already sent a message asking for help from the main army before the siege started. Perhaps in response to this Starhemberg launched an attempt to recapture Tortosa, which blocked the route into Valencia, by a surprise lunge. Early on the morning of 3 December Stanhope managed to get close to three of the gates of Tortosa and launched an assault. These were beaten off with considerable loses on both sides. The action dragged on during the day but clearly the attempt had failed and the army withdrew before the main Bourbon forces could intervene. The main armies then went into winter quarters.

The repulse of the attempt on Tortosa and entry into winter quarters meant that the defenders could not hope for relief from this source. As bombardment was impractical the Bourbon forces now settled down to digging a mine through the solid rock under the fortress.

21. Claude François Bidal, Marquis d'Asfeld

This was to be a long process but one that the defenders could do little to disrupt. In January 1709 a Confederate naval squadron arrived but could not find a safe location to land and so sailed off. By the end of February the Bourbon forces were getting close to finishing the mine which they would set off and so blow a hole in the fortress above. Following the practice of the time they informed their opponents of this and arranged for them to see it. The intention was to get the defenders to surrender without having to blow the mine. Yet the garrison commander, Richards, knew that the rock was full of clefts and he hoped that these would negate the effect of the blast. Therefore he resolved to let the mine be exploded and hope that it would not damage the defences too much.

The Bourbons informed the defenders that they would explode the mine on 3 March 1709, once again hoping that the defenders would submit before this time. Instead Richards and many of the senior officers took station in the area above the mine to put resolve into the defenders and await results. At six in the morning the mine exploded and killed Richards and a number of the other senior commanders and defenders of the fortress. This was, of course, a tragic event but did not prove to be decisive in the siege as it did not result in a practical breach once the dust had settled, and so the siege continued. Meanwhile forces were being collected to attempt to bring relief to the beleaguered garrison by amphibious action.

A force of about 4,000 soldier plus sailors and guns was assembled to attempt this and they arrived at Alicante on 18 April 1709. The fortress was still tightly besieged and there seemed no possibility of a landing to secure relief and so its fall was inevitable. Therefore Stanhope, the commander of the land

22. James Stanhope, 1st Earl Stanhope, by Sir Godfrey Kneller. (National Portrait Gallery)

forces, resolved instead to end the suffering of the doomed garrison and seek terms. Stanhope proposed to D'Asfeld that the garrison be allowed to surrender and embark on the Confederate fleet. This was swiftly accepted and so it was that after withstanding a five-month siege the much-depleted garrison handed over the last remaining Confederate fortress in Valencia. The Confederate forces sailed for Catalonia to aid in the ongoing defence of that province.

The Portuguese Front 1708

1708 was another quiet year in Portugal. The Portuguese army was still in chaos from the results of the previous campaigns. With the original regular army now mainly either lost or cut off from Portugal in the Catalonia area the process of rebuilding the army continued. At this point in the process the Portuguese seem to be aiming to field a force of 30 infantry regiments of a single battalion of 420 men each, 11 cavalry regiments of 420 men each and probably two Dragoon regiments of 600 men.[16] Yet only 13 battalions and 24 squadrons were actually capable of taking the field. In addition to these forces there were some Portuguese militia battalions and squadrons. There were already four British battalions in Portugal and these were joined by a further two units.

British Infantry Regiments in Portugal
Pearce's (later the 5th Foot)
Newton's (later the 20th Foot)
Sankey's (later the 39th Foot)
Stanwix's (later disbanded)
New arrivals in 1708:
Barrymore's (later 13th Foot) – this unit was converted into Pearce's Dragoons in 1706 and had just been re-raised
Paston's (later disbanded)

The field army amounted to about 3,000 cavalry and 9,000 infantry. The army was under the command of the Portuguese Marquis de Fronteira and the British under Galway. Galway was sick and so in fact took little part in the campaign.

---

16 *Österreichische militärische Zeitschrift 1840*, Band 4, pp.22–23.

The Bourbon army facing this force under Bay had about 4,000 cavalry and 8,000 infantry along with other supporting forces. The opposing armies were roughly of the same size but neither had much incentive for decisive actions, a recipe for inactivity. The Portuguese troops were still very raw and in need of training, while for the Bourbon forces it was enough to keep the Portuguese army occupied while the decisive action of the year took place in Valencia and Catalonia.

The campaigning opened with raids by both sides across the border. These caused distress but achieved very little. In late May the two opposing armies gathered near to each other on either side of the River Guardiana. For the rest of the campaigning season the two sides essentially sat and watched each other. The raids continued and occasional movements occurred but all to no purpose. Two positions at Moura and Serpa were abandoned by the Bourbons after being razed. The Portuguese then took over these positions and started to rebuild them. Both sides entered winter quarters as soon as they could and ended a campaign in which nothing significant happened.

11

The Palatine Forces

The Electorate of the Palatine supplied troops to the Confederate cause under a series of contracts and they served on many fronts. Six infantry regiments with a total of 11 battalions and four cavalry regiments with a total of eight squadrons served in Spain. These units were mainly in the pay of the Dutch but the Leibregiment zu fusss and Efferen infantry regiments were in British pay. In the later part of the war the Dutch were reluctant to commit more Dutch regiments to Iberia. Instead the Palatine troops were sent as fulfilment of the Dutch obligation to provide troops. All of these units were experienced, reliable troops who had previously been fighting in Italy along side the Imperial forces there. In 1708 the units were transported from Italy to Catalonia and they served there from then on. They were usually combined with the British and Dutch troops when part of larger armies.

Palatine Organisation and Tactics

The organisation of the units in Spain was different to the theoretical organisation normally used by Palatine troops. It was common for troops that were hired to use a different organisation because of the wishes of the hiring state or as part of the contract. To some extent this seems to the case with the Palatine troops in Spain, particularly the infantry. The following is the organisation used in Spain.

Infantry
Six regiments were sent to Spain. Five of these nominally had two battalions while one, the Schonberg regiment, had just a single battalion. As the size of the battalions dwindled it was common for the two battalion-strong units to fight, officially or unofficially, as a single battalion.

The battalions in Spain seem to have had an official full strength of 480 men. Normally, outside Iberia, Palatine battalions had five companies of 120 or 128 men; one of these companies was grenadiers. No details of the internal structure of the units in Spain are known. It is possible that they retained the five-company structure but presumably with a lower establishment.

Alternatively they may have retained companies of about 120 men but only fielded four companies.

The losses of the infantry forces a reorganisation was carried out in late 1709. The remaining troops were reduced to five regiments each of a single battalion. These battalions were then organised 'on the Dutch footing' and had 10 companies of 66 men.

Little is known about the tactics of the Palatinate troops. It seems most likely that they fired by rank as this was the most common method at the time. Yet they were hired by the British and Dutch who often insisted on hired troops using their platoon firing system and so they may have used this system. It is simply not possible to say for sure.

Cavalry

Four regiments of cavalry were sent to Spain and these were all Horse units. Each unit had two squadrons of three companies of 50 men each. This along with staff gave the units a full strength of 310 men; the Spee regiment had an official strength of 308 men.

As with the infantry little is known of the cavalry's tactics. Many German units during this period charged at a slow trot to maintain order, possibly firing their pistols as they closed with the enemy. It is therefore possible that the Palatine units also did this. The Palatine units were often in commands with the British and Dutch cavalry units and so may have copied their tactics of charging at the trot but without firing. As with the infantry it is impossible to know for sure.

Palatine Uniforms

Infantry

Before 1708 the Palatine regiments had a variety of facing colours but by this time the uniform had been simplified. The Leibregiment zu fusss still wore a uniform with blue facings and white lace and buttons after this time. Barbo's regiment had white facings during the early part of 1708. All other units had red facings and Barbo's had also changed over to red by the end of 1708.

Grenadiers prior to 1708 had worn short caps. By 1708 they had changed to bearskins probably with bags in the facing colour, but it is not clear if the units had changed over by the time they arrived in Spain.

Infantry Uniforms

Unit	Coat	Cuffs	Waistcoat	Breeches	Stockings	Buttons/Hat Lace
Leibregiment zu fusss	Blue	Blue	Blue	Blue	White	White
Barbo's Regiment (early 1708)	Blue	White	White	Blue	White	Yellow
All Other Regiments	Blue	Red	Red	Blue	White	Yellow

Cavalry Uniforms

Unit	Coat	Cuffs	Waistcoat	Breeches	Buttons/Hat Lace	Saddle Cloth/ Edging
Frankenberg's	Grey	Red	Red	White	Yellow	Grey/ Red
Frankenberg's (Stolzenberg's)	Grey	Yellow	Yellow	White	Yellow	Grey/ Yellow
Schellard's	Grey	Yellow	Yellow	White	Yellow	Grey/Yellow
Spee's Mill's	Grey	Blue	Blue	Blue	Yellow	Grey/ Blue

12

The Austrian or Imperial Army

Austria was a major component of the Confederate cause and the Confederate candidate for the king of Spain was Austrian. It is therefore perhaps surprising that at first the Austrians did not send any troops to Spain. The Austrian or Imperial army started to arrive in Catalonia in 1708. This was following the disastrous 1707 Spanish campaign but also after the Italian front had been stabilised. Until this time the Italian, and to a lesser extent other fronts, had been the main focus of the Austrian war effort. Defeat in these areas could lead to an invasion of the Austrian core territories and so they were crucial. By the end of 1707 the campaigns in Italy and southern France had become quiet and stabilised and so troops could be sent to Spain. From 1708 the Austrian units, particularly the infantry, were a key component of the Confederate forces. Starhemberg, an experienced Austrian general, was commander of the army in Catalonia from this time.

Austrian Organisation and Tactics

Infantry
When Austrian infantry regiments were first sent to Spain they each consisted of four battalions and one grenadier company, in theory. In reality all but one of the units sent actually consisted of just two or three battalions. A battalion at this time had four companies of 150 men, 600 in total, and the regimental grenadier company had 100 men. A regiment would have 1,300 men if it had two battalions, 1,900 with three battalions and 2,500 with four battalions. Of course, in common with all armies, it was very rare that units actually had anything like the numbers of men they were supposed to have when they actually took the field. In 1711 the whole army was reorganised and units standardised. Regiments would now have three battalions each and two grenadier companies. The battalions had five companies of 140 men, 700 in total, and the grenadier companies 100 men each. So from 1711 a regiment now had, in theory, 2,300 men. Seven regiments were eventually sent to Spain with a total of 21 battalions.

Austrian units fought in four ranks. They were trained in a system similar to the platoon firing that the British and Dutch used but in theory they only used this when fighting against the Ottomans. Instead, against European opponents, they used a rank firing system. Despite this on at least one occasion, at the Battle of Saragossa (1710), one of the units seems to have used platoon firing. It seems likely that either system could be used depending on what seemed the best at the time. The fact that the use of the platoon firing system was noteworthy on this occasion suggests that it was not commonly used.

Cavalry

Two kinds of cavalry unit were sent to Spain, dragoon regiments and a company of hussars.

The dragoon regiments had 12 companies organised into six squadrons of two companies each. Until 1711 a company was 100 men but after that time it was reduced to 84 men. Therefore a squadron was 200 men, 168 from 1711. A regiment was 1,200 men up to 1711 and 1,000 after this time. Three Dragoon regiments were eventually sent to Spain.

A company of hussars was 100 men but it seems that only a half of a company was sent, probably with additional personnel needed to enable it to operate independently. Thus it numbered 50 to 60 men at full strength.

Austrian dragoons were cavalry who would normally take a supporting or secondary role to the primary battle cavalry, the cuirassiers. In Spain no Austrian cuirassiers were sent so the Dragoons were the battle cavalry of the Austrian contingent. Austrian battle cavalry used a slow advance into combat, firing as they advanced before completing the charge at a trot. This tactic worked well against the Ottomans and in earlier wars but was not as effective in the circumstances of this time. Eugene of Savoy, the gifted commander of the Austrian army of the time, therefore encouraged the battle cavalry to finish off the charge by breaking into a gallop after firing. In effect they were to use similar tactics to their French opponents. This was commonly used in the field rather than the older tactics.

The hussars' tactics were those typical of light cavalry of the period. They were not primarily intended to fight as battle cavalry. Instead their role was to scout for the army, screen movements and skirmish with opponents. For this reason they are often not mentioned in orders of battle as they were usually not particularly involved in battles.

Artillery

Austrian infantry regiments were supposed to have one small 3-pounder regimental gun attached to the regiment for each battalion. These were intended to provide close support to the battalions but were not manoeuvrable enough to perform in the same way as later battalion guns. There is no record of these being present with the units in Spain, although this may be because of a lack of records.

Austrian Uniforms

Infantry Uniforms

Unit	Coat	Cuffs	Waistcoat	Breeches	Stockings	Buttons/Hat Lace
Bagni (1710), Browne	Pearl Grey	Pearl Grey	Pearl Grey	Pearl Grey	Blue	Grey (coat) & Yellow (waistcoat)/ White
Eck, Traun	Pearl Grey	Paille (pale yellow)	Pearl Grey	Pearl Grey	Pearl Grey	White/White
Gschwind	White	White	White	White	White	White/None
Lorraine Lifeguard Osnabruck	Pearl Grey	Green	Pearl Grey	Pearl Grey	Red	Yellow/ White?
Reventlau, O'Dwyer	White	Red	White	White	Red	Yellow/None
G. Starhemberg	Pearl Grey	Blue	Blue	Pearl Grey (Blue 1710)	Pearl Grey	White/None
Toldo	Pearl Grey	Pearl Grey	Blue	Blue	White	Yellow/White

Cavalry Uniforms

Unit	Coat	Cuffs	Waistcoat	Breeches	Buttons/ Hat Lace	Saddle Cloth/ Edging
Battee Dragoons	Blue	Blue	Red	Blue	Yellow	Red/ Blue piped Yellow
Jorger Dragoons (Up to 1709)	Blue	Yellow	Blue	Buff	Yellow	Red/ Yellow
Jorger Dragoons (from 1709)	Red	Black	Red	Buff	White	Red/Yellow
Vaubonne Dragoons	Blue	Red	Blue	Buff	Yellow	Red/ Blue

Hussar Uniforms

Unit	Kalpak Bag	Dolman/Faicng	Breeches	Waistbelt	Cords	Sabretache
Ebergenyi	Red	Whitish/Red	Red	Whitish/Red	Yellow	Whitish/ Red

Artillery

The wood on guns was painted yellow and the metalwork black.

Unit	Coat	Cuffs	Waistcoat	Breeches	Stockings	Buttons/Hat Lace
All	Pearl Grey	Pearl Grey	Pearl Grey	Pearl Grey	Pearl Grey	Yellow

13

The 1709 Campaign: Deadlock in Catalonia, Disaster on the Caya

General peace negotiations had been proceeding for a few years but up to this point only sporadically and with little expectation of success. By 1709 all sides in the war were suffering heavily and there was a growing desire for a peace to end the war. The negotiations were by this time serious and many expected them to bring peace soon. In this climate many leaders were reluctant to take chances that could bring needless losses and possibly also cause problems in the ongoing negotiations. Because of this the campaign of 1709 was notably quiet, especially in Spain.

Forces in Catalonia, Early May[1]

Imperialist: 12 battalions, 6 squadrons, 1 company, 7,933 men

Starhemberg	3 battalions	1,918 men
Reventlau	3 battalions	1,795 men
Osnabruck	3 battalions	1,593 men
Gschwind	3 battalions	1,732 men
Jorger Dragoons	6 squadrons	841 men
Ebengenyi Hussars	1 company	54 men

Spanish: 15 battalions, 12 squadrons, 7,959 men

Ahumada (1st)	1 battalion	296 men
Catalonian Guards (3rd)	1 battalion	488 men
Tattenbach, ex Noyelles (4th)	1 battalion	500 men
Shover (5th)	1 battalion	240 men
Castiglioni (6th)	1 battalion	650 men
La Deputacion (7th)	1 battalion	291 men

---

1   *Österreichische militärische Zeitschrift* 1842 Band 3, pp.198–200.

La Ciudad (8th)	1 battalion	300 men
Ciudad de Cartagena (11th)	1 battalion	150 men
Ciutat d'Alacant (12th)	Disbanded, men placed in 1st regiment	
Ciudad de Zaragoza (13th)	1 battalion	120 men
Ferrer's (14th)	1 battalion	503 men
Whiters' (21st)	Transferred to British pay as Dalziel's regiment, location unknown in 1709	
Taafe (23rd)	2 battalions	1,001 men
Buol (25th)[2]	1 battalion	773 men
Faber (26th)	2 battalions	1,016 men

Note: The Taafe and Faber regiments were later reduced to single battalions.

Zinzendorf's (1st)	2 squadrons	200 men
Morras' (2nd)	2 squadrons	200 men
Sobias' (3rd)	2 squadrons	120 men
Nebot's (4th)	2 squadrons	500 men
Catalonian Gds (8th)	2 squadrons	400 men
Aragon (12th)	2 squadrons	211 men

Note: The Catalonian Guards regiment returned to garrison Sardinia during the year.

British: 2 battalions, 8 squadrons, 1,955 men

Mordaunt's (28th)	1 battalion	450 men
Wade's (33rd)	1 battalion	450 men
Harvey's Horse (3rd)	2 squadrons	
Royal Dragoons (1st)	2 squadrons	
Pepper's Dragoons (8th)	2 squadrons	
Nassau's Dragoons	2 squadrons	

The 8 cavalry squadrons had a total of 1,055 men.

Dutch: 4 battalions, 6 squadrons, 1,973 men

St. Amant's (NL 5)	2 battalions	470 men
Verpoorten, ex Noyelles en Falais' (NL 17)	2 battalions	424 men

Note: These units reorganised into a single battalion each during the year.

Drimborn's (NLC 15)	2 squadrons
Schlippenbach's (NLD 2)	2 squadrons
Mattha (4th Dragoon)	2 squadrons

The six cavalry squadrons had a total of 1,079 men.

---

2   This unit was another former unit from the Bourbon Spanish army in Italy. It was raised in Switzerland from the canton of Grison, and hence is sometimes called the Grison regiment.

Portuguese: 2 battalions, 21 squadrons, 4,305 men

Bouillion	1 battalion	440 men
Albuquerque	1 battalion	460 men
Almedia	3 squadrons	
Meria	3 squadrons	
O'Kelly	3 squadrons	
Castro	3 squadrons	
Miranda	3 squadrons	
Cunea (Acunha?)	3 squadrons	
Sottomayor	3 squadrons	

The 21 cavalry squadrons had a total of 4,305 men. The Meria regiment was absorbed into the others during the year.

Palatine: 6 battalions, 8 squadrons, 3,388 men

Leibregiment zu fuss	2 battalions	780 men
Barbo	1 battalion	400 men
Coppe	2 battalions	771 men
Schonberg	1 battalion	370 men
Frankenbergs, ex Stolzenberg's	2 squadrons	
Spee's	2 squadrons	
Frankenberg's	2 squadrons	
Schellard's	2 squadrons	

The eight cavalry squadrons had a total of 1,067 men.

Note: The losses of the previous campaign, particularly desertion, had forced the temporary reorganisation of the infantry into six battalions. A further reorganisation at the end of the year resulted in these troops being organised into five battalions. In total there were 41 battalions and 61 squadrons, 27,459 men.

As in the previous campaign these troops were divided between two field forces and various garrisons. No details are available but about 15,000 men under Starhemberg assembled once again in the strong positions used in the previous campaign. These were opposed by Bezons in command of a similar number of Bourbon troops. In the north of Catalonia around Ampurdan Count Uhlfeldt commanded a smaller force tasked to repeat the task of the previous year of blocking any movements by the Bourbon army under Noailles. This proved to be an easy task as, apart from descent on an isolated camp by Noailles, the northern front was quiet.

It was broadly similar situation in the south. During the early part of the year the siege of Alicant was proceeding, this fortress finally fell in April. Also in April Bezons moved to take a minor position on the River Noguera, but the garrison put up strong resistance against a less than full-blown attack and after a while Bezons' forces pulled back to its previous positions. In July an additional 3,500 troops joined Starhemberg's army and he launched an advance. On 27 July he arrived at the weakly fortified town of Balageur which surrender the next day. Bezons had been expressly forbidden from risking a major engagement and so did not react to Starhemberg's moves.

Starhemberg also did not want to risk a major engagement and so after taking another minor town Starhemberg retired to quarters. Bezons followed suit, effectively bringing the campaign in Catalonia to an end for this year.

Meanwhile earlier in the year the project to capture Cadiz again resurfaced. This had a lot to recommend it and could be attempted with little risk. If the defences were too strong the task force could just sail away. The main force under Wills consisted of one British dragoon regiment and nine British infantry regiments, about 5,000 men.

Wills' Force: 9 battalions and 2 squadrons
  Rochfort's Dragoons (2 squadrons – 407 men)
  1st Scots Guards Battalion
  Royal Fusiliers (later 7th Foot) – reformed after the siege of Lérida
  Whetham's (later 27th Foot)
  Bowles' – reformed after Almansa
  Dormer's (formerly Mohun's) – reformed after Almansa
  Gore's
  Innchequin's
  Lepel's
  Munden's

23. Adrien Maurice de Noailles

This group was to rendezvous with another group under Stanhope with Harrison's (formerly Southwell's, 6th Foot), an unknown dismounted Spanish cavalry unit and a train at Gibraltar before sailing on to capture Cadiz. Before the expedition could set off further intelligence arrived indicating that the defences of Cadiz had been greatly strengthened. Because of this the expedition was cancelled in October and the decision made to send the units involved to Catalonia instead. This meant the 10 British battalions, the British dragoon regiment and the Spanish dragoon regiment would be available to the army in Catalonia in 1710.

The arrival of this group in Catalonia prompted a reorganisation of the British contingent. Mordaunt's regiment, from the field army, and Hotham's regiment, who had been on garrison duty, were reduced and their personnel used to fill out the other units. Syburg's Huguenot regiment, now commanded by Bourgay and which had been on garrison duty, was strengthened and bought into field service. Innchequin's regiment went on garrison duty.

The Battle of La Gudina, 7 May

On the Portuguese front the 1709 campaign was more active. The Portuguese Marquis de Fronteira was once again in overall command and the British were under Galway. These officers commanded an army of 26 Portuguese battalions, six British battalions, 50 Portuguese squadron and 20 guns.[3] According to O'Callaghan this amounted to 49 regiments.[4] Given that the infantry were all a single battalion per regiment this implies that there were 17 cavalry regiments. These units totalled about 16 or 17,000 infantry and 5,000 cavalry according to the sources previously mentioned. Parnell says that the army had 12,000 infantry (2,800 British and 9,200 Portuguese) and 3,000 Portuguese cavalry.[5] It seems likely that this reflects the strength of the army by the time of the battle.

As is common with the Portuguese army we do not have a detailed order of battle of their forces. Yet in this case we can perhaps take an educated guess about the composition. Looking at the infantry we know the six British battalions involved:

Pearce's (later the 5th Foot)
Newton's (later the 20th Foot)
Sankey's (later the 39th Foot)
Paston's
Barrymore's (later 13th Foot)
Stanwix's

From the accounts of the upcoming battle we also know that Galway's Spanish battalion, probably misidentified as a Portuguese unit, was also present. The rest of the infantry, 25 battalions, were Portuguese and took no part in the battle. It was therefore, at least in theory, intact for the 1710 campaign. There is a list of the Portuguese battalions in this army in 1710 and there are 25 of them – see the chapter on the 1710 campaign. It therefore seems likely that in 1709 this army had the 25 Portuguese battalions with the army in 1710, Galway's Spanish battalion and the six British battalions listed above.

The army in 1710 could also help with reconstructing the cavalry present with the army. In 1710 this army had 38 squadrons in 17 cavalry regiments, some of the regiments having less squadrons than they were supposed to. See the 1710 campaign chapter for details of the army at that time. Unlike the infantry the Portuguese cavalry was involved in the upcoming battle and suffered considerable losses. If the 17 cavalry regiments in the 1710 army were present in 1709 but with the full number of squadrons they were supposed to have that adds up to 50 squadrons. This would be one guard regiment with a single squadron, one dragoon regiment with four squadrons and 15 cavalry

---

3   *Österreichische militärische Zeitschrift* 1842 Band 4, p.237.
4   O'Callaghan, J.C., *History of the Irish brigades in the service of France, from the revolution in Great Britain and Ireland under James II, to the revolution in France under Louis XVI* (Glasgow: Cameron and Ferguson, 1885), p.271.
5   A. Parnell, *The War of Succession in Spain: 1702–1711*, p.267.

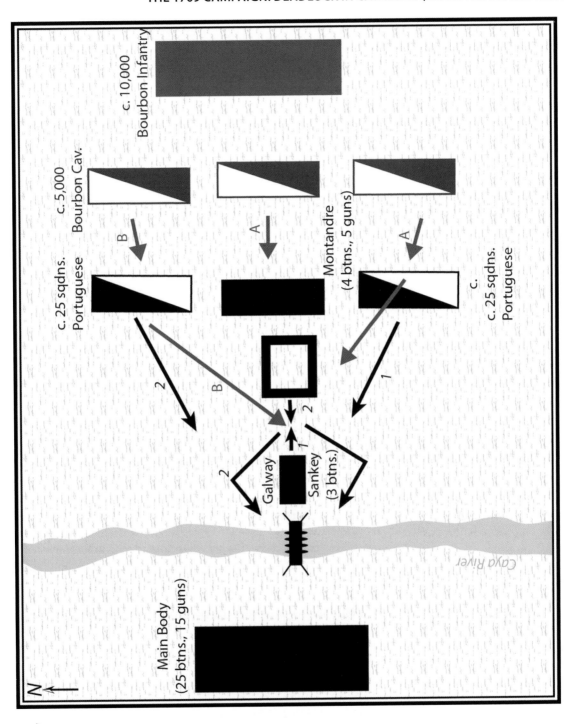

Map 8
The Battle of La Gudina,
7 May 1709

regiments with three squadrons each. It therefore seems possible that the 1709 army contained the same 17 cavalry regiments as in 1710 but with the 12 extra squadrons needed to make them up to full regiments according to the regulations.

Speculative Order of Battle of the Portuguese Army

Cavalry: 50 squadrons – 3,000 (or possibly 5,000) men
Guard Cavalry Regiment (1 squadron)
15 horse regiments (3 squadrons each)
1 dragoon regiment (4 squadrons)

Infantry: 32 battalions – 12,000 (or possibly 16 to 17,000) men
25 Portuguese battalions
Galway's Spanish battalion
6 British battalions

Artillery: 20 guns

The Portuguese army assembled near the border at Campo Major on the River Caya in April. It was ready to try to undertake offensive actions after being rebuilt following the events of 1706. Opposing the Confederates once again was the Bourbon Spanish commander De Bay. De Bay had about 5,000 cavalry and 10,000 infantry on his side of the border over the Caya. Leaving the infantry of the army behind on 3 May De Bay advanced onto the plain opposite Fronteira's army with his cavalry. The intention of this move was to try to tempt the Portuguese to cross the River Caya and it soon proved to be successful at doing that. Galway objected to the move but despite this Fronteira decided to cross the river to confront the Bourbons.

On 7 May the army moved up to the river and used pontoons to bridge the Caya. Once the pontoon bridges were completed all of the Portuguese cavalry, five guns and a brigade of four British battalions under Montandre crossed over the river. The rest of the army was intended to follow but events were to intervene in this plan. They deployed with the infantry in the centre flanked on each side by the Portuguese cavalry. According to Parnell these amounted to 4,700 men but if the other sources are correct they would have numbered more like 6,000 or 7,000 men. These faced the approximately 5,000 Bourbon cavalry led by De Bay.

At noon the five Portuguese guns across the river opened fire on the Bourbon cavalry. This led to De Bay taking control of the Bourbon left and leading them forward in an aggressive attack. The completely inexperienced Portuguese cavalry on the right immediately turned and ran. Sources often mention that they did this without even firing a shot, perhaps an indication of the usual tactics of the Portuguese. The flight of the Portuguese cavalry allowed the Spanish cavalry to capture the five Portuguese guns and exposed the flank of Montandre's brigade. Montandre could see the situation was critical and immediately tried to pull back but De Bay reacted as well and launched three vigorous attacks on this exposed group.

Meanwhile Galway, who appears to have been in the rear when the battle started, had also noticed what was happening. Taking personal control of Sankey's brigade of two British and his own Spanish battalion, he advanced to help the beleaguered advance party. This advance allowed the recovery of the lost five guns and gave Montandre time to form a large square with his four battalions. Reacting to this the Bourbon cavalry attacked the Portuguese cavalry on the left and these too fled rapidly. This left the infantry battalions amidst the victorious Bourbon cavalry without any cavalry support. Galway was caught up in this catastrophe but managed to struggle back to the main army across the river. Montandre's force was also able to slowly withdraw in square, which under heavy attack they proceeded to do. Sankey's group were not so lucky, and was completely caught by the events. Surrounded on all sides, with no time to form a square and cut off they had little choice but to surrender, incidentally once again losing the five guns which had crossed the river.

Montandre's Brigade
    Pearce's (later the 5th Foot)
    Newton's (later the 20th Foot)
    Sankey's (later the 39th Foot)

Paston's

Sankey's Brigade
    Barrymore's (later 13th Foot)
    Stanwix's
    Galway's Spanish

About 1,000 men were taken prisoner and another 500 killed and wounded in the battle, five guns were also lost. The pontoon bridge was taken down and the Portuguese army resumed its defensive posture. It was an object lesson in how unprepared the Portuguese army was for offensive action. Galway was convinced that the army was not fit for action and Fronteira, who had previously not listened, was now inclined to agree. A few days after the battle the army pulled back from the forward position previously occupied on the Caya. De Bay then attempted a half-hearted advance but was quickly blocked. With this burst of activity both armies settled down into quarters to await events.

1709 had been a strangely quiet campaign year in Iberia, but it was the quiet before the storm that was to be the 1710 campaign.

14

The 1710 Campaign: Last Chance of Victory Lost

The campaign of 1707, and the Battle of Almansa, is generally seen as the decisive year of the war in Iberia. Yet 1710 was arguably at least as important and possibly more so. The Battle of Almansa and the 1707 campaign certainly halted the Confederate progress in this theatre. After this time the Confederates were on the defensive but it was not until the failure of the 1710 campaign that defeat in this theatre seemed certain. The events and disappointments of this campaign precipitated the crisis in Britain that led to the downfall of the Duke of Marlborough and Britain withdrawing from the war. This in turn was a major factor in ending the war.

At first it looked like the 1710 campaign was going to be similar to the previous campaign. On the Portuguese front both sides were content to limit their actions. In Catalonia the Confederates faced two threats. The Bourbon forces had reorganised and now had a wholly French area poised along Catalonia's northern border. Meanwhile a wholly Spanish army faced the Catalonia's western border. The Confederates could not match these forces and so, along with smaller garrisons, they posted a strong garrison in Gerona, on the northern frontier, to block the French army. The main army was stationed around Balaguer facing the Spanish army.

The Confederate army was 19 to 20,000 strong and outnumbered by the 22,000 to 23,000 men fielded by the Spanish army facing it. It looked like it was to be another campaign where the Confederates would be limited to trying to restrict their enemy's gains. After some initial manoeuvring around the River Segra in the early months of the campaign the situation was suddenly transformed by two events. The first of these was a raid into the French territory of Languedoc. The raid itself made achieved little physically but it had the effect of throwing that area of France into confusion. The French army to the north of Catalonia abandoned its planned attack on Catalonia and dispersed to defend vulnerable areas from further attacks that were expected. Thus one of the armies threatening Catalonia was temporarily neutralised.

At around the same time the army in Catalonia also received much needed reinforcements. These were mainly in the form of recruits and replacement from Italy but also a few additional units. There were about 4,600 men from

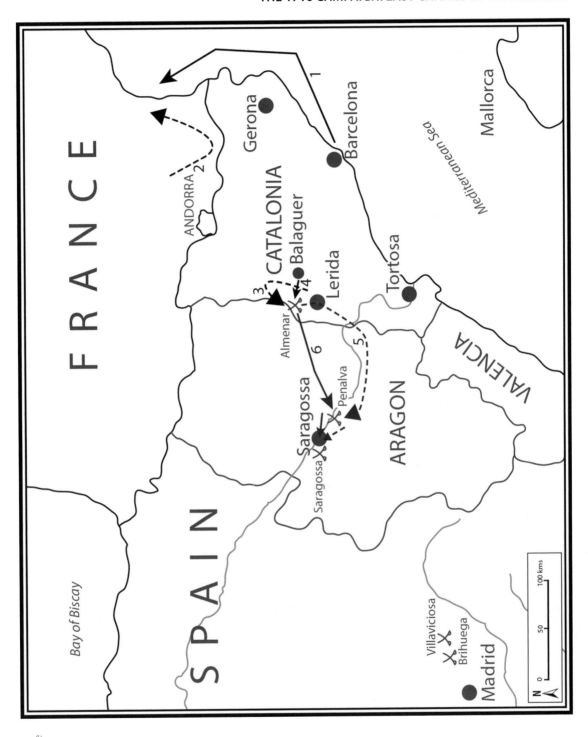

Map 9
Catalonia, 1710 – the
first phase of the
campaign46

Italy and another 1,400 from the raid. Using these troops the Confederate field army was now 25 to 26,000 strong. Comfortably stronger than their Spanish opponents, the Confederates advanced to take advantage of their position.

The army in the Catalonia area consisted of 51 infantry battalions and 60 cavalry squadrons with an independent Hussar company. Of these 35 battalions, 52 squadrons and the independent Hussar company were in the field army. The other 16 battalions and eight squadrons were in various garrisons.

The breakdown of the various contingents was as follows.

Imperialist: 14 battalions, 6 squadrons, 1 company
All units were in the field army.

Starhemberg	3 battalions	
Reventlau	3 battalions	
Osnabruck	3 battalions	
Gschwind	3 battalions	
Eck	2 battalions	Newly arrived from Italy
Jorger Dragoons	6 squadrons	
Ebengenyi Hussars	1 company	

Spanish: 15 battalions, 12 squadrons.
In the field army: 5 battalions, 6 squadrons.

Ahumada (1st)	1 battalion	
Catalonian Guards (3rd)	1 battalion	
Ferrer's (14th)	1 battalion	
Taafe (23rd)	1 battalion	
Buol (25th)	1 battalion	
Zinzendorf's (1st)	2 squadrons	
Morras' (2nd)	2 squadrons	
Aragon (12th)	2 squadrons	

In garrisons: 10 battalions, 6 squadrons

Tattenbach (4th)	1 battalion	
Shover (5th)	1 battalion	
Castiglioni (6th)	1 battalion	
La Deputacion (7th)	1 battalion	
La Ciudad (8th)	1 battalion	
Ciudad de Cartagena (11th)	1 battalion	In Gerona
Ciudad de Zaragoza (13th)	1 battalion	In Gerona
Carles Llorach (24th)	1 battalion	On Sardinia
Faber (26th)	1 battalion	
Granada (27th)	1 battalion	Newly raised, in Gerona
Sobias' (3rd)	2 squadrons	
Nebot's (4th)	2 squadrons	
Catalonian Gds (8th)	2 squadrons	On Sardinia

British: 13 battalions, 10 squadrons
In the field army: 10 battalions, 10 squadrons.
Guards Battalion   1 battalion (a combined battalion from all the Guards' regiments but mainly from the Scots Guards)

Harrison's (later 6th Foot)	1 battalion	
Wade's (later 33rd)	1 battalion	
Bourgay's (ex Syburg's)	1 battalion	
Bowles'	1 battalion	
Dormer's	1 battalion	
Gore's	1 battalion	
Munden's	1 battalion	
Richards' (ex Lepel's)	1 battalion	
Dalziels' Spanish	1 battalion	
Harvey's Horse (3rd)	2 squadrons	
Royal Dragoon (1st)	2 squadrons	
Pepper's Dragoon (8th)	2 squadrons	
Nassau's Dragoon	2 squadrons	
Rochfort's Dragoon	2 squadrons	

In garrisons: 3 battalions

Tyrawley's or Royal Fusiliers (later 7th Foot)		1 battalion
Whetham's (later 27th Foot)	1 battalion	
Innchequin's	1 battalion	

Dutch: 2 battalions, 6 squadrons
All units were in the field army.

St. Amant's (NL 5)	1 battalion
Verpoorten's (NL 17)	1 battalion
Drimborn's (NLC 15)	2 squadrons
Schlippenbach's (NLD 2)	2 squadrons
Mattha (4th Dragoon)	2 squadrons

Portuguese: 2 battalions, 18 squadrons
All units were in the field army.

Bouillon	1 battalion
Albuquerque	1 battalion
Almedia	3 squadrons
O'Kelly	3 squadrons
Castro	3 squadrons
Miranda	3 squadrons
Cunea (Acunha?)	3 squadrons
Sottomayor	3 squadrons

Palatine: 5 battalions, 8 squadrons
In the field army: 2 battalions, 6 squadrons

Leibregiment zu fuss	1 battalion
La Marck (ex Barbo)	1 battalion
Frankenbergs, ex Stolzenberg's	2 squadrons
Spee's	2 squadrons
Frankenberg's	2 squadrons
In garrison (all in Gerona):	3 battalions, 2 squadrons
Coppe	1 battalion
Greber	1 battalion

| Schonberg | 1 battalion |
| Schellard's | 2 squadrons |

The army was divided into two wings, left and right, and a cavalry reserve. The left wing consisted of the British, Dutch and Palatine units – 14 battalions and 22 squadrons. The cavalry reserve consisted of six squadrons of Portuguese cavalry. The right wing consisted of the Austrian, Spanish and rest of the Portuguese troops – 21 battalions and 24 squadrons. The army was supported by 26 guns and the independent Hussar company.

Confederate Order of Battle[1]

(Units listed from left to right)

Army Command: Charles III of Spain and Starhemberg
  Quartermaster General: Peroni
  Artillery Commander: Beauregard
  Artillery: At least 14 guns and probably 26 guns in total

Left Wing: The British, Dutch and Palatine contingents

  Left Wing Cavalry: 22 squadrons
    Cavalry (1st Line): Stanhope assisted by Frankenberg and Rochefort.
    12 squadrons: Queen Anne's Dragoons (2), Nassau's Dragoons (2), Harvey's Horse (2), Mattha's Dragoons (2), Drimborn's Horse (2) and Frankenberg's Horse (2)
    Cavalry (2nd Line): Carpenter assisted by Pepper and Nassau.
    10 squadrons: Pepper's Dragoons (2), Rochefort's Dragoons (2), Schlippenbach's Dragoons (2), Spee's Horse (2), Frankenberg's Horse (2)

  Left Wing Infantry: 14 battalions
    Infantry (1st Line): Belcastel: 7 battalions
    Wade's Command: Wade and Lussy: 5 battalions
    British Guards (1), Bowles' (1), Dalziel's (1), Bourgay's(1) and Wade's (1)
    Saint Amant's Command: Saint Amant: 2 battalions
    Saint Amant (1) and Leibregiment zu fusss (1)

    Infantry (2nd Line): Wills assisted by Lepell.
    7 battalions: Harrison's (1), Munden's (1), Gore's (1), Richards' (1), Dormer's (1), Verpoorten (1) and La Marck (1)

Right Wing: The Austrian, Portuguese and Spanish contingents
  Infantry (1st Line): Puebla: 13 battalions

---

1   *Feldzüge des Prinzen Eugen von Savoyen, 12. Band (1710)* (Vienna: K.K. Kriegs-Archiv, 1887), p.621.

Ahumada's Command: Ahumada and Albuquerque: 9 battalions
Ahumada (1), Luccini (1), Albuquerque (1), Gschwind (3), Reventlau (3)
Eck's Command: Eck: 4 battalions
G.Starhemberg (3) and Catalonian Guard (1)

Cavalry (1st Line): Atalaya: 13 squadrons
Hamilton's Command: Hamilton: 8 squadrons
O'Kelly (3), Miranda (3) and Morras Horse (2)
Galves' Command: Galves: 5 squadrons
Jorger Dragoons (3) and Del Rey Dragoons (2)

Right Wing (2nd Line): Wetzel: 8 battalions and 11 squadrons
Infantry (2nd Line): Luccini and Bouillon: 8 battalions
Ferrer (1), Buol (1), Bouillon (1), Osnabruck (3) and Eck (2)

Cavalry (2nd Line): Gondrecourt: 11 squadrons
Sottomayor (3), Acuna (3), Cordua Horse (2) and Jorger Dragoons (3)

Cavalry Reserve: Almeyda: 6 squadrons
Almeyda or Almeida (3) and Castro (3)

The army numbered 25 to 26,000 men. This meant that on average the infantry battalions were 520 to 540 men strong, while the cavalry squadrons were around 130 to 135 strong on average.

The Battle of Almenar, July 27[2]

By late July the Confederate army was near Balaguer and the Bourbon Spanish army was near Lérida, both on the River Segra. Both armies had been essentially inactive for some time when the Confederate reinforcements arrived. Seizing the opportunity that had opened the Confederate high command decided to launch an offensive and on 25 July they initiated the opening phase of the campaign. They planned to march west towards the main crossing point of the River Noguera and so get behind the opposing army. The following day the advancing army heard that the Bourbon Spanish army had heard of their movement and was on the move to block the Confederate advance. Unless something was done the Confederates would have to launch an attack over the Noguera, a significant obstacle, against an enemy army defending the opposite bank to continue their move. It was clear that something had to be done to avoid this and so it was decided to cross the Noguera further south than originally intended and block the Spanish army's advance.

The Confederates organised an advanced guard of under Stanhope which consisted of four dragoon regiments, 20 companies of grenadiers, six

---

2   N. Dorrell, *Marlborough's Last Chance in Spain: The 1710 Spanish Campaign*, pp.56–71.

24. The Battle of Almenar,
27 July 1710

cannons and the necessary pontoons and equipment to build a bridge over the Noguera for the rest of the army to use. The dragoon regiments were the Dutch regiments of Schlippenbach and Mattha along with two British regiments, Pepper's and the 'Guard's' – probably the Queen Anne Dragoons. The grenadiers were drawn from the battalions in the army and organised into two ad hoc battalions. One battalion was from the British, Dutch and Palatine units of the left wing while the other was from the Austrian, Portuguese and Spanish units of the right wing.

This force moved to the River Noguera near Alfaras and quickly built a pontoon bridge to the other side. Crossing over on the morning of July 27 the advanced guard spotted the Spanish advance guard to the south near the village of Almenar. The Confederates had managed to cross the river in front of the advancing Spanish army and now had a chance of an open engagement with their opponents. Both advanced guards settled into defensive positions to await the arrival of the rest of their army. Over most of the rest of the day parts of both armies arrived piecemeal. The Spanish army arrived slower than the Confederates as they had not expected this turn of events and also the high command did not understand the situation or react to it positively. In contrast the Confederates had planned this move and the high command hurried the marching columns forward.

By six in the evening all of the Confederate army except for 12 of the guns, probably the heavier guns, had arrived on the battlefield. In contrast all of the 28 Spanish guns, most of their infantry and some of their cavalry were yet to arrive. Eight out of 60 cavalry squadrons and 35 of the 44 infantry battalions had yet to arrive, although they were just entering the edge of the area by this time. The light was starting to fail and so the Confederates decided to strike while they had the advantage.

The Spanish advance guard had deployed around the village of Almenar in the river valley. The Spanish reinforcements, the bulk of the cavalry, had taken positions alongside the position taken by the advance guard but on the high ground to the west of Almenar. As the Confederate army had arrived it had moved up to the high ground facing the gathering mass of the Spanish cavalry, 42 squadrons and two infantry battalions. The units of the

Barranquа

3

2

4

Almenar

B

C

A

Alfaras

1

Noguera River

N

Map 10
The Battle of Almenar,
27 July 1710

advance guard rejoined the commands they came from as these arrived on the battlefield. The grenadiers continued to operate as two ad hoc battalions, one per wing of the army. For the attack the Confederates formed up into eight lines of troops. The first two lines were the British, Dutch and Palatine cavalry from the left wing of the army. The third and fourth lines were the Austrian, Portuguese and Spanish cavalry of the right wing and reserve. The next two lines were the battalion of the left wing, including the ad hoc grenadier battalion and these were followed by the seventh and eight lines consisting of the right wing infantry and their grenadier battalion.

This mass of men and horses bore down on the Bourbon Spanish cavalry and quickly put them to flight. For some reason the waiting Bourbon cavalry were in disorder before the Confederate attack and so unable to put up much resistance. The Bourbon cavalry collapsed almost immediately with only the units on their right, the best regiments of the army and also those nearest friendly support, putting up any kind of serious resistance. The routing Bourbon cavalry hotly pursued by the Confederate cavalry crashed into the supporting Bourbon advance guard and into the bulk of the Bourbon infantry which was finally arriving. By this time the light was getting bad and the Bourbon army was in complete disarray. The Confederate cavalry was rampant and threatening to totally destroy the enemy army. Seeing that something needed to be done to check the Confederates and save the army. The rearguard of the Bourbon army was the eight squadrons that were not on the field at the start of the action. These had been caught up in the ongoing disaster hitting the army but their commander managed to rally five groups of Bourbon cavalry. These he valiantly charged into the pursuing Confederates. This charge, and the growing darkness, halted the Confederate pursuit but at a heavy cost, including the death of the commander. This sacrificial charge had done its job and given the rest of the army time to escape.

The Spanish had lost 1,700 to 1,800 in direct losses, about 1,500 killed and wounded and 200 to 300 captured. The army was scattered and so many more than this were absent, at least temporarily. The Confederate losses were only some 400 men but they did lose two units commanders, Rochfort and Nassau the commanders of two of the British cavalry regiments.

The Combat at Penalva, August 15[3]

The Bourbon army regrouped back at Lérida but clearly needed to put more distance between itself and the Confederate army. So after a short stay the Bourbon army moved back towards Saragossa on 12 August where they hoped to recover properly. The Confederates soon set off in pursuit and after a few days were again within striking distance of the Bourbon army. To check this pursuit the Bourbon Spanish cavalry were once again deployed. A group of 13 or 17 Bourbon squadrons, possibly with a small amount of infantry support, planned to spring a trap on the advancing Confederates.

---

3   Ibid., pp.72–76.

The Confederate forces involved were all 24 of the cavalry squadrons of the right wing, probably in two groups of 12 squadrons. An extra four squadrons joined these troops at the end of the action. These were probably Pepper's and Lepell's (ex Rochefort's) British Dragoons.

The action took part in a mountainous area in some defiles. Initially 12 squadrons from the Confederate right wing encountered a small number of Bourbon cavalry, possibly four squadrons. The Bourbons played on what had happened at Almenar and 'routed' when the Confederates advanced. This was a ploy and the 'routing' Bourbon cavalry led the Confederate cavalry into the trap set by the waiting remaining cavalry. The ambushing cavalry promptly charged and routed the hoodwinked Confederate cavalry. The routers rallied when the remaining 12 squadrons of the right wing arrived. All 24 squadrons of the right wing now launched another attack to clear the defile but this was again driven off. At this point the four British cavalry squadrons arrived and the Bourbon cavalry withdrew. It does not seem that the British units were involved in the action although it is not clear.

The Bourbons seem to have lost about 300 men in this action and may have inflicted up to 1,000 casualties on the Confederates. The exact loses are disputed but what was clear was that the action had bought time for the Bourbon Spanish army to continue its march to Saragossa. The Confederates were not far behind and by 19 August the Bourbons had been forced to once again confront their enemy.

The Battle of Saragossa, August 20[4]

The two armies were facing each other outside the town of Saragossa. Both sides deployed with one wing, the Bourbon left and the Confederate right, on the plain in front of Saragossa. The rest of both armies were deployed on two ridgelines facing across a valley. By this time the Confederate army had been reduced to 22,000–24,000 strong but the Bourbon army was down to 17,000–20,000 men. The Bourbon army had deployed conventionally with the infantry in the centre and flanked by two cavalry wings. The wing on the plain was bent back towards Saragossa, which was behind this command, and so was further away from the Confederate army. The Bourbon army seems to have consisted of 54 squadrons, 38 battalions and 27 guns. A further six squadrons and four battalions seem to have been posted in Saragossa, and hence took no part in the battle, to strengthen the garrison and guard the Bourbon Spanish king who was there. By the time the Confederate army arrived on 19 August there was not time to deploy and fight the battle. So the Confederates deployed opposite to the Bourbons and conventionally like the Bourbons for the night ready for combat the following morning.

After a nervous night both sides started a bombardment of their opponents at eight in the morning of the 20th. During the early stages it became clear to the Confederates that the Bourbon deployment was not as conventional

---

4   Ibid., pp.77-91.

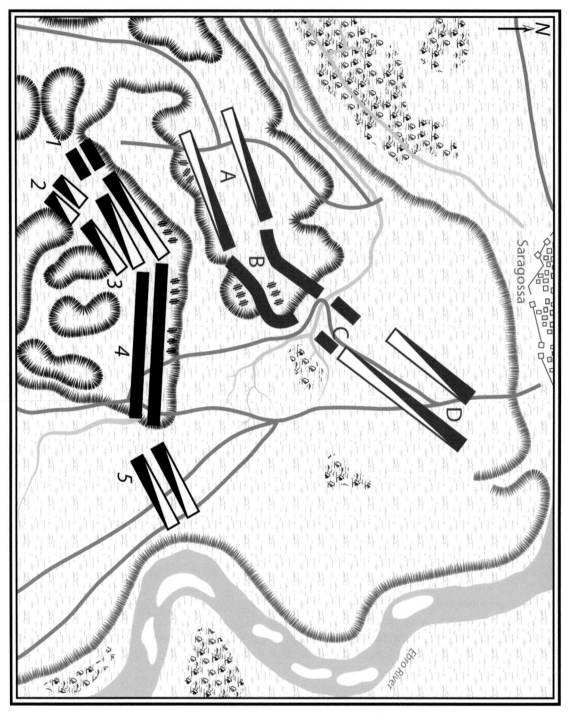

Map 11
The Battle of
Saragossa, 20 August
1710

as it had at first seemed. The Bourbon left wing, the one furthest away, was weaker than the right, 24 squadrons on the left compared with 30 on the right. In addition 10 squadrons from the left were detached from this wing and sent reinforce the right wing. In short the Bourbon high command was concentrating their cavalry on this side.

The Confederate army consisted of the same units that were at Almenar, probably including the two ad hoc grenadier battalions. In response to the Bourbon deployment the Confederates changed their deployment to strengthen their left, which was clearly threatened by the Bourbon redeployment. The army had initially been deployed in two lines and according to the nominal organisation – i.e. with the left wing on the left, etc. The six squadrons of the cavalry reserve were moved in behind the two lines of the left wing cavalry as a third line. Four British battalions were taken from the infantry centre and posted in support of the left wing cavalry. Six Portuguese squadrons that were taken from the right wing cavalry in turn supported these.

Confederate Deployment
Extreme left wing cavalry: 6 Portuguese squadrons
Infantry supporting left wing: 4 British battalions
Left wing cavalry: 22 squadrons from the left wing in two lines and six Portuguese squadrons from the cavalry reserve in the 3rd line.
Centre: 33 infantry battalions in two lines and supported by 26 guns.
Right wing cavalry: 18 squadrons from the right wing in two lines.

After an ineffective mutual bombardment the numerically superior Confederates started a general attack at about midday. The Spanish army had clearly been waiting for this as the Bourbon right wing immediately launched a ferocious attack on the Confederate left wing. Despite being outnumbered the Bourbon cavalry drove their opponents back but did not manage to break them. The support of the four British battalions hindered the attack but the decisive intervention was by the six Portuguese squadrons on the extreme left. The Spanish did not seem to be aware of these at first and so they had freedom to act. The aggressive Bourbon cavalry were only checked and so they reorganised for a second attack. This second attack was two pronged. The largest group renewed the attack on the Confederate left wing cavalry while a smaller group attacked the six squadrons of the extreme left group.

The larger group was now even more outnumbered because of the diversion of some of the squadrons to attack the extreme left group and as more Confederate infantry came to the assistance of their cavalry. Despite this the Bourbon cavalry once again drove their opponents back but could not achieve complete victory and so once again the attack stalled. Meanwhile the smaller group routed the six Portuguese squadrons and pursued them into the Confederate baggage. This group of Bourbon cavalry was beaten off by an improvised force guarding the baggage and their attack also ran out of steam. Once again the Bourbon right wing cavalry paused and reorganised. To aid them 10 squadrons from the so far inactive left wing were dispatched to help achieve a breakthrough.

25. The Battle of Saragossa,
20 August 1710

The Confederates were struggling on their left but now the infantry centres started to become engaged. The left of the Bourbon line was largely composed of Walloon regiments and many of these only put up a token resistance before running. The Walloon units were good troops but they were discontented because they had been sent away from their homeland and because of the way the campaign had progressed. The rout of the Walloons took some of the other Bourbon units with them and left a massive hole in the Bourbon line.

The flight of the Walloons gave the Confederates fresh heart and they eagerly seized the opportunity they had been presented. Using the large hole in the Bourbon line the Confederates started outflanking the enemy units either side of the gap. It was time for the remaining Bourbon units to withdraw from the battle if they could. The success of the Bourbon right wing cavalry meant that some of these cavalry were deep into the Confederate positions. Yet their opponents were badly shaken and so not really capable of taking advantage of the change of fortunes. Also at this point the reinforcements from the left arrived to help out and so these started an orderly withdrawal. The remaining infantry units in the centre now dissolved with their flank turned and as their cavalry support withdrew. At least there was little enemy cavalry around to add to their problem but for the Bourbon left wing this was not the case. A small number of infantry battalions on the extreme left had managed to survive the rout and also the remaining squadrons of the left wing cavalry. These units faced completely fresh and largely unengaged superior forces, including cavalry. While other Confederate forces now moved to attack their open flank. These beleaguered units combined together to perform a noteworthy fighting retreat against the Confederate hoards seeking to eliminate this group. The Bourbon cavalry made repeated charges and the infantry repeated stands to stave off the Confederate pursuit to withdraw from the battle relatively intact.

The battle had been a disaster for the Bourbons. The Confederates had suffered heavily, perhaps more than 2,000 casualties but the Bourbon army had effectively been destroyed. Exactly casualty figures are unknown but could have been as high as 12,000 dead, wounded and captured along with 22 of their guns. Much of the rest of the army was scattered and would be incapable of resistance for some time. The situation had been totally changed and the Confederates had a chance to decisively alter the situation in Spain. Soon the bloodied but victorious Confederate army was on the march to Madrid, the Spanish capital.

Madrid Regained and Lost Again[5]

The Confederates had secured control of Madrid earlier in 1706 but lost it along with a golden opportunity to decisively change the war. They now had a second chance to do the same but once again they would fail to do so. After securing Saragossa the Confederates marched for Madrid and advanced elements reached that city on September 21. Unlike their entry in 1706 there was little enthusiasm, a bad start to their attempt to decisively change the course of the war. The Confederates were at the end of a long supply route from Catalonia and isolated. The Spanish and their French allies had by this time started to react to the reverses they had suffered. Two new French commanders were appointed. Noailles, who was relatively junior at this point but destined to become a senior French commander, was sent to southern France to get the French army involved in the campaign, while the highly respected and experienced senior commander Vendôme was dispatched to take command of the Spanish forces. The Confederate forces in Madrid clearly needed aid and the obvious source for this was, as in 1706, the Portuguese army. In 1706 this army had marched from the Portuguese border to join the Confederate army at Madrid. The Confederate needed it to perform a similar march again now.

The Portuguese field army at this time consisted of 31 battalions and 41 squadrons, around 16,000 men, under the command of Villaverde.[6] Galway was still in command of the British forces but he was not well and Portmore replaced him later in the campaign.

The army mustered the following 25 Portuguese infantry battalions:

Acuna	Pireira
Alarcao	Pires
Alcanforado	Saa
Almaden	Sezar
Brito	Tavares
Botelho	Telles
Cabral	Titua
Caldera	Tragozo
Carvalho	Vasconcellos
Estevas	Veyga
Mansal	Villena
Mello	Xavier
Morars	

---

5   Ibid., pp.92-98.
6   *Feldzüge des Prinzen Eugen von Savoyen*, 12 Band (1710), p.625.

In addition, there were six British infantry battalions. These were:

Pearce's (later the 5th Foot)
Barrymore's (later the 13th Foot)
Newton's (later the 20th Foot)
Paston's
Stanwix's
Bladen's

There were 38 squadrons of Portuguese cavalry in 17 regiments. 16 of these regiments were of 'horse' and one regiment were of dragoons. These were as follows:

Garde (1 sqn)
Antas (3 sqn)
Arcos (1 sqn)
Aveyras (3 sqn)
Bandeira (2 sqn)
Baran (3 sqn)
Barrett (2 sqn)
Bastos (1 sqn)[7]
Bastos (1 sqn)[7]
Costa (2 sqn)
Henriquez (3 sqn)
Lagos (3 sqn)
Lehbo (3 sqn)
Pinheiro (2 sqn)
Quintal (3 sqn)
Texeira (3 sqn)
Dragoons (3 sqn)

There were three squadrons of British cavalry:

Galway's Dragoons (3 sqns)

An advance by this army from Portugal to Madrid would be a potent addition to the Confederate position, but it would also be a great risk for the Portuguese. Just as in 1706 it would leave Portugal wide open. The Spanish Bourbon's had an army along the Portuguese border and Portugal's defences were not significant. The Portuguese were still trying to recover from the setback of 1709. The combat effectiveness of the field army was doubtful while the militia that would have to be relied on to defend Portugal were not expected to be very useful. Suitable horses remained a problem or at least an excuse not to do anything. Prior to this time the Portuguese front had been quiet as both sides had little incentive to do more.

---

7   These appear to be two different units, perhaps with colonels that shared the same name.

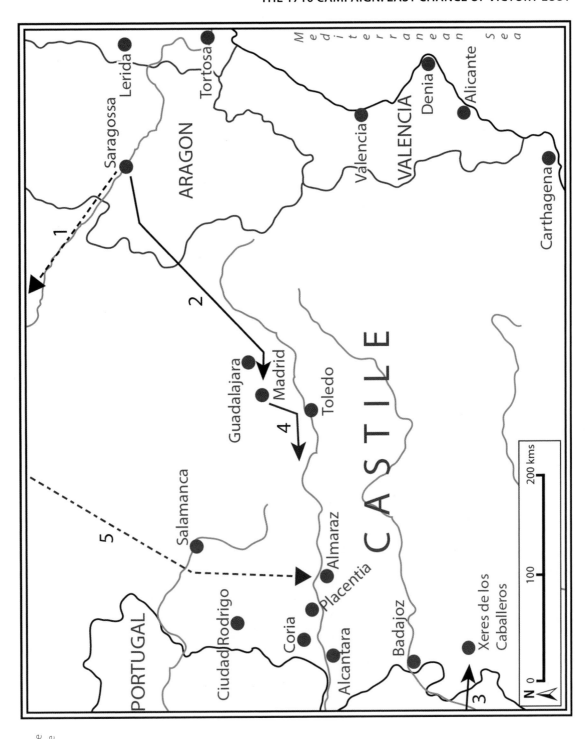

Map 12
Catalonia, 1710 – the
second phase of the
campaign

The Confederate advance prompted heavy diplomatic pressure to get the Portuguese army to advance. Stanhope with a contingent of the Confederate army also moved west towards Almaraz. At Almaraz was a key bridge that the Portuguese would need to reach Madrid. So on 30 September the Portuguese reluctantly crossed the frontier. Their heart was not in the task and they quickly moved to the small, unimportant fortress of Xeres de los Caballeros. This they laid siege to while Villaverde sent back what amounted to a list of reasons why he could not continue his advance. The Portuguese high command accepted Villaverde's view and he then pulled back, in theory to organise for a later advance. Meanwhile the Bourbon commander Vendôme had acted and shown the quality of his leadership. Gathering up forces wherever he could he rushed to the vital bridge at Almaraz and secured it. Any Portuguese advance would now be a lot more difficult. The Portuguese undertook a series of minor attacks across the border as part of their preparations for the march but it was clear that they would do nothing further in this campaign. Stanhope's force pulled back to rejoin the main part of the army which would have to tackle the situation on its own.

Meanwhile in Madrid the situation was becoming bleaker. The Confederates were not attracting any support from the local population or Spanish high society, supplies were short and desertion growing. A small unit of pro-Confederate cavalry was raised at this time but it was very small and quickly disappeared when the Confederates moved away. The news from Catalonia was also not good as it was clear that the French army over the border was preparing for action. The end of the campaign season was approaching and there was seemingly little threat in the Madrid area. It was decided that Charles III and 14 cavalry squadrons would return to Catalonia to led and strengthen the defences there.

Regiment	Nation	Squadrons Escorting the King	Squadrons Remaining with the Army
Jorger Dragoon	Austria	2	4
Morras Horse	Spain	1	1
Acuna	Portugal	2	1
Almeida	Portugal	1	2
Azevedo (ex O'Kelly)	Portugal	2	1
Castro	Portugal	2	1
Miranda	Portugal	2	1
Sottomayor	Portugal	2	1
TOTAL		14	12

At the same time the bulk of the Confederate army dispersed to areas outside Madrid to ease the armies supply problems, cut down desertion and help relations with the local population. By the end of November the Confederate army had stripped the original area they had dispersed to, south-west of Madrid, to also be able to aid the Portuguese if needed. The normal end of the campaign season was now very close so it was decided to relocate the army again. This time they would move to the east of Madrid to be closer to Catalonia and aid lines of communication. On 3 December they started moving in various columns, marching separately so that they could scavenge for supplies as they travelled, and some distance apart. The Spanish Bourbon army was nearly 200 miles away and so not a threat. At least that is what the Confederates thought, but events were to prove they were wrong.

The Battle of Brihuega, 8–9 December[8]

Showing the difference that a good commander could make, Vendôme had not been idle. By reorganising his existing forces and exchanging battered units for fresh units elsewhere he had rebuilt the Bourbon army. Vendôme had assembled 32 battalions, 80 squadrons and 28 guns, a total of about 21,000 men. Unknown to the Confederate with this force he had been closing on Madrid. When news arrived that the Confederates were moving east he sensed an opportunity and advanced rapidly. Vendôme's easiest target was the contingent of British troops under Stanhope that was acting as the rearguard of the army and making for the small town of Brihuega. This command had eight battalions and eight squadrons, all British, and reached Brihuega late on 6 December.

26. Louis Joseph, Duke of Vendôme, by Murat

The British at Brihuega
Guards Battalion: 1 battalion
Harrison's (later 6th Foot): 1 battalion
Wade's (later 33rd): 1 battalion
Bowles':1 battalion
Dormer's : 1 battalion
Gore's: 1 battalion
Munden's: 1 battalion
Dalziels' Spanish: 1 battalion
Harvey's Horse (3rd): 2 squadrons
Royal Dragoons (1st): 2 squadrons
Pepper's Dragoons (8th): 2 squadrons
Nassau's Dragoons: 2 squadrons

---

8   N. Dorrell, *Marlborough's Last Chance in Spain: The 1710 Spanish Campaign*, pp.99–106.

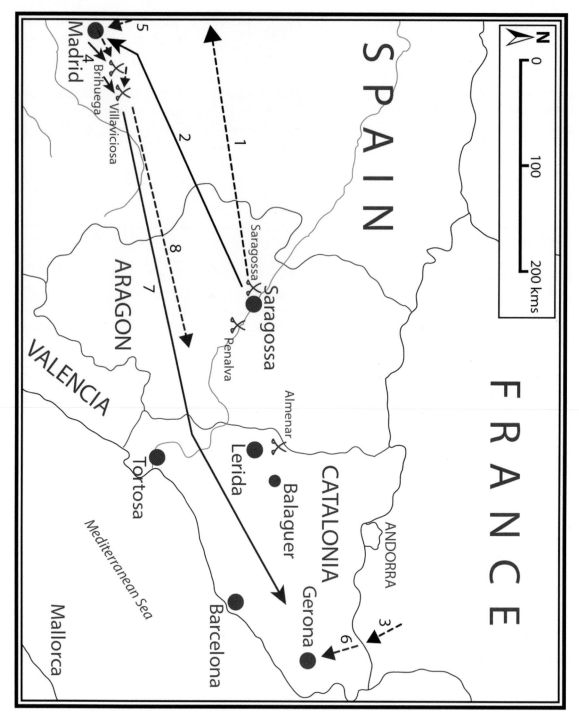

Map 13
Catalonia, 1710 – the
third phase of the
campaign

The remainder of the British contingent was with the rest of the Confederate army, which was 14 miles away around the town of Cifuentes. The British force had been contacted by Bourbon cavalry a few days before but these seemed to be just isolated forces as the Confederates were still unaware of what Vendôme had done. Stanhope was not worried until early in the morning of December 8. Starting with the cavalry Vendôme's army, which had marched 170 miles in a week, arrived at Brihuega and bottled them up in the town. Stanhope was stunned by this turn of events and urgently made defensive preparations, including sending to Cifuentes for aid from the rest of the army. The town of Brihuega was surrounded by a high Moorish wall but the wall only had firing parapets in some places and some old towers. There was a small old castle but neither the town defences nor the castle had any artillery. The defences had been strong in the time they were built but were now out of date and of limited effectiveness at the time. This was not helped by the weak geographical position of the town; the town was in a hollow overlooked by surrounding hills.

The Bourbon forces moved into position and waited for the artillery to arrive. This arrived in the evening of the 8th and fired a few shots as a backdrop to a demand that the British surrender. This failed and so a general assault was organised for the following day. After another attempt to obtain a surrender the Spanish guns opened fire on two points on the wall and also, unknown to the defenders, the Bourbons were using some buildings next to the wall to cover them mining a whole in the wall. By 3 o'clock in the afternoon the walls had been breached by the artillery. The first assault followed shortly after and was repulsed. The Spanish did not rest and a second assault followed which succeeded. The British had built makeshift fortifications behind the breaches and these stopped this second assault. Joined by troops that had filtered through the by now mined wall the Spanish renewed the assault and carried the makeshift entrenchments. The British had fought hard with the cavalry fighting dismounted alongside the infantry. Yet the Spanish had been equal to the task and there was now no other realistic defensible point for the British. The old castle was considered but it was clearly inadequate and so the British sent word that they would surrender.

Reliable figures for loses of both sides are difficult to find but the numbers suggest a heavy and bloody action. The Spanish losses are put at between 300 and 1,500 which are high from an assault force that would have numbered no more than 13,000 men. The British suffered 500 to 1,000 casualties during the assault and the entire British force was captured. In total the forces at Brihuega probably numbered around 4,000 men, thus the loss was a heavy blow for the Confederates. Nor was the bloodshed over, too late help was arriving for the forces at Brihuega.

The Battle of Villaviciosa, December 10[9]

While events were being played out at Brihuega the main army, some 14 miles away, received word of what was happening there. Starhemberg collected the scattered army together and set off to rescue Stanhope's troops in the morning of 9 December. At about 6:30 in the evening, at about four miles from Brihuega, the Confederate army encountered the bulk of the Bourbon cavalry blocking the road near to Villaviciosa. It was late in the day and thinking that the British at Brihuega were being besieged and so that he had time to act Starhemberg halted for the night. In this he was of course mistaken as became clear the next morning.

On the morning of 10 December the rest of the Bourbon army marched to Villaviciosa. The Confederates soon realised the real situation and deployed for battle. The losses and detachments from the army had reduced the army to 27 battalions and 30 squadrons, probably about 14,000 men. The losses also forced a reorganisation of the army as follows.[10]

Army Commander: Starhemberg
  Right Wing Cavalry: Lieutenant General Atalaya: 16 squadrons
    1st Line: 9 squadrons
    Hamilton's Command:
    Jorger (2 sqns), Morras (1 sqn)
    Almeyda's Command:
    Castro (2 sqns), Miranda (2 sqns), Azevedo (ex O'Kelly) (2 sqns)
    2nd Line: Gondrecourt: 7 squadrons
    Jorger (2 sqns), Almeyda (1 sqn), Acuna (2 sqn), Sottomayor (2 sqn)

  Centre
    1st Line: Lieutenant General Wetzel: 16 battalions

    Right Wing Infantry
    Major General Eck and Brigadier Albuquerque: 10 battalions
    Catalonian Guard (1 btn), G. Starhemberg (3 btns), Reventlau (3 btns) and Gschwind (3 btns)

    Left Wing Infantry
    Major General St. Amant and Brigadier Albuquerque: 6 battalions
    Albuquerque (1 btn), Luccini (1 btn), Ahumada (1 btn), Leibregiment zu fuss (1 btn) Saint Amant (1 btn) and Bourgay's (1 btn)

    2nd Line: Lieutenant General Villaroel: 11 battalions

    Right Wing Infantry: Major General Luccini: 6 battalions
    Eck (2 btns), Osnabruck (3 btns) and Bouillon (1 btn)

---

9   Ibid., pp.107-124.
10 *Feldzüge des Prinzen Eugen von Savoyen,* 12. Band (1710), p.623.

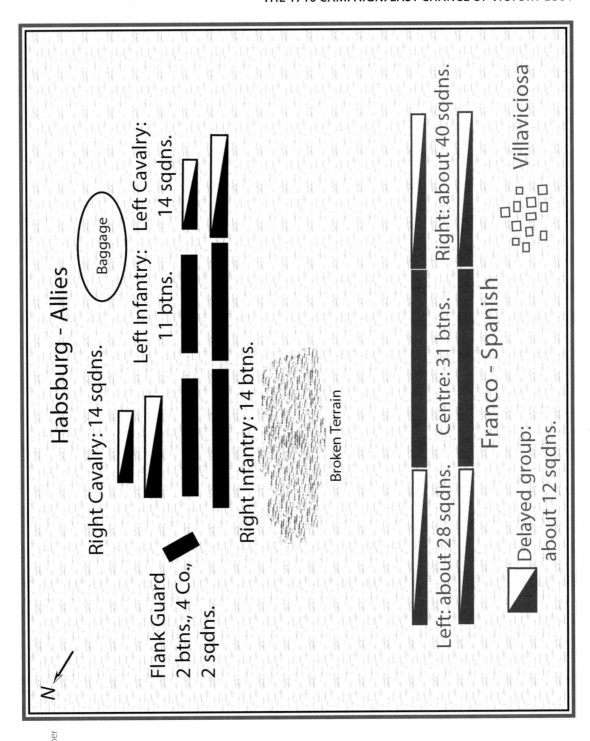

Map 14
The Battle of
Villaviciosa, December
10 1710

Left Wing Infantry: Major General Coppe: 5 battalions
Buol (1 btn), Ferrer (1 btn), La Marck (1 btn), Verpoorten (1 btn) and Richards' (1 btn)

Left Wing Cavalry: Lieutenant General Belcastel: 14 squadrons
1st Line: Major General Frankenberg: 8 squadrons
Frankenberg (2 sqns), Drimborn (2 sqns), Matha (2 sqns) and Lepell (2 sqns)

2nd Line: Major General Lepell: 6 squadrons
Frankenberg (2 sqns), Spee (2 sqns) and Schlippenbach (2 sqns)

Artillery: 20 or more guns, at least 9 in a battery supporting the right wing infantry. Probably the 26 guns used previously.

They were facing 32 battalions and 80 squadrons, although at least one of the battalions seems to have taken a support role guarding the artillery and baggage. In addition, 12 squadrons had not arrived at the time the battle started. The Bourbon army had about 12,000 infantry, 6,800 cavalry and 22 guns at the beginning of the battle, with about 1,200 cavalry en route. With 19 to 20,000 troops the Bourbons had a substantial numeric advantage and were confident after their recent success. Yet they had also recently completed a long rapid march and had the day before fought a hard action so they must also have been tired.

The battle that followed was a confused affair which both sides had reason to claim as a victory. This makes the closing stages in particular difficult to follow. The Bourbon army deployed in the usual fashion for the time, the infantry in the centre with cavalry wings either side. Because 12 squadrons of the army had not yet arrived the left wing was only 28 squadrons compared to 40 on the right. The outnumbered Confederates deployed with their left wing in two lines and the open flank covered by the River Tajuna. The left wing cavalry were next to the river and the infantry alongside them. Between the two armies were a lot of small ravines, remains of small walls and other rubble. These were particularly thick, and so significant, in the part of the battlefield where the Confederate right were. To take advantage of this Starhemberg deployed the bulk of the right wing behind the worst of this terrain in four lines. Two lines of infantry with two of cavalry behind so they could act as a reserve. To secure the open right flank two battalions, four grenadier companies and two squadrons were detached from the main line to face any attempt to outflank the line. The infantry were probably one battalion and two grenadier companies each from the Starhemberg and Osnabruck regiments.

After the customary mutual bombardment Vendôme received word that the late arriving 12 squadrons were close to the battlefield. So to give his army a greater chance of achieving a decisive victory before night fall Vendôme issued the general order to attack. On the Bourbon right the cavalry moved up into position to attack the British, Dutch and Palatine cavalry of the Confederate left. In a reversal of the events at Almenar it was the turn of the Confederate cavalry to flee after minimum resistance. Indeed the British cavalry seem to have routed before the Bourbon cavalry even attacked and their rout carried away the rest of the cavalry on that wing. Seizing this unexpected turn of events the Bourbon right wing cavalry rushed forward. Part of the cavalry chased the fleeing Confederate cavalry and attacked the Confederate baggage which was positioned behind the army, while others slammed into the exposed flank of the Confederate left wing infantry. Seven of the eleven battalions of the left wing were swept from the field to join the cavalry in rout and another three were driven back but managed to rally.

Only Buol's battalion of the left wing managed to stand its ground. These combined with Bouilion's battalion, one battalion of Osnabruck's and three squadrons of Portuguese cavalry from the right wing, attempted to block the rampant Bourbon cavalry which were threatening to sweep the whole army away. The intervention of this group of three battalions and three squadrons was enough to stall the flank attack. The now disorganised Bourbon cavalry turned to easier targets such as the fleeing Confederate troops and especially the temptation of the unguarded Confederate baggage. The area still thick with Bourbon cavalry and the flank would have to be secure. To do this four battalions, probably the four surviving battalions from the left wing, formed into a single large square to protect the flank. This sealed the now exposed flank for the rest of the battle.

While these events were happening on the Confederate left, the right was also under attack. The Bourbon cavalry on this flank were trying to get to the Confederate cavalry but they were at the back of the army and difficult to reach. The Bourbons on the Confederate right swung out to avoid the bad terrain and then ran into the Confederate flank guard on this side which further disrupted their advance. The attack faltered and with perfect timing the Confederate cavalry launched a counter-attack spearheaded by some of the Portuguese cavalry. This attack drove the Bourbon left wing cavalry in confusion. As chance would have it the two senior Bourbon commanders of this wing became casualties at this time. While both Philip, the Bourbon King of Spain, and Vendôme were behind the Bourbon left wing at the time and got caught up in the confusion. Effectively the command of the Bourbon left wing cavalry and the army command itself were unable to command for some time.

Once again, with great timing, Starhemberg seized the opportunity presented. The Bourbon Spanish infantry had been advancing across the broken terrain to engage the Confederate right wing infantry. The combination of the difficult terrain and Confederate fire had slowed the advance, and also led to some disorder in the attacking units. Despite this the attacking Spanish continued to advance and indeed had reached the Confederate gun line. At this point the Confederate left had been secured by the square formed there and the right had, if only temporarily, pushed the enemy back. This was the time to counter-attack and Starhemberg took it. Some of the Confederate right wing cavalry attacked the now partially exposed left wing of the advancing Bourbon infantry. Then the Confederate infantry of the right joined in the attack.

After a hard fight the Bourbon infantry were thrown back in confusion and swept back beyond their own gun lines. The Confederates followed up and even turned round the Bourbons own guns to aid their cause. At least initially the Bourbons were hampered by the lack of senior commanders to coordinate the armies actions. By this time darkness was falling and it starts to get very difficult to reconcile the various accounts of the battle. Both sides later claimed that in this final phase they managed to hold the field and so could claim victory. It seems likely that with the confusion of the fighting, the difficult terrain and the darkness that units or small groups of units on both sides did achieve success against similar local opponents. Therefore parts of both armies did feel they had won the battle. Probably some of the Bourbon left wing cavalry, possibly the late arriving group, managed to intervene before the Bourbon infantry could be completely defeated. The fighting then seems to have broken down into smaller confused actions which continued into the night. To add to the uncertain result of the battle at some point during the night the Confederates started to pull back. It had been a hard battle and both sides had reasons to believe they had done enough to claim victory.

The truth was that the Confederate army had done well after the initial set back of most of their left wing being swept away. Whether they had then managed to drive some or all off the Bourbon army after this it did not actually matter in the longer term. The Confederate army was in no state to continue the campaign and had been defeated strategically. It would have to retreat, abandoning the gains made and all it could do now was hope it could limp back to Catalonia. The Confederates had lost about another 4,000 men and many senior officers during the battle. They had to abandon all but 10 guns because of a lack of horses, which had been lost when the baggage was looted. The Bourbons also lost heavily, probably around 3,000 men and maybe as many as 6,000 or 7,000 men along with a number of senior officers, but the Confederate now had about 9,7000 very disheartened men to face 16 or 17,000 buoyant enemy.

The Confederate army pulled off the battlefield and immediately marched as quickly as it could for Barcelona. During the march a half of the Verpoorten battalion was left with the wounded and the Ferrer battalion was later left in Saragossa. Vendôme did not rest on his laurels and he set off in pursuit of the wounded Confederate army. The Bourbon army was exhausted after the long march they had already completed and after fighting two tough actions a few days later. Because of this the Confederates were able to make good their escape as the Bourbons were too tired to mount an effective pursuit. Early in Vendôme's army recaptured Saragossa but on 6 January 1711 the Confederate army safely arrived at Barcelona.

The 1710 campaign had been transformed by the arrival of Vendôme. After a promising start it had turned into a disaster for the Confederate cause and was to have a wider impact on the course of the war. Once again the Confederates in Catalonia would have to try to rebuild their army to continue the campaigns, that is if the political situation gave them the chance to do this.

15

The 1711 Campaign: Deadlock at Prats del Rey and Disillusionment

As the battered Confederate army limped back to Catalonia the situation worsened. News arrived that the French forces north of the border had finally crossed it to attack Gerona, the key Confederate fortification blocking access from the north. On 15 December 1710 a French army under Noailles arrived at the fortifications but it was not until 23 December that serious operations started. Tattenbach was the Confederate commander of the garrison and he led an active defence.

Garrison of Gerona: 5 battalions (possibly also a sixth battalion), two squadrons and unknown number of irregulars.

Spanish:

Ciudad de Cartagena (11th)	1 battalion
Ciudad de Zaragoza (13th)	1 battalion
Granada (27th)	1 battalion

The Granada battalion had been raised in Gerona earlier in the year and could still have been in the garrison.

Palatine:

Coppe	1 battalion
Greber	1 battalion
Schonberg	1 battalion
Schellard's	2 squadrons (probably fighting dismounted)

Outer works were taken by the end of 1710 but then bad weather delayed the siege until 14 January. When better weather arrived the French continued to make progress despite the best efforts of the defenders. A breach was made in the defences and on January 23 the French assaulted and secured this breach. The garrison now had no choice but to surrender and they did so on 24 January 1711. The Bourbon armies now had an important foothold in

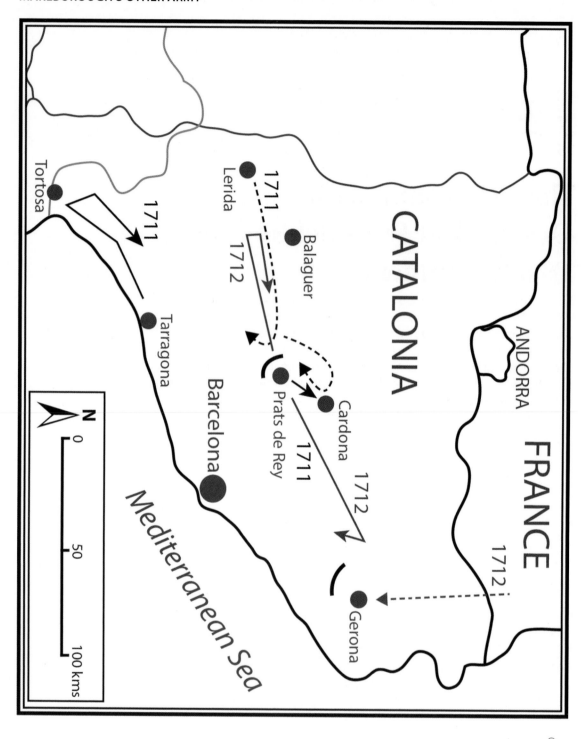

Map 15
Catalonia, 1711–12

the north of Catalonia. This greatly weakened the Confederate position in Catalonia and was a further loss that can be attributed to the failure of the 1710 campaign.

The other important development since the army left Catalonia was the defeat of the British government in elections in October 1710 and the impact of this. The pro-war Whigs were defeated by the Tories who were less enthusiastic about the war. Initially, at least in public, the new British government was committed to continuing the war but also to seeking peace as soon as possible. This initially included the core British commitment to 'No peace without Spain'. The disastrous events of the later part of the 1710 campaign and growing discontent with the worsening situation in Spain started to undermine the support for this idea and the commitment to this principle. The seeds had been sown for the eventual outcome of the war in the events of this time in Spain.

On 6 January 1711 the Confederate army reached Barcelona and safety. At this time the army had 25½ battalions of infantry, 30 cavalry squadrons and 10 guns. There were 6,563 infantry and 2,151 or 2,251 cavalry fit for service. In addition another 1,294 or 2,058 (it varies according to different sources) infantry and 764 cavalry were with the army but not fit to fight. This gives a total of between 10,872 to 11,636 men (probably around 12,000) with the addition of the artillery and other personnel. About 1,500 cavalry of the original army was already in Catalonia and so the army had lost nearly 50% of its original 25 to 26,000 strength at the start of the campaign. The army had been effectively destroyed. The army at around this time was as follows.

Infantry

Nationality	Fit Men	Wounded Men*	Battalions	Regiments
Austrian	3,887	692	14	Starhemberg (3), Reventlau (3), Gschwind (3), Osnabruck (3), Eckh (2)
Spanish	1,119	320	4	Catalonian Guard, Luccini, Buol, Ahumada
British	600	-	2	Bourgay's, Richards
Portuguese	548	52	2	Albuquerque, Bouillon
Palatine	119	62	2	Leib, La Marck
Dutch	290	168	1½	St. Amant, Verpoorten (1/2)
TOTAL	6,563	1,294	25½	

* These figures are for 27 December 1710.

Cavalry

Nationality	Fit Men	Wounded Men*	Squadrons	Regiments
Austrian	333	155	4**	Jorger
Spanish	300	-	1	Morras
British	100	-	1	Lepell
Portuguese	1,017	405	18**	Acuna (3), Almeida (Secuira) (3), Azevedo (3), Castro (3), Miranda (3), Sottomayor (3)
Palatine	214	85	6	Frankenberg (ex Stolzenberg), Frankenberg (ex Leiningen), Spee
Dutch	287	119	6	Mattha (2) Schlippenbach (2), Drimborn (2)
TOTAL	2,251	764	36	

*   These figures are for 27 December 1710

**   In addition there were about 40 hussars.

The most urgent task was to rebuild the army so that it could take the field again. The Austrians had already sent extra forces to Catalonia, most of these arrived in January but some did not arrive until July. These amounted to an extra six battalions and 12 cavalry squadrons along with replacements for the units already in Catalonia. Two extra battalions were also raised for two of the Italian units in the Spanish army, at least on paper. From Britain a new commander of the British contingent arrived in May, the Duke of Argyll. Argyll was a very experienced commander who had fought at Ramillies, Oudernaarde and Malplaquet. He was later to fight as the commander of the British army against the Jacobites in the 1715 uprising. To replace the massive British loses of the previous campaigns General Wheatham arrived in Lisbon in February with six battalions from Britain and Ireland. A few months later, despite Portuguese protests, these troops sailed for Catalonia with one of the British battalions formally in Portugal. Going via Gibraltar where this force picked up another battalion and arrived in Catalonia with eight battalions. These troops with the addition of three battalions withdrawn from other duties brought the British up to 13 battalions in Catalonia.

To balance these gains there was some reorganisation of the survivors of the 1710 campaign. The Austrian Jorger Dragoons were reduced by two squadrons to four squadrons. The two remaining Portuguese battalions in Catalonia were amalgamated into a single battalion. Similarly two of the Portuguese cavalry regiments were amalgamated into a single unit and used to rebuild the strength of the other regiments. The Dutch St. Amant's battalion was also absent from Catalonia for this campaign but it is not clear why. Possibly it was sent to operate with the navy as the unit was a marine regiment. Alternatively it may have gone to rebuild its strength, perhaps having left most of its personnel in Catalonia to build up the remaining Dutch troops. Regardless, the St. Amant battalion would return for the 1712 campaign.

By July the forces available were as follows.

Imperialist: 20 battalions, 16 squadrons, 1 company.

Unit	Organisation	Strength (Horses)	Notes
Starhemberg	3 battalions	1,634	
Reventlau	3 battalions	1,448	
Osnabruck	3 battalions	1,562	
Gschwind	3 battalions	1,450	
Eck	2 battalions	1,014	
Browne (ex Bagni)	2 (3) battalions *	1,009	Arrived late 1710
Toldo	4 (3) battalions *	1,775	Arrived July 1711
Jorger Dragoons	4 squadrons	628 (528)	2 squadrons disbanded
Vaubonne Dragoon	6 squadrons	800 (777)	Arrived late 1710
Battee Dragoons	6 squadrons	866 (748)	Arrived late 1710
Ebengenyi Hussars	1 company	49 (30)	

* Initially Browne's regiment had two battalions and Toldo's had 4 battalions. In December the units were all reorganised as three-battalion units.

Total Infantry: 9,892   Total Cavalry (Horses): 2,343 (2,083)

Spanish: 17 battalions, 12 squadrons, 1 company.

Unit	Organisation	Strength (Horses)	Notes
Ahumada (1st)	1 battalion	407	
Catalonian Guards (3rd)	1 battalion	431	
Tattenbach (4th)	1 battalion	480	
Shover (5th)	1 battalion	512	
Castiglioni (6th)	1 battalion	801	Known as Luccini
La Deputacion (7th)	1 battalion		
La Ciudad (8th)	1 battalion		
Ciudad de Cartagena (11th)	1 battalion	381	Known as Alcantarilla
Ciudad de Zaragoza (13th)	1 battalion	286	Known as Pertus
Ferrer's (14th)	1 battalion	345	
Taafe (23rd)	2 battalions	1197	
Carles Llorach (24th)	1 battalion		On Sardinia
Buol (25th)	1 battalion		Known as Grisons
Faber (26th)	2 battalions	1100	
Granada (27th)	1 battalion	575	
Zinzendorf's (1st)	2 squadrons	379 (378)	'the King's Dragoons'
Morras' (2nd)	2 squadrons	297 (247)	
Sobias' (3rd)	2 squadrons	248 (209)	
Nebot's (4th)	2 squadrons	339 (304)	
Catalonian Gds (8th)	2 squadrons	350 (275)	Known as Clariana
Aragon (12th)	2 squadrons	404 (309)	Known as Cordova
Don Antonio Prats *	1 company	40 (34)	

* Described as a 'Free Company' it is probably the remnants of the attempt to raise a unit in Madrid in 1710.

Total Infantry: 6,515   Total Cavalry (Horses): 2,057 (1,756)

Dutch: 1 battalion, 6 squadrons

Unit	Organisation	Strength (Horses)
Verpoorten's (NL 17)	1 battalion	522
Drimborn's (NLC 15)	2 squadrons	226 (262)
Schlippenbach's (NLD 2)	2 squadrons	345 (372)
Mattha (4th Dragoon)	2 squadrons	351 (390)

Total Infantry: 522   Total Cavalry (Horses): 922 (1,024)

Portuguese: 1 battalion, 15 squadrons

Unit	Organisation	Strength (Horses)	Notes
La Cerda	1 battalion	667	Reorganised Albuquerque and Bouillon battalions
Azevedo	3 squadrons	396 (304)	
Castro	3 squadrons	396 (304)	
Miranda	3 squadrons	397 (304)	
Sottomayor	3 squadrons	398 (304)	
Revelo	3 squadrons	494 (401)	Reorganised Cunea and O'Kelly regiments

Total Infantry: 667   Total Cavalry (Horses): 922 (1,024)

Palatine: 5 battalions, 8 squadrons

Unit	Organisation	Strength (Horses)
Leibregiment zu fuss	1 battalion	502
Coppe	1 battalion	476
Bentheim (ex Greber)	1 battalion	584
Schonberg	1 battalion	504
La Marck (ex Barbo)	1 battalion	289
Schellard's	2 squadrons	282 (275)
Frankenberg's	2 squadrons	235 (235)
Frankenberg's (ex Stolzenberg's)	2 squadrons	231 (231)
Mill's (ex Spee's)	2 squadrons	230 (230)

Total Infantry: 2,355   Total Cavalry (Horses): 978 (972)

British: 13 battalions, 2 squadrons.

Unit	Organisation	Strength (Horses)	Notes
Pearce's (5th)	1 battalion	595	From Portugal
Tyrawley's or Royal Fusiliers (later 7th Foot)	1 battalion	534	
Livesays (12th)	1 battalion	593	From Britain & Ireland
Whetham's (later 27th Foot)	1 battalion	643	
Bourgay's (ex Syburg's)	1 battalion	480	
Elliot's	1 battalion	559	From Gibraltar
Mark Kerr	1 battalion	606	From Britain & Ireland
Molesworth (ex Allen's)	1 battalion	663	From Britain & Ireland
Rich's	1 battalion	549	From Britain & Ireland
Richards' (ex Lepel's)	1 battalion	439	
Rooke's	1 battalion	544	From Britain & Ireland
Slanes'	1 battalion	595	From Britain & Ireland
Stanhope's (ex Innchequin's)	1 battalion	503	
Lepel's (ex Rochfort's) Dragoon	2 squadrons	260 (260)	

Total Infantry: 7,303   Total Cavalry (Horses): 978 (972)

Starhemberg and the Confederates were given time to recover because of a combination of events. First of all, while the Confederate forces were in a lot worse shape than their opponents, the 1710 campaign had still been an exhausting one for the Bourbons as well. So they also needed time to rest and reorganise. More importantly, the change of government in Britain gave new impetus to peace negotiations. Peace negotiations had been ongoing for some years but with little chance of a conclusion. The new circumstances meant that at last peace was a realistic possibility. This was especially true when Charles III's brother the Austrian emperor died on 17 April. Charles was the heir to his brother and now would be the Austrian emperor. This was another key event in the outcome of the war. The prospect of the Habsburg's gaining control of the Spanish throne was nearly as unpalatable to the supporters of the war as was the prospect of the Bourbon's doing the same. A lot of the incentive to put a non-Bourbon rival on the Spanish throne had disappeared along with a lot of the desire to continue a war that was going badly and very expensive. Everyone now expected a negotiated end to the war and indeed the process was now underway which would lead to the end of the war, although it would not happen yet.

There had been some campaigning on the Portuguese front early in 1711. In March, 11 infantry battalions and five cavalry regiments marched to

2728.. John Campbell, 2nd Duke of Argyll, by William Aikman. (National Portrait Gallery)

Miranda do Douro, a Portuguese position that had previously been lost. After a short siege this position was recaptured and the Portuguese army settled into inactivity for a short while as an attempt to negotiate a local agreement was tried. When this did not work out the Portuguese collected together its army and marched again. With 20 battalions and 46 squadrons[1], about 17,000 men, they again campaigned in Portuguese territory they had previously lost, possibly eventually aiming at Badajoz. De Bay, the opposing Spanish commander, reacted to this by launching a similar campaign towards Elvas. This proved to be enough to halt the half-hearted Portuguese advance.

The new British commander in Portugal was the Earl of Portmore and he soon came to understand little would happen in Portugal that year. The British contingent in Portugal consisted of 2,738 men in February - probably these were the six infantry battalions and three cavalry squadrons stationed there the previous year. One of the battalions, Pearce's, left Portugal with Wheatham's force going to Catalonia and another, Barrymore's, went to Gibraltar later in the year. In 1709 five or six new cavalry regiments were authorised to be raised – consisting mainly of Portuguese personnel, they were to be paid directly by the British. They proved to be difficult to raise and only now were they in any shape to take the field.

New 'British' Cavalry Regiments in Portugal
Withers' Dragoons
Plus either
Poissac's, Desbordes', Magny's, Trapaud's/Gually's and Montandre's/Saarlande's Dragoons
or
Tavora's, Gama's, Mello's and Sousa's Dragoons

Information on these regiments is very difficult to find and often vague. It is likely that none of them every achieved full strength, if only because of the shortage of horses. It is not known if, in addition to Withers' unit, there were four or five other units. It seems likely that Galway's and Withers' unit had a total of five squadrons, probably Galway's three and Withers' two. The other units probably had a total of 10 squadrons spread amongst the units. There was a continuing shortage of horses in Portugal and those that were available were poor quality. By the time the autumn campaigning season arrived no

---

1   Hughill, J.A.C., *No Peace without* Spain, pp.334-335.

one in Portugal was keen, with peace negotiations continuing, for serious campaigning. So once again after some brief manoeuvres the activity on the Portuguese front died down as both sides retired to winter quarters.

Prats del Rey and Cardona

By the time the autumn campaign was about to start it was clear that the Bourbon forces in Catalonia were going to actively campaign. Vendôme was preparing to campaign with about 19,000 troops and two obvious objectives, Barcelona and Tarragona. Starhemberg also had to secure Cardona, which could be a secondary target, and some forces would be needed to observe the so far inactive French forces in the north around Gerona. Thus a 'flying corps' was sent to observe the troops in the north. Also Tarragona, Cardona and a number of smaller fortresses were garrisoned. The bulk of the army would move to a position at Prats del Rey. This was a strong position where the Confederates could hope to block any advance on Barcelona or Tarragona.

The following is a breakdown of the army at this time.[2]

Northern 'Flying Corps': Sormani: 6 battalions, 12 squadrons: 2,869 men
    Infantry
        Ahumada
        Catalonian Guards
        Castiglioni
        Ciudad de Cartagena
        Ferrer's
        Granada
    Cavalry
        Zinzendorf's (2 sqns)
        Morras' (2 sqns)
        Sobias' (2 sqns)
        Nebot's (2 sqns)
        Catalonian Guards (2 sqns)
        Aragon (2 sqns)
        Don Antonio Prats (1 company)[3]

Garrison of Tarragona: Wetzel: 8 battalions, 300 dismounted dragoons: 2,600 men
    Infantry
        Tattenbach
        Faber (2 battalions)
        Leibregiment zu fusss
        La Marck
        Tyrawley's Fusiliers
        Livesays'
        Whetham's

---

2   See *Feldzüge des Prinzen Eugen von Savoyen, 13. Band (1711)* (Vienna: K.K. Kriegs-Archiv, 1887), pp.529-530; *Österreichische militärische Zeitschrift* 1844 Band 2, pp.256–257.

3   Don Antonio Prats is not mentioned but was probably here with the rest of the Spanish cavalry.

Dismounted Dragoons
300 dismounted British dragoons, sometimes identified as from Lepel's.

Garrison of Cardona: 2 battalions: 800 men
Infantry
Taafe (2 battalions)

Various Smaller Garrisons: 4 battalions: 1,200 men

Infantry
Shover
La Deputacion
La Ciudad
Ciudad de Zaragoza

Field Army: 36 battalions, 44 squadrons, 16 3 pounder guns and 2 howitzers:[4]
15 to 20,000 men depending on source.
Commander: Starhemberg
Second in Command: Argyll
Commander of the First Line: Atalaya
Commander of the Second Line: Battee

Left Wing Cavalry: 16 squadrons
1st Line: Pepper and Drimborn: 10 squadrons
Lepel's Dragoons (2 sqns)
Mattha's Dragoons (2 sqns)
Drimborn's Horse (2 sqns)
Schellard's Horse (2 sqns)
Frankenberg's Horse (2 sqns)

2nd Line: Frankenberg: 6 squadrons
Schlippenbach's Dragoons (2 sqns)
Frankenberg's Horse (2 sqns)
Mill's Horse (2 sqns)

Infantry Centre: 34 battalions
1st Line: MonTessé, Eck and Toldo: 17 battalions
Slanes' (1 btn)
Mark Kerr (1 btn)
Molesworth (1 btn)
Rich's (1 btn)
Elliot's (1 btn)
Verpoorten's (1 btn)
Bentheim (1 btn)
Coppe (1 btn)

---

4   Francis, D., *The First Peninsular War: 1702–1713*, p.359.

Gschwind (3 btns)
Reventlau (3 btns)
Starhemberg (3 btns)

2nd Line: Windham and Browne: 17 battalions
Rooke's (1 btn)
Pearce's (1 btn)
Stanhope's (1 btn)
Richards' (1 btn)
Bourgay's (1 btn)
Schonberg's (1 btn)
Eckh's (2 btns)
Browne's (2 btns)
Osnabruck's (3 btns)
Toldo's (4 btns)

Right Wing Cavalry: 22 squadrons
1st Line: Gondrecourt: 12 squadrons
Castro Horse (2 sqns)
Jorger Dragoons (4 sqns)
Battee Dragoons (3 sqns)
Vaubonne Dragoons (3 sqns)

2nd Line: Almeyda and Hamilton: 10 squadrons
Azevedo Horse (2 sqns)
Miranda Horse (2 sqns)
Battee Dragoons (3 sqns)
Vaubonne Dragoons (3 sqns)

Reserve: Bouillon: 2 battalions, 6 squadrons and 1 company[5]
Revelo Horse (3 sqns)
Buol (1 btn)
La Cerda (1 btn)
Sottomayor Horse (3 sqns)
Ebengenyi Hussars (1 company)[5]

On 27 September Charles III left Barcelona to become the Austrian Emperor, an event that was symbolic of the declining fortunes of the Confederates. By the time Charles left Vendôme had already made some advances. From July small Bourbon detachments operated against minor positions to clear the approaches to the Confederate position at Prats del Rey. By 16 September the Bourbon army had reached the Confederate position. This position was difficult to attack and for the attacking Bourbons there was little water in the area where they were based. Over the next few weeks the Bourbons periodically bombarded the Confederate positions and launched at least one, unsuccessful,

---

5 The Hussar company is not mentioned but was probably present.

attempt to assault part of the position.

With the Bourbons tied up in front of Prats del Rey the Confederates attempted a counter-move. General Wetzel was sent with a small force to try to recapture Tortosa. This force consisted of the Ferrer, Shover and Ciudad de Zaragoza battalions and possibly others. Tattenbach's battalion was moved from Tarragona to the Flying Corps at around this time, possibly to replace Ferrer's which had previously been part of that group. The garrison of Tortosa had been warned of the Confederate attempt by informants so when Wetzel attempted to assault Tortosa his force was bloodily repulsed and had to make a hasty retreat. This diversion had little impact on the situation at the Prats del Rey position where all of Vendôme's efforts were fruitless as the position was too strong for the forces at his disposal. Vendôme wished to continue to try and take the position but was convinced to withdraw by wiser council. The Bourbon forces therefore pulled back from direct confrontation with the Confederate position.

At the end of October the effective strengths of the Austrian and Flying Corps units were as follows:[6]

Unit	Strength	Unit	Strength (Horses)
Starhemberg	1,477	Tattenbach	447
Reventlau	1,322	Jorger Dragoons	639 (334)
Osnabruck	1,402	Vaubonne Dragoon	793 (453)
Gschwind	1,269	Battee Dragoons	892 (500)
Eck	839	Zinzendorf's Dragoons	368 (318)
Browne (ex Bagni)	728	Morras' Horse	272 (163)
Toldo	1,838	Sobias' Horse	247 (145)
Ahumada	738	Nebot's Horse	328 (221)
Catalonian Guards	409	Catalonian Guard Horse	272 (168)
Castiglioni	686	Aragon Horse	354 (203)
Ciudad de Cartagena	397	Don Antonio Prats	38 (36)
Granada	554		

At the same time a force of 3,000 men was detached from the Bourbon army to take Cardona. This force under de Muret arrived on 12 November and was ready to bombard Cardona on 15 November. The garrison of Cardona was under the command of Eckh and consisted of the following troops:[7]

Buol	596 plus 77 grenadiers
Taafe	729 plus 71 grenadiers
La Deputacion	252 plus 44 grenadiers
Commanded battalion[8]	310
Total:	1,887 plus 192 grenadiers

---

6   *Feldzüge des Prinzen Eugen von Savoyen*, 13 Band (1711), pp.534–536.

7   Ibid., pp.537–539.

8   This was a mixed unit of men from the 7 Austrian infantry regiments and 19 Portuguese soldiers.

These troops were joined by a group of grenadiers led by Count Gehlen in mid-November, presumably before the town fell. These were 81 Austrian, 59 British and 29 Dutch/Palatine grenadiers – 169 in total.

After two days of bombardment the outer defences and the town were in ruins. The Bourbon forces then assaulted and met fierce resistance from the defenders. Despite inflicting, and taking, heavy casualties the Confederates were forced back into the citadel but they were not yet beaten. The garrison continued to resist valiantly and so a further assault was forgotten. An attempt to mine the citadel was tried but bad weather foiled this. Fresh Bourbon troops arrived, probably an additional 3,000 men or more. By now the besiegers were also being harassed by Confederate miquelets irregulars under Nebot and progress was slow.

The resistance of the defenders of Cardona and the inactivity at Prats del Rey prompted Starhemberg to make an attempt to relieve the siege. To do this a force of 4,000 to 4,300 men under Battee were detached from the main force and sent to Cardona along with a lot of supplies to re-supply the garrison. The exact composition of this force is uncertain but seems to have consisted of the following.

- 200 grenadiers. From the Starhemberg regiment and probably other units, most likely the Austrian units.
- 550 men under Stanhope. Probably two grenadier companies from the Osnabruck and Gschwind regiments, 200 British grenadiers and 150 men from Stanhope's regiment.
- 1600 Palatine and Austrian infantry. The Schonberg and Bentheim Palatine regiments and one battalion each from the Austrian Osnabruck and Gschwind regiments.
- 600 cavalry. Mill's Palatine Horse, Battee's Austrian Dragoons, Ebengenyi's Hussars and the Casanova volunteers.
- 850 Miquelets irregulars in two groups.
- 500 Vaubonne's Dragoons dismounted.

These were joined by 500 more irregulars, including 100 cavalry, under Nebot at Cardona on 19 December. At five in the morning of 21 December the Confederate relief force attacked the besiegers from two directions. Initially they were repulsed but in a hard-fought action a further attack succeeded in breaking through to the garrison. Both sides suffered in this hard-fought and confusing action but the relieving force managed to deliver supplies and reinforcements to the citadel. There was now no prospect of success for the Bourbon forces. Consequently, early in the morning of 25 December De Muret led his forces away from Cardona and back to the main army. All forces now went into winter quarters bringing the campaign to an end.

At this time the Austrian infantry was reorganised so that each of the seven regiments now had three battalions of five companies and two grenadier companies. By the end of December the Austrian units, and a few Spanish, had the following strength:

Unit	Strength
Starhemberg	1,560
Reventlau	1,460
Osnabruck	1,461
Gschwind	1,324
Eck	1,301
Browne (ex Bagni)	1,723
Toldo	1,552
Taaffe	581
Faber	583

Despite the reasonably successful defensive campaign in Catalonia the situation for the Confederates had been transformed by events outside Iberia. During 1711 very few funds were sent by the British government to finance the war as disillusionment with the war grew. Disgusted by the lack of support Argyll left Catalonia early in the campaign and sailed to Minorca with some of the British troops from Catalonia to see if anything could be achieved there. Meanwhile disillusionment with the war was growing in Britain, fuelled by the disastrous 1710 campaign in Spain and continuing lack of progress there. This discontent was fanned into change by Charles III becoming the Austrian emperor. On 7 December 1711 a debate was held in the British Parliament on the motion that 'No peace could be safe or honourable to Great Britain or Europe, if Spain and the West Indies were allotted to any branch of the house of Bourbon'.[9] This motion was brought by the opposition, the party in favour of the war, and was defeated after a great effort by the new government. This was the abandonment of the key principle of British policy of 'No peace without Spain'. It was a clear signal that the new British government now wanted peace at any price. The end of the war was now only a matter of time.

---

9   G. Holmes, "The Commons' Division on 'No Peace without Spain, 7th December 1711", *Bulletin of the Institute of Historical Research*, 3 (1960), pp.223–224.

16

The 1712 and 1713 Campaigns: Peace At Last, For Some

In January 1712 peace negotiations started again and it was clear to everyone that there was a good chance they would be successful. The peace talks were to drag on for some time and when peace arrived it was not a general armistice between all combatants straight away. Instead the peace was to come in stages - for the Catalans the war was to continue in earnest further. Most commanders were happy to watch their opponents and wait for peace to come. Yet for some this gave an opportunity to strike a final blow and perhaps get a better deal in the peace talks.

In Catalonia Vendôme had initially been enthusiastic to campaign actively but was talked out of it by his subordinates who wanted to wait. Vendôme was ill at this time and would die on 15 June from an indigestion problem. This was a great loss for the Bourbon cause as Vendôme was undoubtedly one of the best commanders of this time. So it was that Starhemberg was the person to initiate action in this area. There were some minor changes on the forces available. The Confederates had received more replacements for the Austrian regiments and the foreign regiments in the Spanish army. Five British battalions had left Catalonia for various reasons and the Portuguese cavalry had been reorganised. The Portuguese cavalry had been reorganised at some time and now had five regiments with two squadrons each, rather than the three they previously had. Small-scale attacks into Aragon and Valencia provinces along with an attack on Rosas on the frontiers were all undertaken, but with little long-term impact. From April the French garrison in Gerona was blockaded. The main Confederate force under Starhemberg moved to capture Cervera and then threatened Lérida. This move was easily blocked by Tserclaes von Tilly, the new commander of the Bourbon forces west of Barcelona.

Starhemberg now concentrated his forces to make a serious attempt to recapture Gerona. Gerona was defended by the Bourbon general Fiennes with 15 battalions and 20 squadrons, about 10,000 men. By 28 July the concentration of the Confederates had brought together 28 battalions, 31 squadrons and at least 15 guns, about 18,000 men.

Left Wing Cavalry: 15 squadrons
1st Line
Miranda Horse (2 sqns)
Revelo Horse (2 sqns)
Sottomayor Horse (2 sqns)
Castro Horse (2 sqns)

2nd Line
Lepel's Dragoons (1 sqn)
Schlippenbach's Dragoons (2 sqns)
Drimborn's Horse (2 sqns)
Wassenaar's (ex Mattha's) Dragoons (2 sqns)

Centre Infantry: 28 battalions
1st Line:
Gschwind (3 btns)
Toldo's (3 btns)
Osnabruck's (3 btns)
Reventlau (3 btns)
Starhemberg (3 btns)

2nd Line
Tyrawley's Fusiliers (1 btn)
Mark Kerr (1 btn)
Stanhope's (ex Richards') (1 btn)
Rooke's (1 btn)
Nassau's (ex Stanhope's) (1 btn)
Verpoorten's (1 btn)
Coppe (1 btn)
Bentheim (1 btn)
La Marck (1 btn)
Schonberg's (1 btn)
Leibregiment zu fuss (1 btn)
Luccini (probably Taaffe's) (1 btn)
La Cerda (1 btn)

Right Wing Cavalry: 16 squadrons
1st Line
Nebot's Horse (1 sqn)
Jorger Dragoons (4 sqns)
Battee Dragoons (2 sqns)
Aggregirte Cavalry (1 sqn)[1]

---

1   This was a squadron composed of surplus officers from other units.

2nd Line
> Frankenberg's Horse (2 sqns)
> Frankenberg's (ex Stolzenberg's) Horse (2 sqns)
> Mill's Horse (2 sqns)
> Schellard's Horse (2 sqns)

With these troops Starhemberg moved to threaten Gerona more directly. Although the Confederate army was not strong enough for a more formal siege they could now properly blockade it and hope to retake the fortress at some point. Meanwhile an armistice had been signed in August between Britain, Holland, France and Spain and news of this arrived in Barcelona on 2 October. Following this the British and Dutch units withdrew from the front and prepared to leave Catalonia. This armistice did not cover the remaining troops and so for them the war continued. It did encourage the French and Spanish to be more active as they now faced fewer opponents. The small gains made earlier by Starhemberg were now reversed and, worse, a relief force for Gerona started to be assembled.

The French general Berwick was assigned the task of relieving Gerona and he slowly assembled a force of 34 battalions, 41 squadrons and 30 guns at Toulon. To counter this Starhemberg striped Catalonia of as many troops as he dared and assembled 36 battalions and 37 squadrons. Although understrength he now had enough troops to try a more direct attack on Gerona before the relief force from Toulon could arrive. Starhemberg tried to persuade the beleaguered garrison to surrender, probably hoping the extra numbers would overawe them, but this failed. Following this the Confederates made three assaults but all failed. By 1 January 1713 Berwick's army from Toulon was approaching the position and over the next few days they brushed aside Confederate blocking forces. Starhemberg did not have enough troops to seriously contest Berwick's advance and so the Confederate army pulled back to Barcelona. Berwick marched into Gerona on 8 January 1713 with enough supplies to withstand a very long siege, the city was now controlled by the Bourbons.

On the Portuguese front a similar sequence of events were being played over this period. Early in the year the front was quiet as everyone waited for the outcome of the peace negotiations. Portmore, the British commander on this front, was so convinced little would happen that he left in early September, leaving Colonel Pearce in charge of the dwindling British contingent in Portugal. De Bay, the Bourbon commander on this front, received reinforcements during the year as other fronts went inactive. Despite the lack of enthusiasm of most of the army De Bay was determined to strike a blow before peace came.

The target De Bay choose was the key position of Campo Maior. Before the Spanish army could get to Campo Maior the Portuguese managed to reinforce the garrison with 800 grenadiers. Stiffened by these timely reinforcements the garrison of Campo Maior stood firm in the face of the Bourbon challenge. On 17 October the Spanish launched a major assault. The Portuguese defenders not only beat this off this attack but launched a sally of their own afterwards. On 23 October news arrived of the armistice which meant that the British were out of the war. The British contingent were convinced to remain with the army for the duration of the crisis at Campo Maior, although they would not participate in any combat. Shortly after this time the weather deteriorated as heavy rains started. This effectively stopped operations, and after a few weeks of frustration De Bay gave up and on 8 November the Bourbons broke the siege and withdrew.

This was effectively the end of the war on this front. On 5 December an armistice was agreed and the remaining British troops marched to Gibraltar through Spain. The remaining British troops had by this time been concentrated into two regiments, Pearce's and Newton's, with the others being reduced. A final peace treaty involving Portugal was not agreed until 1715 but a series of armistices were agreed from this time until the treaty was concluded. Thus the war ended on this front, although it would take some time to work out the details.

Long before this time, 1715, the Confederate war had finished. The withdrawal from Gerona was effectively the end of the operations on this front. The Austrians were keen to try to keep the war going in all fronts but the Confederate forces were too weak in Catalonia to do anything, while the Bourbon forces were content to sit and wait for an agreement to be made with the Austrians. By the end of May 1713 the total forces in Catalonia were as follows.

Unit	Btns/Sqns	Men	Horses	Notes
Starhemberg	3	1,924		
Gschwind	3	1,749		
Browne (ex Bagni)	3	1,720		
O'Dwyer (ex Reventlau)	3	2,002		
Toldo	3	1,704		
Osnabruck	3	1,651		
Traun (ex Eck)	3	1,609		
Vaubonne Dragoon	6	925	719	
Battee Dragoons	6	940	581	
Jorger Dragoons	6	969	624	
Ebengenyi Hussars	1/2	51	35	
Catalonian Guards		634		
Tattenbach		312		
Ahumada		762		
Ciudad de Cartagena		318		
Granada		611		
Ciudad de Zaragoza		385		
Borda	Probably the La Deputacion and La Ciudad regiments. Unknown size.			
Ibarra				
Faber		395		
Castiglioni		649		Known as Marulli
Taafe	Unknown size			Known as Luccinin
Buol	Unknown size			

Unit	Btns/Sqns	Men	Horses	Notes
Starhemberg	3	1,924		
Gschwind	3	1,749		
Browne (ex Bagni)	3	1,720		
O'Dwyer (ex Reventlau)	3	2,002		
Toldo	3	1,704		
Osnabruck	3	1,651		
Traun (ex Eck)	3	1,609		
Vaubonne Dragoon	6	925	719	
Battee Dragoons	6	940	581	
Jorger Dragoons	6	969	624	
Ebengenyi Hussars	1/2	51	35	
Catalonian Guards		634		
Tattenbach		312		
Ahumada		762		
Ciudad de Cartagena		318		
Granada		611		
Ciudad de Zaragoza		385		
Borda	Probably the La Deputacion and La Ciudad regiments. Unknown size.			
Ibarra				
Faber		395		
Castiglioni		649		Known as Marulli
Taafe	Unknown size			Known as Luccinin
Buol	Unknown size			
Hamilton	Unknown unit and size.			
Zinzendorf's		218	177	Known as King's Dragoons
Morras'		203	135	
Sobias'		218	119	Philipp Cordova Dragoons?
Nebot's		241	118	
Catalonian Guards		254	104	Sormani Dragoons?
Aragon		219	125	
Aggregirte *		427		
Irregular 'Fusileros' and 'Freiwillige'		4,225	519	

* Surplus officers from other units.

By this time it had already been decided to withdraw the Austrian forces from Catalonia as Austria too made peace. On 8 July 1713 the Austrian forces started to leave Catalonia and the Confederate war ended. But this was not the end of the war for Catalonia.

I: Rigaud inv:

The Assault on the an

Aftermath and Afterword

28. The final assault on
Barcelona, 11 September 1714

Catalonia would now have to fight another war to survive as a separate
nation. On 9 July 1713, the day after the last of their allies, left the Catalans
signalled their resolve by putting the area on a war footing and declaring
their intention to fight to the end. For this purpose they authorities raised
a new Catalan army but the core of these forces were ex-Confederate units.
Two of the former Spanish Confederate battalions, the La Deputacion (7th)
and La Ciudad (8th) battalions, now became units in the Catalan army. Of
the five other regular infantry regiments one was mainly composed of former

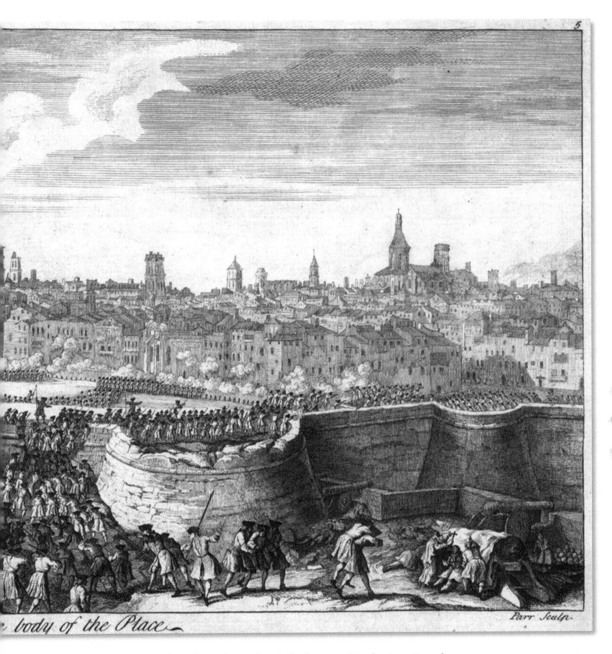

body of the Place

Parr Sculp.

Ahumada (1st) personel and another of mainly former Catalonian Guards (3rd) personell. A third unit contained large numbers of German soldiers from various former Confederate units who did not want to leave Catalonia. It was a similar story with the cavalry. Nebot's (4th) regiment became a Catalan unit and another was largely composed of former personnel of Aragon (12th) regiment.

A large number of other units were raised to try to defend the remaining territory the Catalans controlled. These were both regular and irregular and included veterans of the previous campaigns. In the rest of 1713 and early 1714 the Bourbon forces cleared out minor positions, attempted to control the discontented countryside and put Barcelona under ineffective siege. In the second half of 1714 Bourbon reinforcements and crucially a siege train of artillery arrived at Barcelona. Under the command of Berwick a full siege was established in July 1714. On 12–14 August a series of assaults were bloodily repulsed. After further preparations the final Bourbon assault was launched on 11 September. An overwhelming general assault carried the defences and the Bourbons swept into the city. The final bloody assault led to perhaps 9,000 casualties and crushed the Catalan cause.

The Catalans were disgusted at being abandoned by their allies but the experience of the following months was crucial to the development of Catalonian national feeling. After the end of the conflict the Catalans were subjected to a loss of former privileges and other indignities. The events and memory of the events of this time are factors that have kept Catalonian independence an issue in Spain to this day. To this day 11 September 1714 is celebrated in Catalonia as their national day.

The war had also largely determined some aspects of diplomacy for long periods afterwards. For Spain and France having a Bourbon king meant that until the downfall of that house in France the two nations would be bound together, if only loosely. A tie that would involve both sides in future unwanted difficulties and conflicts. Britain gained Minorca and Gibraltar at the peace and these provided targets for continuing problems. Spain eventually recovered Minorca later in the 18th century but the British enclave at Gibraltar remains to this day. It also remains a problem in the relationship between Spain and Britain, with international tensions periodically rising over it. This in turn meant that it was in Britain's interest to help and support Portugal. Britain and Portugal had often cooperated before this time but from this point on the alliance was close. It is an alliance which, at least in theory, continues to this day.

For the historian or military theorist it offers a useful contrast to other events. The failures of this 'First Peninsular War' are a stark contrast to the way that the more famous Peninsular War was fought in 1808–1814. This campaign also highlights how successful Marlborough's efforts were in the same war. Problems that Marlborough and the high command in Flanders dealt with seemingly effortlessly can be seen to have been major problems to their counterparts in Iberia. Comparison with Marlborough's efforts also points to the relative importance of tactical and other innovations of this period compared to military skill and traditional good military practice. The supposedly decisive Confederate tactical innovations such as platoon firing and improved tactics in a charge had little impact in Iberia.

The campaigns in Spain and Portugal could have been decisive in the war and possibly represent a missed opportunity. Similarly, a lack of scholarly interest in this theatre may be a missed opportunity to gain insights into this fascinating series of campaigns.

Colour Plate Commentaries

Introduction

By illustrator Mark Allen

Contradictory sources abound in researching early 18th Century uniforms, this is particularly true in the case of what were referred to at the time as the 'Confederate' forces. William III's habit of leaving colours and standards in French hands, at the end of any given engagement, may not have been good for morale but was great for research, as was the slower tempo of the 1690s, which allowed details of the dress of the 'resting' armies to be recorded in camp. The success of Marlborough and his allies in the War of the Spanish Succession does mean that in sources like Spofforth we have a great source for the capture colours of the French at Blenheim, but in researching the war in Spain, it is clear that it was viewed, militarily and politically, as a secondary front, in terms of the distribution of resources. Below are some snippets, alluding to the dress of the soldiers on this 'front', it is by no means complete, but gives some reasonable opinions and, sometimes, guesses on the subject.

Plate One: British Infantry

(From left to right, top to bottom). Pre-1707 2nd captain's colour of the Scots Regiment of Foot Guards, post this date it is presumed that the Union flag was carried, though there was likely a considerable delay. Scots regiments were often slow in letting the 'saltire' be replaced, which added to the time lag.[1] Finally, apart from the case of the buffs (see below) there does not seem to have been much evidence of colours being 'altered' to reflect the new politics.

There is some contention over the uniforms of the Guards regiments at this time, with many, modern, illustrations depicting the Scots with white/silver lace. This does not appear to have been the case before the 1720s, with the regiments, at this point, being difference by their unique badges alone.

Colonel's colour 1st Foot Guards, both the English Foot Guard Regiments carried red/crimson colonel's colours with Saint George's cross colour, thereafter, later replaced by the Union flag.

---

1   Stephen Ede-Borrett, 'Colours of the Marlburian Wars', parts 1 and 2. *Miniature Wargames*, 1989.

10th captain's colour 2nd Foot Guards, differenced by a special badge and a Roman numeral in the canton. All Foot Guards companies were issued colours, but only three were carried, per battalion, in the field.

Charles Churchill's Regiment of Foot, probably an altered pre-1707 colour, likely dating from before the death of Queen Mary in 1694, as it carries the monogram of the joint monarchs. The earlier colour was blue, which would have allowed an easy alteration to a Union flag. The drummer, pictured here, wears reverse colours, with the coat buff, the regiment's alternative name.

Lucas' regiment showing a possible pre-1707 pattern flag, the griffin was a family crest which may have appeared on the drums.[2] Modern reconstructions of the dress show a greyish green.[3]

Stanhope's/Hill's speculative colour, during the 1680s and 90s the colours were crimson. Again, a questionable colour, Stuart's regiment were listed as wearing orange linings at early as the 1680s, this is the flag of Cunningham's from that time. The regiment was an early visitor to Spain, so may have carried old fashioned colours into the field.

Both Harrison's and Breton's are shown with post 1707 Major's Colours, which would have been the same for the Foot Guards.

Grenadier caps, Foot Guards and a green-faced line regiment during the reign of Queen Anne.

Plate Two: British Cavalry and Dragoons

A: Major General Harvey's Horse, wrongly depicted with a waist belt, horse units normally wore crossed belts well into the 18th century. We have left it here as it may reflect a more practical usage in Spain.[3]
   i. Cloak

B: Grenadier, Royal Dragoons
   i. Trooper
   ii. Drummer

C: Possibly cornet of horse, Queen Anne's reign
   i Horse Grenadier cap, Queen Anne's Reign

1. Harvey's Horse
2. Carpenter's Dragoons
3. Pearce's Dragoons
4. Conyngham's Dragoons
5. Peterborough's Dragoons
6. Artilleryman, Trayne of Artillery

---

2   M. Barthorp, *Marlborough's Army, 1702–11* (London: Osprey, 1980).
3   X. Rubio, *God Save Catalonia!* (Calafell: Llibres de Matrícula, 2010).

Portraits of the Earl of Peterborough and Lord Stanhope from contemporary images.

Plate Three: Austrian Infantry and Dragoons; Dutch Infantry, Cavalry and Dragoons

Imperial Infantry and Dragoons[4]

1. Serenyi infantry: man/drummer/officer
2. Alt Starhemberg: man/drummer/officer
3. Reventlau/ O'Dwyer: man/drummer
4. Eck: man 1709–man 1714
5. Ahumada: man 1716
6. Toldo: man 1705–1716
7. Osnabrück: man 1708, man 1710
   a. Company flag
   b. Colonel's colour (late)
   c. Colonel's colour (1701)
8. Palffy Dragoons: man/guidon
9. Herbouville Dragoons: man/officer
10. Bayreuth Dragoons: man

Dutch Infantry, Cavalry, and Dragoons

11. Drumborn Horse: man/officer/cornet
12. Slippenbach Dragoons: man/guidon
13. Bruhese Infantry: man
14. Saint Amant: man/drummer
15. Verpoorten: man/drummer
16. Palm/Leefdael: man/drummer/colour (reconstruction)
17. Keppelfox: man/drummer
18. Friesheim: man/drummer/colour
19. Vicouse (Huguenot): man/officer
20. Lislemarais (Huguenot): man/drummer

Plate Four: Catalonian Troops

1. Regiment de la Diputacio General. Regiment flag and uniform
   a. Drummer lace
2. Regiment de la Ciutat de Barcelona. Regiment flag/uniform
3. Regiment de la ImmaculadaConcepcio. Regiment flag/uniform
   a. Drummer lace
4. Regiment Nostra Senyoradels Desemparats. Regiment flag/uniform
5. Regiment Santa Eulalia. Regiment flag/uniform
6. Regiment Nostra Senyora del Roser. Regiment flag/uniform

---

4   Hall, Boeri, *Uniforms and Flags of the Imperial Austrian Army 1683–1720.*

7. Regiment dels Set Delors. Regiment flag/uniform
8. Majorca Reinforcements. Uniform
9. Regiment Santa de Narcis. Uniform.

A. Colonel's Colour (reverse, obverse as 4)
   b. Grenadier cap
B. Cavalry regiment Nebot
C. Regiment de la Fe
D. Regiment de Santa Jordi
E. Regiment de Sant Miquel
   a. Post-1713 uniform

Plate Five: French Infantry

Ordnance colour and uniform of Normandie, Auvergne, du Guast, La Couronne, Vermandois, Royal de Vaisseaux, Angoumois, Berwick, Orléans, La Marche, Blaisois, and Payssac.

All would have carried a plain white colonel's colour, one per regiment. La Couronne carried their Crown onto this colour, Royal de Vaisseaux their Fleur de Lys, in the same pattern, and Berwick, who originally had a red cross, now only had their motto. Regiment Hessy is shown with their particular colonel's colour, the other side bore an ornate cartouche with a fleur de lys on blue.

Central figures show soldiers of the Berwick and Blaisois Regiments equipped with the 'belly box' dating from the middle war years.

Plate Six: French Cavalry and Dragoons

Uniforms of Cavalerie Regiments Anjou, Thury, La Ferronays and Villiers/Croi.
A. Cavalerie Cornet of Anjou
B. Cornet of de Fleshe (reverse)
C. Cornet of Villiers/Croi (reverse, obverse like D, but yellow field)
D. Cornet of de Fleshe (obverse)

Troopers of de Fleshe and Noailles, trumpeter of Villiers/Croi
Dragoon Regiments Saumery, Languedoc and Asfeld

Plate Seven: Spanish (Bourbon) Army Infantry

Spanish Infantry
1/2 colours of the Spanish and Walloon Guards Regiments, newly dressed 'a la Francaise' in a copy of the dress of their French counterparts, the most obvious 'Bourbonisation' of the Spanish Army. Differenced only by a white or black loop to their red cockades.

3. Guards Uniform, usually shown with Red breeches and hose.
A. Post-1707 Napoli regiment
B. Grenadier Valencia Regiment, post-1707

The old Hapsburg Infantry of Spain were dressed in a multitude of colours, with different facings and bore monikers based on their colours and age of formation, these uniforms were worn during the early years of the wars in the peninsula.

4. Sevilla or Old Purples
5. Léon or New Yellows
6. Cordova or Old Greens
7. Post-1707 Milan regiment with colour
8. Post-1707 colonel's colour
9. Pre-1707 colonel's colour
10. Regiment Cueta
11–19 various types of pre-1707 Spanish flags

Plate Eight: Spanish (Bourbon) Dragoons and Cavalry; Portuguese Army

Spanish Cavalry and Dragoons
1. Uniform and Cornet, Milan Regiment
2. Unknown Cavalry Cornet
3. Regiment Poroblanco
4. Regiment Reyna
5. Regiment Estremadura Viejo
6. Regiment Rosella Nuevo
7. Regiment Estella
8. Dragoon Regiment Vallejo, the caps and tricornes seem interchangeable
9. Dragoon Regiment Marimon
10. Dragoon Regiment Osuna

Portuguese Army
11. Regiment Armada
12. Regiment Campo Maior
13. Regiment Chaves
14. Regiment Porto
15. Regiment Lisbon

Much discussion has been had regarding Portuguese flags, the 'Gironne' or windmills designs often being placed after 1740, however they occur in the near contemporary painting of Almanza, and so have been reestablished as possible Spanish Succession colours. The contrary view is that the Portuguese carried flags with horizontal stripes.[5]

16. Unknown regiment
17. Unknown regiment
18. Possibly Regiment Armada
19. Possibly Regiment Lisbon
20. Guardias das Minas
21. Carvelho Dragoons
22. Brito Dragoons
23. Mello de Silva Dragoons

Sources

Barthorp, M., *Marlborough's Army, 1702–11* (London: Osprey, 1980)

Boeri, Mirecki, Palau, Hall, *The Spanish Armies in the War of the League of Augsburg, 1688–97* (Romford: Pike and Shot Society, 2011)

Condray, P., *The Portuguese Army during the War of the Spanish Succession (1704–1715)* (Alexandria: Borkaw, 1992)

Ede-Borrett, S., 'Colours of the Marlburian Wars', parts 1 and 2. *Miniature Wargames*, 1989

Hall, Boeri, *Uniforms and Flags of the Imperial Austrian Army 1683–1720.*

Hall, Stanford, *Flags and Uniforms of the Dutch Army 1685–1715* (Romford: Pike and Shot Society, 2014)

Hinds, J., *The Spanish Army of Philip V* (Alexandria: Brokaw, 1987)

Rubio, X., *God Save Catalonia!* (Calafell: Llibres de Matrícula, 2010)

---

5   Hall, Stanford, *Flags and Uniforms of the Dutch Army 1685–1715* (Romford: Pike and Shot Society, 2014), volume 2.

Bibliography

Anonymous, *An Impartial Account of all the material transactions of the Grand Fleet and Land Forces* (London: Gibson, 1703)

Anonymous, *The Present State of Europe Volume 18* (London: H. Rhodes, 1707)

Anonymous, *An Account of the Earl of Galway's Conduct in Spain and Portugal* (London: J.Baker, 1711, 2nd ed.)

Anonymous, *An Impartial Enquiry into the Management of the War in Spain by the Ministry at Home* (London: J. Morphew, 1712)

Berwick, James Fitzjames, *Memoirs of the Marshal duke of Berwick* (London: T. Cadell, 1779)

Borges, J.V., *Conquista De Madrid 1706* (Lisbon: Tribuna, 2003)

Cleaveland, R.F., *Notes on the Early History of the Royal Regiment of Artillery* (Woolwich: n.p., n.d. [c.1880])

Condray, P., *The Portuguese Army during the War of the Spanish Succession (1704–1715)* (Alexandria: Editions Brokaw, 1992)

Dalton, C., *English Army Lists and Commission Registers, 1661-1714 Volume V: 1702–07* (London: Eyre and Spottiswoode, 1902)

Dorrell, N., *Marlborough's Last Chance in Spain: The 1710 Spanish Campaign* (Sweden: Arnfelts, 2011)

Duncan, F., *History of the Royal Regiment of Artillery, Volume 1* (London: John Murray, 1879, 3rd ed.)

Feldzüge des Prinzen Eugen von Savoyen, 10. Band (1708) (Vienna: K.K. Kriegs-Archiv, 1885)

Feldzüge des Prinzen Eugen von Savoyen, 11. Band (1709) (Vienna: K.K. Kriegs-Archiv, 1887)

Feldzüge des Prinzen Eugen von Savoyen, 12. Band (1710) (Vienna: K.K. Kriegs-Archiv, 1887)

Feldzüge des Prinzen Eugen von Savoyen, 13. Band (1711) (Vienna: K.K. Kriegs-Archiv, 1887)

Feldzüge des Prinzen Eugen von Savoyen, 14. Band (1712) (Vienna: K.K. Kriegs-Archiv, 1889)

Francis, D., *The First Peninsular War: 1702–1713* (London: Ernest Benn, 1975)

Earl of Galway, *An Account of the Earl of Galway's Conduct in Spain and Portugal* (London: J. Baker, 1711, 2nd ed.)

Golberg, C-P., *Die Vereingten Niederlande Heft 3* (Kaltenkirchen: Golberg, 1993)

Hall, R., Stanford, I. & Roumegoux, Y., *Uniforms and Flags of the Dutch Army And The Army of Liege 1685–1715* (N.p.: n.p., 2013)

Holmes, G., "The Commons' Division on 'No Peace without Spain, 7th December 1711", *Bulletin of the Institute of Historical Research*, 3 (1960)

Hughill, J.A.C., *No Peace without Spain* (Oxford: Kensal Press, 1991)

Kamen, Henry, *The War of Succession in Spain 1700–15* (London: Weidenfeld and Nicolson, 1969)

Knighton, C.S. (ed.), *Calendar of State Papers, Domestic Series, of the Reign of Queen Anne Volume 3 1704–05* (Woodbridge: Boydell Press, 2005)

Knighton, C.S. (ed.), *Calendar of State Papers, Domestic Series, of the Reign of Queen Anne Volume 4 1705–06* (Woodbridge: Boydell Press, 2006)

MacKinnon, D., *Origin and services of the Coldstream Guards Volume 1* (London: Bentley, 1833)

Maffey, R.P. (ed.), *Calendar of State Papers, Domestic Series, of the Reign of Queen Anne Volume 1 1702-03* (London: HMSO, 1916)

O'Callaghan, J.C., *History of the Irish brigades in the service of France, from the revolution in Great Britain and Ireland under James II, to the revolution in France under Louis XVI* (Glasgow: Cameron and Ferguson, 1885)

Österreichische militärische Zeitschrift 1838, 1840, 1842, 1844

Parnell, A., *The War of Succession in Spain: 1702–1711* (London: Bell and Sons, 1888)

Sapherson, C.A., *Armies of Spain 1701–1715* (Leigh-on-Sea: Partizan Press, 1997)

Sapherson, C.A., *The Dutch Army of William III* (Leigh-on-Sea: Partizan Press, 1997)

Stanhope, P., *History of the War of the Succession in Spain* (London: John Murray, 1836)

Streffleurs militärische Zeitschrift 1838

Walton, C., *History of the British Standing Army, 1660–1700* (London: Harrison and Sons, 1894)

<http://www.11setembre1714.org/Unitats/b-infanteria-frame.html>

<http://www.11setembre1714.org/batalles/batalla-1708-09-29-menorca-frame.htm>l